Kristeva in Focus

KRISTEVA IN FOCUS

From Theory to Film Analysis

Katherine J. Goodnow

berghahn
NEW YORK · OXFORD
www.berghahnbooks.com

First published in 2010 by
Berghahn Books
www.berghahnbooks.com

©2010, 2014 Katherine J. Goodnow
First paperback edition published in 2014

All rights reserved. Except for the quotation of short passages for the purposes of criticism and review, no part of this book may be reproduced in any form or by any means, electronic or mechanical, including photocopying, recording, or any information storage and retrieval system now known or to be invented, without written permission of the publisher.

Library of Congress Cataloging-in-Publication Data
Goodnow, Katherine J.
Kristeva in focus : from theory to film analysis / Katherine J. Goodnow.
p. cm.
Includes bibliographical references and index.
ISBN 978-1-84545-612-2 (hardback) -- ISBN 978-1-78238-506-6 (paperback) -- ISBN 978-1-84545-794-5 (ebook)
1. Motion pictures--Philosophy. 2. Motion pictures--Social aspects. 3. Kristeva, Julia, 1941---Criticism and interpretation. 4. Motion pictures--New Zealand. I. Title.
PN1995.G579 2009
791.4301--dc22

2009047656

British Library Cataloguing in Publication Data
A catalogue record for this book is available from the British Library

Printed on acid-free paper.

ISBN: 978-1-84545-612-2 hardback
ISBN: 978-1-78238-506-6 paperback
ISBN: 978-1-84545-794-5 ebook

Contents

Acknowledgments vii

Preface ix
    Increasing accessibility x
    Identifying central concepts x
    Demonstrating relevance xii
    Combining a sympathetic and an evaluative stance xiii
    Some aspects of structure xiv

Chapter 1. Introduction to Kristeva 1
    A first general concept: Order and disturbances of order 2
    A second pervasive concern: The text of society and history 12
    Proximal history 19

Chapter 2. Horror – Basic concepts: The abject and its varieties 28
    Introducing *Kitchen Sink* 28
    The abject, borders, and images of pollution 29
    Varieties of the abject 33
    Summary comment 44

Chapter 3. Horror – Specifying the circumstances 46
    The nature of rituals of defilement 47
    The functions of rituals of defilement 48
    Questions about rituals 52
    The knowledge that rituals imply 53
    Differences among spectators 57

Chapter 4. Strangers – Basic concepts: Strangers without and within 63
    Aspects of continuity and change 65
    Introducing two films: *Vigil* and *Crush* 69
    Who is a stranger? What marks the stranger? 72
    What creates the tension? 79
    The representation of tension 85
    What is the narrative function of the stranger? 86
    When are tensions and changes most likely to occur? 88

Chapter 5. Strangers – Expansions: The stranger's story	96
Introducing *An Angel At My Table*	97
The stranger's position	100
The stranger's feelings	103
The stranger's options	107
Angel's impact upon the spectator	110
Chapter 6. Love – Basic concepts	115
Aspects of continuity and change	115
Sweetie and *The Piano*: An introduction	118
What are the forms of love?	121
The difficulties of love	126
Links to change: Steps towards love	133
Times of difficulty and change	136
Chapter 7. Love – Expansions: Old and new discourses	141
Aspects of continuity and change	141
Current discourses and their weaknesses	142
The shape of new tales of love	144
The special case of motherhood and maternal love	154
Chapter 8. The text of society and history	159
The paths for *Kitchen Sink* and *Vigil*	161
A rockier path: *Crush*	164
Campion's first feature: *Sweetie*	166
Campion's second feature: *An Angel At My Table*	168
Campion's third feature: *The Piano*	171
Cross-cutting themes	177
Chapter 9. Women and social change	184
Kristeva's 'generations' of feminist theory	185
On men and women	188
Women's voice, women's writing, women's genius	191
Some reservations	198
A reminder of positives	201
Bibliography	209
Filmography	216
Index	219

Acknowledgments

My debts are several both in number and in kind.

For accounts of Kristeva that first raised my initial interest, I am indebted to Elizabeth Grosz, E. Ann Kaplan, John Lechte, and Toril Moi.

For an understanding of the background to 'New Wave' New Zealand films, I am indebted to Jan Chapman, Bridget Ikin, and John Maynard. The latter two especially gave generously of their time.

Munia Kanna procured videos for me, kept me up-to-date on what was happening on the other side of the world, and unfailingly offered her friendship. So also did my old friend, Florian Bick. Her constant readiness to say 'I don't understand' helped unravel many a sentence.

Above all my thanks go to my friend and partner, Runar Bjaalid, for meals that did more than keep body and soul together, and for listening to desperate concerns over lost footnotes, computer failures, and the general lack of hours in the day.

Preface

KRISTEVA IN FOCUS
From theory to film analysis

The work of Julia Kristeva has attracted attention as a base for examining the general nature of representation, theories of language, and the position of women in society.[1] Most of these analyses, however, have been concerned either with Kristeva's general philosophical position or with its relevance to written texts. In comparison, 'the issue of film ... has so far been neglected by most Kristeva scholars'.[2] Kristeva herself has also written little about film despite the recognition that 'we are a society of the image'.[3] 'The universe of the image ... invades us through film and television: the cinematic image, the central place of the imaginary'.[4]

Kristeva has in fact a great deal to offer for the analysis of film. My aim is to increase the accessibility of her concepts (the extensions that have been made to film tend to assume a previous understanding of these), identify central concepts, demonstrate the relevance of Kristeva's ideas to a number of films, and ask what needs to be added or questioned. Meeting that aim may help make her work easier to understand and appreciate for people starting from other content areas, but the extension to film analysis is my primary concern.

What makes her work of interest, especially to film analysts? To start with, Kristeva's analyses of texts contain a pervasive interest in topics that are often of interest in film analysis. She is concerned with the affective impact of any image or text on the spectator or reader. Her work contains also a strong interest in the emergence of new texts: images and narratives that depart from what has preceded them and that present challenges to established forms of social and representational order. Marking her work is a combination of perspectives drawn from the several disciplines to which film analysis itself often turns: psychoanalytic theory, literary theory and political theory. There is as well a pervasive concern with topics that are often central to film: topics such as the representation of horror, strangers, and love.[5]

Increasing accessibility

Why then the limited use of Kristeva's concepts? As Noëlle McAfee notes, her name may be better known than her actual proposals.[6] One reason has to do with their accessibility. Kristeva's style makes her concepts less accessible than they might be. She makes, as Toril Moi has pointed out, 'few pedagogical concessions ... to the reader' and has 'the unsettling habit of referring to everyone from Saint Bernard to Fichte or Artaud in the same sentence'.[7] She may strike many readers as being 'too French'.[8] Her material is known to be 'daunting and demanding', setting 'an odd limit to her influence'.[9] That style is deliberate. Her aim is to combine the expression of a novel idea with 'stylistic inventiveness'[10]. She also considers that the act of writing should itself be a way of disturbing an established order (literary or political). In this sense, her style is part of her political position.

That fusion of aims, however, creates a particular need for some less stylistically inventive statement of her ideas. In the process of such re-statement, the poetic, allusive quality to Kristeva's writing may be insufficiently represented. Readers, however, should find the re-statement more easily grasped than they may find the originals. They may also find that the change in language then makes it easier to turn to the originals, to what has been written about her work, and to the extensions to film that have been made.[11]

Identifying central concepts

For an examination of Kristeva's work to be broadly useful, we need to identify a central set of ideas. Readers may then use the central concepts both to cut across topics and to develop extensions to new content areas. With this need in mind, I have given particular attention to two concepts that have a central place within Kristeva's work.

These are not the only concepts in her work. They are, however, the building blocks that appear in the early work and that underlie much of the later material: building blocks not only conceptually but also historically.

The first of these concepts has to do with disturbances of order:, with Kristeva's pervasive interest in marginality, subversion, transgression, disruption, and innovation – in effect, with breaks in an established literary or social order. The second is what Kristeva has called the 'text of society and history'. It has to do with the ways in which the accumulated texts and images of a culture provide a background – a storehouse – that writers and readers draw upon to interpret what is encountered and create something new.

These two concepts are a core part of Kristeva's work. The theme of disturbances of order, for example, is central to all her writing about 'revolt'. She uses that term to cover more than political revolution.

> Revolt as I understand it – psychic revolt, analytic revolt, artistic revolt – refers to a state of permanent questioning, of transformation, change, an endless probing of appearances.[12]

> I work from its etymology, meaning return, returning, discovering, uncovering and renovating. There is a necessary repetition when you cover all that ground, but ... I emphasise its potential for making gaps, rupturing, renewing.[13]

That interest in revolt is part of Kristeva's early work. *Revolution in Poetic Language* is one example. It is also central to her later analysis of writing by Arendt, Colette, and Klein: all seen as 'women of revolt', women who reshaped and questioned earlier traditions.[14]

The 'text of society and history' is also a pervasive and continuing theme. To take one early example, her writing about 'the bounded text' (1980) emphasizes the need for analyses that 'define the specificity of different textual arrangements by placing them within the general text (culture) of which they are a part and which, in turn, is part of them'.[15] It appears also in a later comment on works by Picasso: *Les Demoiselles d'Avignon* and *Guernica*:

> Both works transpose the violence of their subject-matter into the field of representation, exerting violence against previous artistic forms and demolishing traditional pictorial codes .... These paintings enact very violent transformations of the codes of representation.[16]

Those transformations, however, can occur only if there are already existing forms of representation: 'There is no revolt without prohibition of some sort. If there weren't, whom would you revolt against?'[17]

Kristeva also uses the texts of society and history to bring out how renovation may be sparked by some more immediate circumstances. Her own closeness to the political revolt in Paris in May 1968, for example, was part of her recognition of the importance of a particular kind of freedom: 'freedom to revolt, to call things into question'.[18] It was also part of the importance she came to give to the way in which individuals questioned and re-examined their own lives. It brought her as well to a stronger interest in Freudian theory – 'the unconscious, dreams, drives: that was just how we were living at the heat of the moment'.[19] The limitations of revolt by 'the *enragé* had to give way to reading Heidegger and above all the wisdom of Freud'.[20]

To take a last example, it was her direct contact in the 1970s with a group based in the 'Women's Bookstore' – a group that prompted her to write *About Chinese Women* – that led to her own questioning look at some forms of feminism. That group 'seemed to magnify the worst aspects of political parties, sects and totalitarian movements'.[21] These movements Kristeva sees as often restricting freedom and deadening questions. Her response was to avoid commitment to particular groups: 'I carried on thinking about the feminine condition though, either on my own or in the context of my academic or clinical work'.[22]

Demonstrating relevance

Some extensions of Kristeva's concepts to the analysis of specific films have already been made. Barbara Creed, for example, focused on horror, and used Kristeva's concept of the abject in her analysis of the film *Alien*.[23] Katherine Goodnow has expanded Creed's work to cover a broader range of instances of horror and the abject in *Alien* and *Aliens*.[24] Tina Chanter has extended the concept of abjection to the analysis of fetishism and the film *Exotica*.[25] Frances Restuccia has picked up Kristeva's concepts of melancholia and depression and extended them to the film *Blue*.[26] Maria Margaroni has focused on the importance Kristeva gives to the speaking subject, the significance of silence, and the necessity of loss from the mother and of giving up impenetrability. She has then used those concepts in an analysis of *The Piano*.[27] In short, the neglect of Kristeva's work in relation to film analysis is far from being total.

These are, however, extensions to single films. At this point the exploration of a larger set of films is needed. If one takes Kristeva's proposals as a vantage point, what do they lead us to notice, to understand, or to ask about the shape, the emergence, and the impact of films?

I have chosen a set of films: *Kitchen Sink, Vigil, Crush, An Angel At My Table, Sweetie,* and *The Piano*. This set has the immediate virtue of containing within it films that deal explicitly with the themes of horror, strangers, and love. Their larger virtue lies in the ways in which they illustrate the two basic concepts: innovation and disruptions of order, and the texts of society and history.

To start with disruptions of order, these films were recognized internationally as distinctive and different. They were certainly different from earlier film styles in New Zealand. Those earlier styles reflected a tradition that concentrated on themes of 'men against the bush' and had 'a naturalistic style'. The title of one earlier film – *The Heart of the Stag* – is nicely indicative. In the new films, the settings were likely to be urban as well as rural, women often had a central place, and the visual style was more 'art-house'. This break from New Zealand film tradition gave rise to the label 'New Zealand New Wave'.

The break from tradition, however, was much broader than the break from New Zealand film alone. It was a break from film styles in general. In the 'new' films, content had more to do with people and their interrelationships. (*The Piano*, for instance, was a deliberate return to the issue of passion in the grand, *Wuthering Heights* tradition.). The new films were also as concerned with the representations, positions, and perspectives of women as they were with those of men – sometimes more so. These women were in themselves often 'different'. They often made breaks from their expected lives and lived out passion through music (*The Piano*) or literature (*An Angel At My Table*). It was those general breaks that attracted international attention and international labelling as 'different'.

These films also illustrate the ways in which new works reflect 'the text of society and history'; of special interest is the way they offer a particular opportunity to look at that text in the form of some immediate, predisposing circumstances.

Some of those more immediate circumstances, for example, had to do with concern about the development of a national image: an image that would foster some sense of national identity in a country where cultural diversity is marked and there is a history of colonialism. The search for a national image was certainly part of government funding for innovation in film. More broadly, the country was, and still is, in the midst of coming to terms with its colonial history, the interrelationships of Maori and Anglo (or pakeha) people, the country's place in the larger world, the limitations of what Jane Campion has termed its 'Presbyterian' ethos[28] and the limits of preoccupation with landscape in itself, with less concern for the interrelationships between landscapes and people, women especially. Questions about who is a 'foreigner', about the place of love and sensuality, and about the true complexities of interpersonal relationships had then a special salience.

At a level closer to production, this was a time and a place when filmmaking could be regarded as a field open to people with a variety of backgrounds rather than limited to people who had been trained at an established film school. It was also a small and youthful industry: small enough to allow people to know each other and to play several roles (to be, for instance both director and script-writer).[29]

The chosen set of films provides as well the right size of arena for an analysis of immediate circumstances, especially since the analysis can be informed by direct comment from the film-makers on what they hoped to achieve and what influenced the way events unfolded. Those capsule histories for each of the films considered will then be interwoven with the dissection of Kristeva's concepts and the demonstration of how these concepts prompt new ways of considering films.

Combining a sympathetic and an evaluative stance

This final concern may be briefly stated. Kristeva cannot be expected to answer every question, to cover every aspect, of the way films come to be made and received. It is, however, reasonable to ask whether gaps occur in the way Kristeva accounts for issues that she herself takes as central, and to consider what aspects film analysts especially would wish to see expanded or questioned.

My evaluative comments will come up in each chapter. In addition, I shall take up in the final chapter a number of questions that have been raised about Kristeva's perspective and that film analysts would also raise. These reservations have to do with the nature of her argument about the position of women, her views about the significance of images and the place of silence, and the extent to which she appears to accept the status quo rather than to challenge it.

That final chapter stems partly from Kristeva's argument that one of the functions of 'new' or 'avant-garde' texts (and one of her own aims) is to produce social change. It stems also from the fact that the strongest reservations about Kristeva's perspective have to do precisely with her own commitment to, and programme for, social change. The social changes of particular concern in theis final chapter have to do with the position of women. Kristeva is widely regarded as one of *the* French feminists. It is nonetheless from feminists that some of the strongest criticism has come. More broadly, the measure of any theory, any perspective, has come to be its treatment of male/female issues – the possible difference of males and females as spectators;, the extent to which differences lie in 'essences' or in social position;, the extent to which a woman's voice is distinctive;, and the feasibility of even considering 'women' as a category rather than emphasizing individuals and their 'particularity'. To use Robert Lapsley's and Michael Westlake's phrase, 'the politics of gender has largely replaced the politics of class in film theory'.[30] It is then appropriate on several counts to make issues of gender the focus for the final chapter in this exploration of Kristeva's concepts.

Some aspects of structure

Chapter 1 introduces the two core concepts: order and disturbances of order, and texts of society and history. Chapters 2 and 3 deal with horror and Kristeva's concept of the abject in relation to horror. The film of particular interest here is *The Kitchen Sink*. Chapters 4 and 5 focus on the concept of strangers and on three films (*Vigil, Crush* and *An Angel At My Table*). Chapters 6 and 7 look at love and desire and the films *Sweetie* and *The Piano*. Chapter 8 cuts across all these films and brings out, for each of them, the circumstances that influenced their production and their final shape. Chapter 9, as noted earlier, focuses on some questions and reservations that have been raised about Kristeva's concepts.

The four concerns – accessibility, identifying core concepts, relevance, evaluation – frame the way I have proceeded throughout the several chapters.

Notes

1. See, for instance, Barbara Creed (1985) 'Horror and the monstrous-feminine: An imaginary abjection'. In *Screen*, issue 27(1); Toril Moi (1985) *Sexual/textual politics*. London: Methuen; Elizabeth Grosz (1989) *Sexual subversions: Three French feminists*. Sydney: Allen and Unwin; John Lechte (1990) *Julia Kristeva*. London: Routledge; E. Ann Kaplan (1992) *Motherhood and representation: The mother in popular culture and melodrama*. London: Routledge; Kelly Oliver (1993b) *Reading Kristeva: Unraveling the double-bind*. Bloomington, Indiana University Press; Anna Smith (1996) *Julia Kristeva: Readings of exile and estrangement*. New York: St Martin's Press; Noëlle McAfee (2004) *Julia Kristeva*. New York: Routledge; or Tina Chanter and Eva Plonowska Ziarek (Eds) (2005) *Revolt, affect, collectivity: The unstable boundaries of Kristeva's polis*. Albany: State University of New York Press. These writers come from a variety of content areas ranging from literary theory to behavioural sciences, philosophy and politics.
2. Chanter and Ziarek (2005, p.5)
3. Julia Kristeva (2002a) *Intimate revolt*. New York: Columbia University Press, p.63.
4. Ibid., p.65.
5. All three are central to Kristeva's work: the first in *The Powers of Horror*, for example, the second in *Strangers to Ourselves* and *Nations Without Nationalism*, and the third in *Tales of Love* and *In the Beginning Was Love*.
6. Noëlle McAfee McAfee (2005) 'Bearing witness in the *Polis*: Kristeva, Arendt, and the space of appearance'. In Chanter and Ziarek, p.119.
7. Moi (1985, p.96).
8. Lechte (1990, p.19).
9. McAfee (2005, p.119).
10. Julia Kristeva (1993) *Nations without nationalism*. New York: Columbia University Press, p.44). That the poetic style is deliberate is indicated by the straightforward style of exposition Kristeva uses in a text written as an introduction to linguistics: Julia Kristeva (1989) *Language the uunknown: An initiation in linguistics* (Kristeva, 1989: New York: Columbia University Press. (Thisa text was first published in 1969 under her married name, Julia Joyaux.). Kristeva also displays concern with increasing the accessibility of her ideas in her writing about strangers. *Nations Without Nationalism* (1993), for instance, contains an essay that condenses much of the argument contained in *Strangers to Ourselves*. It was an essay intended as 'a reflection involving an audience wider than that of academic circles' (p.6). The material is nonetheless not easily grasped on first encounter. Written in a less stylistically inventive fashion, and more easily read, are the books covering the lives and writings of Hannah Arendt, Melanie Klein, and Colette.
11. The extensions include Barbara Creed (1985) 'Horror and the monstrous-feminine: An imaginary abjection'. In *Screen*, issue 27(1); Barbara Creed (1993) *The Monstrous-feminine: Film, Feminism, Psychoanalysis*. London: Routledge); and Maria Margaroni's (2003) analysis of *The Piano* 'Jane Campion's selling of the mother/land: Restaging the crisis of the postcolonial subject'. In *Camera Obscura*, issue 18(2) These extensions, are more accessible than most but even they assume some familiarity with both Kristeva's theory and psychoanalytic theory.
12. Kristeva (2002a, p.120).
13. Ibid., p.85.
14. Julia Kristeva (1984) *Revolution in poetic language*. New York: Columbia University Press; Julia Kristeva (2001a) *Hannah Arendt*. New York: Columbia University Press;

Julia Kristeva (2001b) *Melanie Klein*. New York: Columbia University Press; *Melanie Klein* (2001b); Julia Kristeva (2004) *Colette*. New York: Columbia University Press. The description of 'women of revolt' comes from Kristeva (2002a, p.95).
15. Julia Kristeva (1980) *Desire in language: A semiotic approach to literature and art*. New York: Columbia University Press p.36).
16. Kristeva (2002a, pp.121–122).
17. Ibid., p.31.
18. Ibid., p.12.
19. Ibid., p.20.
20. Ibid., p.26.
21. Ibid., p.30.
22. Ibid., p.30.
23. Creed (1985); Barbara Creed (1993) *The monstrous-feminine: Film, feminism, psychoanalysis*. London: Routledge.
24. Katherine Goodnow (1991a) *Alien/aliens: Analyzing the forms and sources of horror*. Bergen: University of Bergen. Unpublished document, University of Bergen. See also Katherine Goodnow (1991b) 'Mødre, Fødsle, og den kvinnelige tilskuer'. In Z, Issue 38; and Katherine Goodnow (2006) 'Bodies: Taking account of viewers' perspectives'. In K. Goodnow and J. Lohman (Eds) *Human remains and museum practice*. Paris: UNESCO.
25. Tina Chanter (2005) 'The exoticization and universalization of the fetish, and the naturalization of the phallus: Abject objections'. In Chanter and Ziarek.
26. Frances L. Restuccia (2005) 'Black and *Blue*: Kieslowski's melancholia'. In Chanter and Ziarek.
27. Margaroni (2003).
28. Jane Campion (1990f) in interview with Katherine Tulich: 'Jane's film career takes wing'. In *Daily Telegraph Mirror*, 21 September in interview with Katherine Tulich, *Daily Telegraph Mirror* (Sydney), p.63.
29. These were also people who were in themselves part of the search for identity, for a sense of belonging, and, at the same time, a sense of being different. By name they were: Jane Campion, Alison Maclean, and Vincent Ward as directors; Jan Chapman, Bridget Ikin, and John Maynard as producers. They were New Zealand born but most of them were living in Australia. They were then 'strangers' in Australia. As 'pakeha' (white and not Maori) they were also in part 'strangers' within New Zealand. Issues of being a stranger and belonging were then not purely abstract issues for them.
30. Robert Lapsley and Michael Westlake (1988).

Chapter 1

INTRODUCTION TO KRISTEVA

Kristeva, like most postmodernists, does not present herself as offering a grand metatheory:

> Considering the complexity of the signifying process, no belief in an all-powerful theory is tenable; there remains the necessity to pay attention to the desire for language, and by this I mean paying attention ... to the art and literature of our time, which remains alone, in our world of technological rationality, to impel us not toward the absolute but toward a quest for a little more truth ... concerning the meaning of speech, concerning our condition as speaking beings.[1]

That lack of a grand theory – or of a single, central proposition from which all else unfolds – makes for difficulties when one attempts to present any simple synthesis of Kristeva's position. One solution to this difficulty would be to present a chronological account of what she has written. Her work, however, is often recursive rather than linear over time.[2] Film analysts are likely to find it more rewarding if they begin, not with a chronological account, but with a sense of the kinds of questions she has asked, the kinds of perspectives she has used, and the general concerns that cut across her work.

I shall accordingly open this chapter by noting that Kristeva combines in one person a knowledge of the several disciplines – semiotics, psychoanalysis, political theory, and feminist theory – to which film theorists have often looked for borrowable concepts and methods. She is Professor of Linguistics and Director of the doctoral school 'Language, Literature, Image' at the University of Paris. She is a practising psychoanalyst: a career that came after the start of a career in linguistics. She has been, over time, committed to Marxist theory (with reservations based on her having first-hand experience of life in Bulgaria, before coming to Paris in her mid twenties), interested in Maoist theory, disillusioned with political groups, and more oriented towards what individuals – particularly individuals within the avant-garde – can achieve in the destabilization of restrictive social orders or in the preservation of an effective order that is under threat (she is concerned, for instance, with the rise of racial prejudice in contemporary France). Finally, she has long been regarded as one of the leading 'French feminists', although her own self-identification is not as a 'feminist' and the reactions of many feminists to her proposals about the position of women have been far from universally positive.[3]

I shall introduce Kristeva by beginning with two concepts – two grand concerns – that cut across much of her work. These are far from being the only concepts she presents or the only ones of interest to film theorists. At this point, however, presenting a *précis* of each of Kristeva's main ideas would result in a chapter that would be weak on interconnections and so skeletal, so poorly anchored in examples, as to be uninteresting, even if comprehensible. These two large concepts will open the analysis, with others added as the chapters unroll and specific questions arise. That route is a little closer to Kristeva's own style (although still far from it). In many ways, Kristeva often writes as if she expected understanding to emerge in the way it does with the reading of a poem. It is the accumulation of images, of references, that yields at the end the sense of now knowing what is intended. My approach is not poetic in any standard form, but it will be cumulative rather than attempting to touch on all points at the start.

Which concepts, then, to choose as a starting point? Of the two selected, the first has to do with the nature of order and its destabilization. The second has to do with what Kristeva refers to as 'the text of society and history'. The two, it will emerge, are closely inter-related, in the sense that the challenge to any existing order (social order or literary canon) lies often in drawing upon past texts in a way that is novel, that refuses to accept the customary ways, and that displays a 'defiant productivity'.[4]

A first general concept: Order and disturbances of order

The heading Moi chooses for her chapter on Kristeva, in a book on *Sexual/Textual Politics*, is 'Marginality and Subversion'.[5] Kristeva has indeed a long-standing interest in the ways by which any established order is challenged, undermined, or changed, in the necessity for disturbance, and in the risks and promises, the gains and losses, that breaks in an established order bring with them.

This concern is a thread that links Kristeva's early work – *Revolution in Poetic Language*, for example, to later work such as *Strangers to Ourselves* and *Intimate Revolt*. It is a thread that also cuts across the several kinds of representations or texts that Kristeva analyses: from novels to the several versions of the French constitution during the Revolution and works of art by Giotto or Holbein. It is as well part of Kristeva's image of her own position, her own suspicion of established theory. Asked at one point, for instance, about her connection to a Marxist 'line of thought', her response was: 'I never intended to follow a correct Marxist line, and I hope I am not correctly following any other line whatsoever'.[6] Léon Roudiez, the translator of several of Kristeva's books, describes Kristeva in similar terms:

> She is nearly always, if ever so slightly, off-centred in relation to all established doctrines .... Her discourse is not the orthodox discourse of any of them; the vocabulary is theirs but the syntax is her own.[7]

Conscious of her own position as a foreigner in France, a woman in a world dominated by men, a speaker who stands outside language in order to study it, Kristeva must indeed have been pleased with Barthes's description of her:

> Julia Kristeva changes the place of things. She always destroys the latest preconception, the one we thought we could be comforted by .... [S]he subverts authority, the authority of monologic science.[8]

From Kristeva's several expressions of concern with order and its destabilization, I shall draw out several propositions. I do so with an awareness that this way of proceeding violates Kristeva's own style, and runs the risk of losing the richness of her thought – of 'domesticating the alien'.[9] At the same time, as I noted in the preface, I wish to make Kristeva's argument accessible to those who may have no other knowledge of what she has written. I shall accept the risk, with the promise that the later chapters will undo any appearance of reductive or simplistic thought on Kristeva's part.

The reader will recognize that these propositions place Kristeva within a line of thought that includes Althusser, Barthes, Derrida, and Lacan, and it is certainly not part of my argument to present Kristeva as being without precedent. What distinguishes her, however, and makes her ideas particularly attractive for film analysis, is the combined set, and in particular, the later propositions within the set.

Order takes a variety of forms

Some of these forms have to do with the nature of texts or representations. The expected forms of written texts or works of art, for instance, specify what can be named or pictured, and how this should be done. Change then may be in either of these aspects. In Kristeva's view, for instance, 'Western painting' departed from 'Catholic theology' first by its 'themes (at the time of the Renaissance) and later, [by] its norm-representation (with the advent of Impressionism and the ensuing movements)'.[10]

Other forms of order have to do with the relationships expected to apply between individuals, either as lovers or as residents of one country. 'Self' and 'other' are expected to be separate, but the degree and the nature of separateness – or, as in the case of marriage, 'oneness' – are codified rather than left to chance or to mood.

Another form of order refers to relationships within parts or aspects of the individual. This form of order again involves a distinction between 'self' and 'other'. 'Not yourself' or 'beside myself', for instance, are phrases indicating that there are some parts of oneself that are expected to occupy only a certain place. Dreams, fantasies, violent feelings, or the state of being 'in love', for example, are in contemporary times accepted as part of one's self, as part of one's 'unconscious' or 'dream life' (in earlier times they might well have been exteriorized as the result of witchcraft or possession). They are, however, not typically seen as part of one's 'usual self' and they are expected to be under the control of one's 'usual self'.

Finally, 'order' refers to the general state of affairs that applies in a society. It is possible, for instance, to describe a society as dominated by the values of a bourgeoisie, with little or no dissenting voice. It is also possible to describe a society as marked by patriarchy. For Kristeva the major distinction is between social orders that allow differing amounts of space for the dissenting voice: the voice that she sees as part of a 'semiotic' rather than the 'symbolic' register or form of experience. The social order that is dominated by the symbolic is, in essence, one marked by the valorization of rationality, technology, evaluative judgments, strict logic, naming, and the delineation of opposites (man/woman; rationality/emotionality; prose/poetry, etc.). In contrast, a social order with some space for the semiotic is one with a place for rhythm, 'pulses' and colour, a feeling for the 'unnameable' and for the flow of opposites into one another, and a desire for *'jouissance'* rather than for control, clarity, and the observance of rules.

That societies differ in the extent to which they allow a dissenting voice is a proposal that passes without challenge. The extension to identifying this voice as semiotic, however, is a different point: one that has raised some degree of concern. Among some critics, there is a degree of concern with the way Kristeva moves from terms originally developed to describe the nature of language to a use of the same terms to describe a social order. Nancy Fraser, for instance, objects to 'a quasi-structuralist conflation' of 'a register of language – symbolic/semiotic – with a social order'.[11] For the moment, however, I shall let the analogy stand.

The several forms of order are related to one another

Two such links stand out in Kristeva's work. In the first link, the way in which parts of oneself are interrelated (the internal 'self' and the 'other') is regarded as parallel to, and giving rise to, the way in which we regard strangers. (Hence the title *Strangers to Ourselves,* for a book that begins with concern about the rise of xenophobia in contemporary France.) The same kind of link is also part of the argument that in order to love others we must be able to love ourselves (but also to go beyond self-love), and that we find unsettling or 'uncanny' encounters with the 'alien double'. This link will be recognized as having a classic psychoanalytic base.[12]

The second link is between the social order and the literary order. This linking actually has several parts to it, each attracting varying degrees of comment, and it will be worth separating them from the start. The first part – the notion that there are links of various kinds between forms of social order and the forms that texts or representations take – receives the widest support. It is a pervasive proposal in the field of humanities: one that may be found in work ranging from historical analyses of art to analyses of horror films.[13] It is when the move is made towards specifying the nature of the link that agreement diminishes.

The second part – the notion that challenges or changes to established forms of speech or representation can give rise to reflection upon a social order and perhaps to changes within it – would also receive a fair degree of support. It is, in many ways, the assumption behind the insistence by feminists that the generic term 'he' (with its implication that 'he' refers to both male and female, to all people) should give way to the double term 'he or she' or to the pronoun 'they'. Even Fraser – a feminist who argues that 'feminists should have no truck with Lacan and ... only the most minimal truck with Julia Kristeva' – agrees with this part of Kristeva's position, endorsing the view that 'the formation of social groups proceeds by struggles over social discourse'.[14]

It is the third part of Kristeva's position – the notion that the changes introduced by the avant-garde into established forms of representation are analogous to, or give rise to, changes in social order – that is usually the source of negative comment. It is this part of the proposal that leads, for instance, to Fraser's objection to Kristeva as making 'the avant-garde the privileged site of innovation',[15] and to Moi's more detailed comment:

> [I]t is still not clear *why* it is so important to show that certain literary practices break up the structures of language when they seem to break up little else. She seems essentially to argue that the disruption of the subject, the *sujet en procès* displayed in these texts, prefigures or parallels revolutionary disruptions of society. But her only argument in support of this contention is the rather lame one of comparison or homology. Nowhere are we given a specific analysis of the actual social or political structures that would produce a homologous relationship between the subjective and the social.[16]

For my present purposes, this part of Kristeva's argument is fortunately not critical. I wish primarily to know how a change from one kind of written or visual text to another can be defined, and to ask: what is an innovation? I also wish to know some of the specific circumstances that allow or facilitate a change in text or image. But I do not need to prove that changes in written or visual texts produce changes in the social order. For that matter, I am not completely convinced that Kristeva consistently thinks in such causal terms, although some of what she writes implies that she does so. The interpretation I prefer is similar to that of Grosz, who sees Kristeva as proposing that:

> Art is a kind of index of social stability. Upheavals, transformations or subversions of artistic norms and canons do not exactly reflect or cause symbolic/social transformations; rather, they anticipate and accompany them. Kristeva refuses to reduce representations to the socio-economic order .... Economic and social relations do not directly produce artistic transformations nor do artistic and representational upheavals incite social rebellion. This is to consider socio-economic relations in isolation from representations, as two distinct systems: one does not simply represent the other or act as its symbol or substitute. On the contrary, the mode of production necessarily implies the mode of sign-production.[17]

Order is maintained by the construction of borders or boundaries

For Kristeva, the boundaries of particular interest are the divisions and contrasts we draw between meanings, rather than the physical boundaries of national frontiers, prison walls, quarantine zones, or segregated ghettos. We construct and maintain a sense of personal and social order, she comments, by the distinctions we draw between opposites: self/other, me/not me, living/dead, male/female, infant/child, and citizen/resident. The point is not completely unique to Kristeva. The work of Cixous, for example, contains a strong emphasis upon the way the patriarchal system involves a series of binary oppositions that overlap with the dichotomy of male and female (active/passive, sun/moon, culture/nature, day/night, head/heart, and logos/pathos. A similar point is made by the anthropologist Michelle Rosaldo who, like Cixous, remarks on the way the 'feminine' side of the dichotomy is consistently seen as the less powerful side of the pair but, unlike Cixous, sees the primary dichotomy as 'public/private' with 'male/female' mapped on to this basic dichotomy.[18]

Kristeva draws attention, however, to a further way in which customary boundaries are maintained. The usual texts – images, narratives, tales – tell us what is reasonable or possible to speak about or to represent and what is not. They tell us not only how things shall be named, but also what is not to be covered: the unnameable, the unrepresentable, the areas of silence.

The usual texts tell us also how we should interpret or 'read' what we encounter. One of the first dissatisfactions with a social order may then appear in a discontent with the customary tales: with the extent to which they reflect or address current concerns; with the outcomes or the contracts that they offer as proper or inevitable. To take an argument from *Tales of Love*, we assign meanings to any experience or narrative of love in the light of the tales we know: tales that range from Romeo and Juliet to the more recent Scarlett and Rhett. These tales frame our understanding: they tell us what it means to be 'in love'; where love's difficulties lie in waiting; what the probable course of love will be; and how we should recognize what is seemly, what is reasonable, possible, outrageous, or inevitable. These same conventional tales, however, may become the targets of our dissatisfaction when the feeling arises that the narratives and the feelings represented are too strongly formed upon women as inevitably making sacrifices or are too orientated towards an easy sexuality, neglecting the caring side of love.

Where Kristeva stands out also is in the next proposition: in her insistence that borders are inherently unstable and in the reasons she gives for their being so.

Borders and divisions are inherently unstable

The reasons Kristeva offers for this proposition are threefold. One reason is that distinctions, dichotomies, and borders are socially constructed rather than being 'given' or 'natural', and so 'fixed'. On this basis, any fixed distinction between 'masculinity' and 'femininity' – any 'essentialist' position – cannot be maintained. What is regarded as 'feminine' at one time or in one place, for instance, will not be the same as the definition offered at another. Even the apparently biological line of divisions between living and dead – or the point at which a foetus becomes 'truly human' – can be debated and be open to change.[19]

The second reason for instability has to do with the way in which societies contain competing codes, the relative strengths of which vary from one point of time to another. I shall anticipate Chapter 4 a little by taking an example from Kristeva's analysis of increased tension with regard to foreigners in today's European world. Our response to strangers, Kristeva argues, is regulated by two competing codes: one universalist (e.g., 'love your neighbour as yourself') and one particularist (e.g., 'look after your own'). The dominance of one of these codes over the other is never constant. Their relative strengths inevitably change from time to time as changes occur in the need for foreigners, the degree of power that foreigners are perceived to have, or the extent to which foreigners are prepared to accept quietly the price of being allowed to stay, the price of the sociosymbolic contract that usually regulates their presence and their acceptance.

The third reason – and at first glance the most complex reason for borders being inherently unstable – has to do with the nature of people. We are, first of all, not all-of-a-piece within ourselves. Becoming a member of adult society means that some desires have to be foregone, some earlier states of being left behind. The forbidden/excluded/repressed/

abandoned, however, remains a part of us, even if it is often outside awareness. It also remains attractive, in part because it represents a state to which one was at an earlier stage deeply attached. The argument is part of many versions of psychoanalytic theory. In classic Freudian terms, repression is never complete. In Lacanian terms, there is always nostalgia for the state before the separation from the mother, a state in which there was complete oneness, and no sense of lack.[20] In Kristevan terms, the semiotic order may be followed by entry into the symbolic but is never completely superseded. It remains present, for instance, in the pleasure felt in the rhythms and sounds of words over and above our interest in their referential meanings and their syntax.[21]

More subtly, the entity that one calls 'I' is not fixed. 'I' refers always to a person occupying for the moment a particular social position – a position that is open to change – and to a person who, in the moment of reproducing a form of speech, also changes it: inflects it, marks it, transforms it in some way. This proposal is part of Kristeva's concept of 'the speaking subject', and it requires some amplification.

Briefly, the concept is part of a general European move towards undoing 'the logic of identity': the notion of a stable, continuing, rational 'I' that knows what it does and what it thinks (the kind of 'I' implied by *'cogito, ergo sum'*). One of Kristeva's contributions to this move, as Elizabeth Grosz points out, was to 'reveal the wayward functioning' of both 'the unified, rational being' and 'the coherent, meaningful text'.[22] Another – the contribution on which I shall concentrate – was to treat change, innovation, disruption, and transformation as a given, as a process that is an intrinsic part of language rather than an extra to be accounted for by some special magic or by some extra mechanisms. Rather than think only in terms of a person who is shaped by, and subjected to, the given forms of language, Kristeva argues for the need to think of speakers as people who use that system, who act upon it, and who create and modify it in the course of everyday practice. This active user and modifier is 'the speaking subject', engaged in a 'signifying process' or a 'signifying practice'.[23]

Some further statements by Kristeva, and one by Fraser, may help fix the concept. Here, for instance, are some of Kristeva's statements on this score. The first of these is part of her looking back at changes in the field of linguistics:

> As soon as linguistics was established as a science (through Saussure to all intents and purposes) its field of study was ... hemmed in; the problem of *truth* in linguistic discourse became dissociated from any notion of the *speaking subject*. Determining *truth* was reduced to a seeking out of the object-utterance's internal coherence .... Any attempt at reinserting the Cartesian subject or any other subject of enunciation more or less akin to the transcendental ego ... resolves nothing as long as that subject is not posited in the place, not only of structure and its regulated transformation, but especially of *its loss*.[24]

The A second comment from Kristeva comes from her summary of the sixties 1960s as a time that led people to 'question the metaphysical premises on which rest not only the sciences of language but their exportation to other domains'.²⁵ Part of that move:

> involved a questioning of meaning and its structures, giving heed to the underlying *speaking subject* .... That means that references to 'dialectics', 'practice', 'subject' etc. are to be understood as *moments* within an analytic process, one involving the analysis of meaning, structure, their categories and relationships – not at all in the purity of the source from which they sprang.²⁶

A third comment underlines the connection between disruption and renewal:

> [T]he subject of the semiotic metalanguage must, however briefly, call himself into question, must emerge from the protective shell of a transcendental ego within a logical system, and restore his condition within that negativity – drive-governed, but also social, political and historical – which rends and renews the social code.²⁷

The last comment I shall quote comes from Fraser, noting the one part of Kristeva's proposals that she finds attractive, even 'brilliant', and offering a more conventional form of statement. The speaking subject is for Fraser a subject who:

> is socially and historically situated, to be sure, but is not wholly subjected to the reigning social and discursive conventions. It is a subject, rather, who is capable of innovative practice .... Her general idea is that speakers act in socially situated, norm-governed signifying practices. In so doing, they sometimes transgress the established norms in force. Transgressive practices give rise to discursive innovations and these in turn lead to actual change. Innovative practice may subsequently be normalized in the form of new or modified discursive norms, thereby 'renovating' signifying practices.²⁸

In sum, all speaking subjects transform language as they speak. Kristeva's 'revolutionary subject', then, is not a completely new individual, but one who stands at the end of a range that embraces us all.

The state of borders is related to 'affect' and action

This is the fifth proposition with regard to order that I shall abstract from Kristeva's writing. It is not enough, she argues, to observe that societies and individuals are held together by various forms of order or to conceive of order as constantly being transformed in the process of being enacted. We must also take account of the fact that people respond to the presence of order and to moments of destabilization with 'affect', and with actions. To say that texts – words, paintings, images – need to be considered in terms of the feelings they evoke, however, is only a first step. In Kristeva's analysis, the links to emotion (and to the consequences of emotion) are of several kinds.

I shall start from what is likely to happen when borders are settled and the status quo seems assured. This state brings a sense of safety, of security, and of predictability. Its imperfections are at least known and calculable. At the same time, a settled state may easily bring a feeling of dullness, of boredom and sterility, and of there being something 'missing'. A search may then begin for some form of excitement, preferably within the bounds of 'safety', with a guaranteed return to the safe state. This is the kind of sequence that Kristeva proposes as leading to our fascination with what is horrific and our flirtations with horrifying experiences.

A search may also begin for what is missing: what is excluded here? Why does this account seem insufficient? In many ways, this is Kristeva's own search in the field of linguistics. Dissatisfied with the limitations of any line of thought that concentrates on referential meanings – on the logic, the rationality, the fixed grammatical order of language – she asks: what is missing here? Part of what is missing, she answers – to use the title of one of her books – is 'desire in language'. No theory of language is adequate, she argues, unless it accounts for the pleasure of poetry as well as for the nature of grammar.[29] A similar type of theme emerges in Kristeva's analysis of love. Women especially, she argues, feel dissatisfied with the 'tales of love' that are offered to them: tales of romance that ignore the wear and tear of everyday life, or tales of maternal love that cover only the extremes of mothers as monsters or mothers as victims. Their search is then for new discourses that will supply what they feel is missing from those currently available.

What may also happen is that the individual develops a sense of resentment and anger when the cost of maintaining the usual borders becomes too high; when the contracts they call for become too demanding, too sacrificial in style. Then the search may begin for new codes, new contracts. Foreigners, to take part of Kristeva's analysis, may question the legislative codes that restrict them; they may resist the insistence that they change, that they become invisible, and that they accept always being in an inferior position, as an 'other'.

Clearly states of order – both by their stability and their destabilization – can give rise to a variety of consequences. Fortunately, Kristeva goes on to ask: what are the specific circumstances that give rise to one degree of feeling rather than another? And what are the specific circumstances that give rise to one effect rather than another: to horror, for instance, rather than to suspicion, aggression, or a pleasurable thrill?

The nature of the specific circumstances is a large part of what I plan to unfold by considering in turn Kristeva's analyses of horror, foreignness, and love. At this point, however, it is essential to note two subpropositions contained within the general one I have given as a heading. These subpropositions are addressed to the sources of differences and similarities among people in the way they feel about any text. The two subpropositions form a somewhat uneasy combination but both are contained in Kristeva's work.

Of the two, attention to differences among members of an audience – among readers or viewers – is the minor theme. Kristeva's main proposal is that people differ in their feelings about a destabilizing event in relation to their position in society. More precisely, they differ in relation to their vested interests in the maintenance or subversion of an established order. The established class, for instance, is likely to respond to a new and 'shocking' film or novel with alarm at this sign of deterioration in the moral fibre of a society, at this potential source of corruption for the unprotected or unwary reader. In contrast, for Kristeva's 'revolutionary subject', bent on changing literary norms and on challenging bourgeois society, the dominant emotion may be a sense of freedom, joy, liberation, and exhilaration. In another version of this type of argument, Kristeva proposes that mothers may be particularly disturbed by political destabilization (may even be especially vulnerable to the appeal of fundamentalist positions) because their vulnerable position calls for the protection of a stable society, perhaps even the preservation of 'the couple'.[30] The particular argument is debatable, but I cite it as an instance of Kristeva's tendency to think of individual differences in the form of who stands to win or lose by a change in order.[31]

The second subproposition is that people are united in their feelings about a destabilizing event by virtue of a common history: a history of shared texts that inclines us to interpret and feel about what we see similarly. It is this proposal that underlies, for instance, Kristeva's interest in the way we bring to any new tale of love a knowledge of past love stories. It underlies as well her attention, in the analysis of horror, to the Judaic and Christian traditions that shape our sense of purity and of abomination.

This second proposal brings us face-to-face, however, with the second large, general concept that is a necessary part of any introduction to Kristeva. The notion of a history of texts goes well beyond its use as a way of helping to account for shared (and unshared) feelings or interpretations in the face of a novel, a painting, or a film. It is also an essential part of Kristeva's analysis of any representation. As we shall see, it is not completely separate from the first concern: Kristeva's attention to order and its maintenance or destabilization. In fact, one critical connection between one text and another lies in the way a later text criticizes or subverts the form of order represented by another. Moreover, a successful challenge calls for a knowledge of past texts. If I am to challenge, transgress, or subvert an established order, I need to have some knowledge of what that order is. I also need to have a way of making the challenge: a way that will be noticed and attended to by those upholding the established order. Refusing to speak, Kristeva argues, or speaking in a voice that is not heard, is not enough.

I begin to anticipate a little the second goal for this chapter: providing a sense of what Kristeva means by her references to 'the text of society and history'.[32] Let me take up that large and basic concept more directly and lay out the essentials.

A second pervasive concern: The text of society and history

Part of Kristeva's approach to any topic consists of outlining the historical context. Her account of poetry in language, for instance (*Revolution in Poetic Language*), considers the emergence of the novel from epic stories. Her account of *The Powers of Horror* outlines the change from Judaic to Christian views of 'impurities' and 'abominations'. Her analysis in *Strangers to Ourselves* offers descriptions of the ways in which foreigners have been regarded and regulated in biblical times, in ancient Greece, in France at the time of the French Revolution, and during contemporary times. Her analysis of love goes through the *Tales of Love* in various centuries and the images of motherhood dominant at various periods of Christianity.

What are the main points to be abstracted from Kristeva's accounts of historical contexts? I shall draw out three, stating these again in the form of propositions. The first takes the form: any text needs to be considered in the light of the texts that have preceded it. Of the three, this is the proposition that has attracted the most attention from film analysts, taken up under the label of 'intertextuality'. The second proposition is less familiar. It takes the form: placing a text historically is a way of distinguishing one text from another. This proposition comes, as Kristeva points out, from Bakhtin and is part of a set of criticisms of structuralist positions. For my analysis, its main importance lies in the way it leads on to the critical third proposal. This takes the form: the essential part of any historical placement lies in asking about the *quality* of the connection between one text and another. It is here that Kristeva contributes the concept of change in the form of 'transposition'. It is here also that she makes particular use of Bakhtin's distinction between monologic and polyphonic texts. And – most particularly – it is here that she takes Bakhtin's concept of 'Menippean discourse' and uses it as a basis for selecting 'major' works for analysis: works that criticize, mock, transgress, subvert, or replace established forms of narrative or visual order.

I shall proceed in turn through the three propositions. The terms 'text' and 'word', it may be noted, are used throughout in a generic sense. Bakhtin and Kristeva are primarily interested in the analysis of verbal productions. The term does cover, however, any form of representation – verbal or visual – and the reader interested in films might readily substitute 'film' in any place where the terms 'text' or 'word' occur.

Any text needs to be considered in the light of the texts that have preceded it

The description of this proposition may well begin with Kristeva's comments upon Bakhtin's position:

> Bakhtin was one of the first to replace the static hewing out of texts with a model where literary structure does not simply *exist* but is generated in relation to *another* structure. What allows a dynamic dimension to structuralism is his conception of 'the literary word' as an *intersection of textual surfaces* rather than as a *point* (a fixed meaning), as a dialogue among several writings: that of the writer, the addressee (or the character), and the contemporary or earlier cultural context.[33]

> Bakhtin situates the text within history and society, which are then seen as texts read by the writer, and into which he reinserts himself by rewriting them.[34]

> [T]he three dimensions or coordinates of dialogue are writing subject, addressee, and exterior texts. The word's status is thus defined *horizontally* (the word ... belongs to both writing subject and addressee) as well as *vertically* (the word in the text is oriented towards an anterior or synchronic literary corpus ...). In Bakhtin's work, these two uses, which he calls *dialogue* and *ambivalence*, are not clearly distinguished. Yet what appears as a lack of rigor is in fact an insight ...[:] any text is a mosaic of quotations; any text is the absorption and transformation of another.[35]

This kind of proposition has a powerful simplicity to it. History and society, to repeat part of the second statement, become a mosaic of texts drawn upon by the writer or the reader to produce or interpret any particular word, sentence, or story. These additional texts, moreover, do not have to be in the same medium as the specific text one is considering: books for books, for instance, or films for films. Those may be the background texts that one thinks of first. That this limitation is not intended, however, is indicated by Bakhtin's example of the 'deep generating series' drawn upon by Shakespeare. In Bakhtin's description, Shakespeare drew upon 'semantic treasures' that were created and collected through the centuries and even millennia: they lay hidden in the language, and not only in the literary language, but also in those strata of the popular language that before Shakespeare's time had not entered literature, in the diverse genres and forms of speech communication, in the forms of a mighty national culture (primarily, carnival forms) that were shaped through millennia, in theatre-spectacle genres (mystery plays, farces, and so forth), in plots whose roots go back to prehistoric antiquity, and, finally, in forms of thinking.[36]

One part of Bakhtin's proposals – the notion that 'any text is the absorption and transformation of another' – has been widely taken up. Here, for instance, are several statements describing what the term 'intertextuality' has come to mean in the world of film analysis:

> In the broadest sense, intertextual dialogism refers to the infinite and open-ended possibilities generated by all the discursive practices of a culture, the entire matrix of communicative utterances within which the artistic text is situated, and which reach the text not only through recognizable influences but also through a subtle process of dissemination.[37]

> Dialogism operates, then, within all cultural production, whether literate or non-literate, verbal or non-verbal, highbrow or lowbrow. The contemporary film artist, within this conception, becomes the orchestrator, the amplifier of the ambient messages thrown up by all the series – literary, painterly, musical, cinematic, commercial and so forth. A film like *The Band Wagon*, as Geoffrey Nowell-Smith points out (in *Narremore*, 1991: 16–18), is a virtual melting-pot of 'high' and 'low' artistic discourses, with references to ballet, folk art, Broadway, Faust, Mickey Spillane and *film noir*. This inclusive view of intertextuality would see a film like Woody Allen's *Zelig* as the site of intersection of innumerable intertexts, some specifically filmic (newsreels, archival material, home movies, television compilation films, 'witness' documentaries, cinema verité, film melodrama, psychological case-study films like *Spellbound*, 'fictive documentaries' like *F for Fake*, and more immediate fiction-film predecessors like Warren Beatty's *Reds*); others literary (the Melvillean 'anatomy'), and some broadly cultural (Yiddish theatre, Borscht-Belt Comedy). The film's originality, paradoxically, lies in the audacity of its imitation, quotation and absorption of other texts, its ironic hybridization of traditionally opposed discourses.[38]

Those two quotations are from a 1993 'vocabulary for semiotics' written by Robert Stam, Robert Burgoyne, and Sandy Flitterman-Lewis. They note as well Michael Riffaterre's 1979 definition of intertextuality, as the reader's perception of the relation between a text and all the other texts that have proceeded it. Thus the intertext of a film such as Kubrick's *The Shining* could be said to consist of all the genres to which the film refers, for example the horror film and the melodrama, but also to that class of films called literary adaptations with the attendant literary affiliates such as the Gothic novel, and extending to the entire canon of Kubrick films, Jack Nicholson films, and so forth. The intertext of a work of art, then, may be taken to include not just other artworks in the same or comparable form, but also all the 'series' within which the singular text is situated.[39]

Such broad-brushstroke backgrounds, however, are surely too gross. They are a step beyond the treatment of texts in isolation but the connections noted begin to read like the unrelated items of a shopping list. Was this really what Bakhtin or Kristeva had in mind? The answer, I propose, is 'no'. Their real concern was with specifying the quality of connections among texts, either within a defined piece of work or across them. This is the heart of what I shall extract as the second and the third propositions contained within Kristeva's analysis of connections among texts.

The historical placement of a text serves to distinguish one text from another

During the 1960s, there arose what Kristeva has described as 'a critique' of structuralism: 'a critique of Hegelian, Heideggerian, Marxian, or Freudian derivation'.[40] During this time, as Moi points out, there emerged a recognition that meaning depended upon context, and that this recognition meant facing the question: what is this 'context' that one should pay attention to? One might simply refer to 'culture', 'society', or 'history'. This, however, evades the issue: 'It does not follow ... that "context" should be understood as a unitary phenomenon, to be isolated and determined once and for all'.[41] In fact, Moi comments, the essence of Derrida's argument is that 'inscribing a specific context for a text does not *close* or *fix* the meaning of that text once and for all: there is always the possibility of reinscribing it within other contexts'.[42]

In short, one should not expect to find, for the way an utterance or a text is interpreted, any single context or any fixed and static context. Short of analysing each statement or each image within that situation in which it is used, heard, or viewed, how can one proceed? One way forward lies in a goal expressed by Bakhtin and Kristeva. This is the goal of coming up with new ways of differentiating among texts: new ways of conceptualizing the links between one text and other texts in the culture or between one part of a text and other parts of the same text. This goal is part of Kristeva's general programme for semiotics:

> One of the problems for semiotics is to replace the former, rhetorical division of genres with a *typology of texts*: that is, to define the specificity of different textual arrangements by placing them within the general text (culture) of which they are a part and which, in turn, is part of them.[43]

That same goal is also what Kristeva sees as one of Bakhtin's major achievements: his 'radical undertaking – the dynamic analysis of texts resulting in a redistribution of genres'.[44] In Kristeva's account, it was with this end in mind that Bakhtin undertook an 'entire historical inventory'[45] of written texts, and that he argued for distinctions between epic and carnivalesque traditions and for some particular divisions within the latter. To take some statements along these lines:

> Situated within the carnivalesque tradition, and constituting the yeast of the European novel, these two genres are Socratic dialogue and Menippean discourse .... Socratic dialogue did not last long, but it gave birth to several

dialogical genres, including Menippean discourse, whose origins lie also in carnivalesque folklore.[46]

Menippean discourse ... includes all genres (short stories, letters, speeches, mixtures of verse and prose) whose structural signification is to denote the writer's distance from his own and other texts.[47]

I shall come back to Menippean discourse in a moment. The points to note for now are that the term refers to a genre rather than to the original work of Menippus of Gadara (a third century BC philosopher/satirist), and that the distinction between Menippean and non-Menippean discourse is one of the distinctions that Bakhtin – and Kristeva – propose as superseding more conventional distinctions among genres.

If one sets aside conventional distinctions among genres, however, what is to take their place? What are the dimensions that Bakhtin and Kristeva now use in order to distinguish among texts? The dimensions have to do with the quality of the connection between texts. It is not enough, the argument runs, to show that texts have a history. We now need concepts that differentiate among the several ways in which a text is 'inserted' into its past or transforms it. This is the step that avoids the 'shopping list' quality of any recital of antecedents. It is the heart of the third proposition.

The essential part of any historical placement lies in asking about the quality of the connection between one text and another

We may extract from Kristeva's writings three particular ways of describing the quality of interconnections. The first is by way of 'transposition'. I note it primarily because of its relevance to that much used term 'intertextuality'. The second is by way of asking whether the move is from a monologic to a polyphonic text (the latter being a text that allows for competing voices, for contrary subtexts). The third is by way of asking whether a text displays the features of 'Menippean discourse': in particular the features of the writer being aware of his or her distance from other texts and taking a critical stance towards those other texts and the established forms of order that they represent. I shall consider in turn each of those approaches to specifying the quality of the connection.

Connection by transposition. I shall take one written statement from Kristeva and then offer a film example of what I understand to be its meaning. The statement is from the glossary of terms offered by Kristeva's translator Léon Roudiez at the start of *Desire in Language*:

> INTERTEXTUALITY (*intertextualité*). This French word was originally used by Kristeva and met with immediate success; it has since been much used and

abused on both sides of the Atlantic. The concept, however, has been generally misunderstood. It has nothing to do with matters of influence by one writer upon another, or with the sources of a literary work; it does, on the other hand, involve the components of a *textual system* such as the novel, for instance. It is defined in *La Révolution du Langage Poétique* as the transposition of one or more *systems* of signs into another, accompanied by a new articulation of the enunciative and denotative position.[48]

Where can one observe such transpositions, such shifts in meaning? I shall take a small but concrete example from *Vigil* (a New Zealand film considered in more detail in a later chapter). The example has to do with part of the rituals accompanying death. The child in the film watches her father being given a religious burial. His body is returned to the earth; his soul is commended to God; the language is one of 'offering to God'. The child then makes her own respectful offering. She plants a tree near the site where her father fell, and she keeps watch (her 'vigil') over that site, still with the conviction that 'God cares', that God will notice what she offers. The next offering she makes has a complete shift in quality. With a taunting cry – 'Beans to God!' – and a jig that is the opposite of her previously subdued respect, she hurls towards the sky the remnants of her plate of beans. God does not care, a newcomer has argued. She has accepted his argument and makes a new derisory offering that signals her change of heart. Without the previous offerings, however, this new action would lose a great deal of its meaning. The earlier offerings to God have now been given a change of key: they have been transposed from one into another.

Shifts from monological to polyphonic texts. The example taken from *Vigil* is within a film rather than across films. It might well qualify for what Genette has termed 'intratextuality' as against 'transtextuality'.[49] At first glance this way of distinguishing one kind of connection among images from another is appealing. Kristeva, however, uses the term 'intertextuality' to refer to transpositions both within and across novels. More seriously, this way of differentiating one form of interconnection from another is not the primary intention of either Bakhtin or Kristeva (this way of proceeding would, in effect, return one to conventional distinctions).

What, then, is the more dynamic alternative? One that stands out comes from Bakhtin's distinction between 'direct' or 'object-oriented' words and 'ambivalent' words. The former 'refer back to the object':[50] they have 'direct, objective meaning'.[51] In the latter, 'the writer can use another's word, giving it new meaning while retaining the meaning it already had'.[52] Parody is one example; 'polemical confessions' are another.[53] The dimension at stake is the extent to which a word is used with a recognition of its having more than a direct, denotative meaning.

The same type of dimension appears again in Bakhtin's distinction between 'monological' and 'polyphonic' texts. 'Monological' texts are those that assert a single truth (authoritative Bibles provide one example;

science textbooks which assert a single truth without any indication that a contrary view is possible provide another). Polyphonic texts contain within themselves two or more voices, two or more perspectives. Moreover, these voices or perspectives 'contest' or compete with one another. It is not enough for two or more voices to be set beside one another, as in a film such as *Rashomon*, where three perspectives of the same event are presented in sequence. In a polyphonic text, two or more voices compete with one another, or become interwoven with one another. There is, one might say, 'a text' and a 'subtext', but they must compete with one another.

The novel, for Bakhtin, is the prime text for the analysis of such polyphony.[54] It is par excellence the 'genre in which ambivalent words appear'.[55] The concept again is by now not unfamiliar. Without it, for instance, there could not be analyses of novels for the hidden theme, or of films for the way they might be read 'against the grain'. Only the accepted presence of polyphony makes such analyses possible.

Menippean discourse. Is the competing presence of two or more voices – and the reflection of one upon the other or upon itself – sufficient to distinguish one text from another? Or one relationship between a text and its culture from another? Not quite, it seems. One needs to ask as well about the social position of one text in relation to another. Is a novel, for instance, of the type claimed by the bourgeoisie as its own, or is it 'on the fringe of official culture'?[56] Is it respectful of traditional forms, even while it offers changes, or does it look upon traditions with scorn and either ignore them or happily trample upon them?

Kristeva offers a list of several features for novels in the Menippean genre (Joyce, Kafka, and Bataille are among those she regards as producing modern works in this category). Some of these have to do with the way the narrative blends the real and the unreal:

> Phantasmagoria and an often mystical symbolism fuse with macabre naturalism. Adventures unfold in brothels, robbers' dens, taverns, fairgrounds, and prisons, among erotic orgies and during sacred worship .... Elements of the fantastic, which never appear in epic or tragic works, crop forth .... Pathological states of the soul, such as madness, split personalities, daydreams, dreams, and death become part of the narrative.[57]

A further set of features has to do with the position taken towards earlier forms, earlier uses of words:

> They often appear as an exploration of language and writing .... Its language seems fascinated with the 'double' (with its own activity) as well as with what it denotes.[58]

It frees speech from historical constraints .... The word ... becomes free from supposed 'values' .... The 'inopportune' expression, with its cynical frankness, its desecration of the sacred, and its attack on etiquettes, is quite characteristic.[59]

Finally, a third set of characteristics has to do with the connection between the written text and the politics of the day:

> [T]hrough the status of its words, it is politically and socially disturbing: it is a kind of political journalism of its time. Its discourse exteriorizes political and ideological conflicts of the moment. The dialogism of its words is practical philosophy doing battle against idealism and religious metaphysics, against the epic. It constitutes the social and political thought of an era fighting against theology, against law.[60]

I have given these comments on Menippean discourse a fair amount of space. That is in part because they help account for Kristeva's selection of some novels as more important than others. A 'major' writer, in her view, should make major breaks with earlier forms, should show a visible concern with the activity of language and not be restricted to its surface referents, should use words or narrative structures in ways that are socially and politically disturbing, and should be 'on the fringe of official culture'.[61] It is also because these statements emphasize again the critical point that what matters is not the simple presence of connections within texts or across texts but the *quality* of the connection, with a particular importance given to connections that undo or subvert an established order in one way or another.

Proximal history

In addition to past texts, texts are related to present circumstances. (It would be surprising if a text were connected only to the past.) The challenge begins when one asks: how is any text related to the present?

To bring out this connection, let me first note that Menippean discourse involves a relationship to both past and present. The concept tells us that a text is related to what precedes it and surrounds it in some specific ways: ways that have primarily to do with the relationship of the new text to (a) the forms of textual order that precede it or are part of its time, and (b) the general society of which all these texts are a part. Menippean discourse, for instance, displays an awareness of traditional forms and deliberately disrupts them (by its language, for example, or by its narrative – e.g. the setting in brothels, robbers' dens, etc.). Menippean discourse also displays a political attitude towards the people who are in power and who form a set of potential readers or addressees. It mocks them, it attacks their etiquettes, and it does not wish to be taken up by them.

Are there some further ways by which the present circumstances come into play? To bring these out, I shall turn to Kristeva's concept of productivity: a concept involving a changing relationship between the speaker and the text, and also between the speaker and the addressee. The term 'productivity' is in general a means of stepping away from the view of the world as based upon fixed structures and unchanging differences. Rosalind Coward and John Ellis comment that the overall sense of the term is conveyed by the social *productivity* of the world, the fact that it is constituted of complex relations that are in constant flux, disappears beneath a system of essences. The real is the immediately visible, and this visible does not appear to be a form of representation. Such is the work of myth.[62]

More timely, the concept for Kristeva implies links between the speaker and the text, and between the speaker and the addressee. Suppose we begin with the relationship between the speaker/writer and what is said. Language, the argument runs, does not exist outside of a subject:

> [L]anguage does not exist outside the *discourse of a subject* .... The subject *is* not, he makes and unmakes himself in a complex topology where the other and his discourse are included .... The subject and meaning are not, they are produced in the *discursive* work .... It is not a production as defined by generative grammar – which doesn't produce anything at all itself (for it doesn't question the subject and meaning) .... The production of meaning is instead an actual production that traverses the surface of the *uttered* discourse, and that engenders in the *enunciation* ...[;] a particular meaning with a particular subject.[63]

This understanding of meaning Kristeva attributes partly to Roman Jakobson, in particular his concept of 'shifters'. Shifters such as *here*, *there*, *this*, or *that* set a context, but their meaning is also a product of the context.[64] A broader attribution is to the evidence from psychoanalysis of the unconscious and its logic, and of the ways in which meanings are altered in the course of 'dreamwork':

> From then on, it became difficult to talk about a subject without following the various configurations revealed by the different relations between subjects and their discourse.[65]

The speaker and the text, however, do not exist except in relationship also to the addressee. To repeat part of an earlier quotation and to add to it:

> The subject ... makes and remakes himself in a complex topology where the other and his discourse are included. One cannot possibly talk about the *meaning* of a discourse without taking this topology into account.[66]

The very term 'topology' – 'the study of spaces and forms' – is used by Kristeva to mark 'the discursive space of the subject with respect to the other and to discourses'.[67] More fully:

> The story, like Benveniste's concept of 'discourse' itself, presupposes an intervention by the speaker within the narrative as well as an orientation toward the other .... By the very act of narrating, the subject of narration addresses an

other; narration is structured in relation to this other. (On the strength of such a communication, Francis Ponge offers his own variation of 'I think therefore I am': 'I speak and you hear me, therefore we are'.)[68]

More concretely, what needs to be considered as part of any productivity is the way in which what is produced fits with what the addressee expects and finds understandable. Kristeva offers an example from music:

> The degree of communicability of a particular musical text (that is, its possibility of reaching the addressee) would depend upon its resemblance to a difference from the musical code of his time. In monolithic societies, like primitive societies, musical 'creation' requires strict obedience to the rules of the musical code, which is considered as a given and as sacred. Conversely, the so-called *classical* type of music testifies to a tendency toward variation, so that each musical text invented its own laws and did not obey more of the common 'language'. This is the famous loss of 'universality' attributed to Beethoven. For such a musical text to break off ties with common musical language it had to be organized on the inside as a regulated system. Hence the reason for the exact repetition of parts of the melody, which traced the coordinates of a musical oeuvre as a particular system in and of itself, which were different, for example, in Bach and succeeding composers.[69]

Two questions stand out when one reads such comments upon the necessarily dynamic connection between speaker and addressee. One takes the form: what is the nature of the relationship between the two? The other asks: where is there the attention one would expect to the materialist/economic/social circumstances of this relationship?

The nature of the link between speaker and addressee

Two possibilities are suggested by Kristeva. One has to do with the extent to which the speaker 'makes sense to' or can be heard by the addressee (the comments on music are an example of this). The other has to do with the extent to which what is said is welcomed or rejected (the bourgeoisie, for instance, may embrace a novel as 'their own' or consign it 'to the fringe of official culture').

The addressee, however, is unlikely to be in any fixed position to the speaker, or for that matter, to be a single person. Among those relationships and among those addressees, there surely needs to be room for addressees who are in a position to make official judgements not only about what is produced but also about whether it is produced at all. Giotto, to take one of Kristeva's examples of a change in representational order, needed the church's approval in order to gain the spaces and the support he required. The presence of this power relationship is one that Kristeva alludes to in her comments upon the Medieval Church's attitude to painting in general:

Western painting professed to serve Catholic theology while betraying it at the same time .... Several theoretical statements bear witness to high spiritual leaders' distrust of painting, which they perceive as 'not elevated enough' spiritually, if not simply 'burlesque'.[70]

Such comments are not restricted to the analysis of Giotto's painting. The novel, Kristeva notes, was also suspect to others who were in the social position of judges and controllers:

[T]he novel has been considered as an inferior genre (by neoclassicism and other similar regimes) or as subversive (I have in mind the major writers of polyphonic novels over many centuries – Rabelais, Swift, Sade, Lautréamont, Kafka, and Bataille – to mention only those who have always been and still remain on the fringe of official culture).[71]

The materialist circumstances attending moments of production

Kristeva is especially attracted to the broad sweep of circumstances. To anchor my comment again in the analysis of Giotto's painting, it is the broad sweep of changes in the use of colour that lead her to favour a statement by Matisse:

When the means of expression have become so refined, so attenuated that their power of expression wears thin, it is necessary to return to *the essential principles which made human language* .... Pictures which have become refinements, subtle gradations, dissolutions without energy, call for beautiful *blues, reds, yellows* – matters to stir *sensual depths in man*.[72]

Less prominent in Kristeva's analysis is attention to the circumstances that are closer to the moment. She does note, for instance, that Giotto's contemporaries did not follow his lead. For them, the need to break through contemporary restrictions was either not felt at all or was restrained by other considerations. Kristeva also makes reference to the importance of the circumstances of the time. She notes with approval, for instance, 'Autal's detailed analysis of the economic and ideological foundations of the pictorial experience examined here'. She then sets it aside, however:

I would simply emphasize that one cannot understand such practice without taking its socioeconomic foundations into account, nor can one understand it if one chooses to reduce it only to these foundations, thereby bypassing the signifying economy of the subject involved.[73]

Taking account of socioeconomic conditions, however, does not necessarily mean that one regards these circumstances as all that matters. Perhaps Kristeva's relative lack of attention comes about because she perceives a closer look at the socioeconomic circumstances as part of the 'sociology' of texts. [74] In addition, the texts she takes as examples – great works of writing or painting – are from periods from which the people involved are no longer accessible for comment. For whatever reason, one does not find within Kristeva's analyses accounts of the immediate circumstances surrounding the emergence of a text. It is not that she is unsympathetic. She would not otherwise merit from Coward and Ellis the comment that she represents 'the real beginning of a materialist theory of language, signification, and ideology'.[75]

If I follow her lead, however, and ask her own question – what is missing here? – then one answer needs to be in the form of accounts of the ways in which a text comes to emerge from its immediate or proximal history, comes to take the particular shape that it does and to have the impact that it does. What would such accounts look like?

To start with, one would expect them to take into consideration the variety of addressees that may be involved and the several relationships in which they and the speaker may become engaged. In addition, one would expect these accounts to include some consideration of competing forces. Discursive spaces that contain the orientations of narrators and addressees towards one another may make it sound as if the relationships between the two were eventually neutral. That this is not what Kristeva has in mind is indicated by Kristeva's general references to the ways in which the emergence of a new text or a new mode of thinking reflect the changing relative strengths of competing forces. A creative push towards undoing an established order, for instance, competes with some kind of code or ideology that holds down this push. The likelihood of the experience of horror, for instance, reflects the relative strengths of the pull towards the excitement of the abject and of the rituals that restrict, surround, and contain one's encounters with what is unsettling. The extent to which being a foreigner or encountering foreigners is a cause for unease stems in part from the relative strengths of competing ideologies: the universalist ethos 'love your neighbour as yourself' and the particularist ethos 'first look after your own'. The extent to which narratives and experiences of love are found satisfying reflects the extent to which they meet the demands for new roles in new circumstances. This argument of tension from competing codes or powers will be unfolded in later chapters, but for now, here is one example of it:

> In the Middle Ages, Menippean tendencies were held in check by the authority of the religious text; in the bourgeois era, they were contained by the absolutism of individuals and things. Only modernity – when freed of 'God' – releases the Menippean form of the novel.[76]

The notion of competing influences represents for film theorists an attractive way of specifying how it is that a new text comes to have the particular shape and impact that it does. There are, for instance, several authors who have been concerned with the impact of the nature of the film and television industry upon what is produced, and with the 'negotiations' among several parties that shape the form of what finally emerges.[77] These particular circumstances receive less attention from Kristeva than does the competition of larger codes or ideologies. They are, however, part of Kristeva's argument.

The reader, then, may expect to find, in the subsequent chapters, two general lines of analysis. One will be an examination of the ways in which Kristeva's analyses of forms of order and the text of society/history prompt particular ways of reading a set of films: prompt questions especially about the nature of the narrative, its affective impact, and the emergence of the text. The other will be a closer look at the emergence of the text in terms of the circumstances surrounding its production and distribution.

With this much introduction, let us see, then, in the next chapter, how Kristeva's baseline concepts, and the expansions upon these, are worked out in the course of analysing a specific experience – horror – and a specific product of the New Zealand film industry: Alison Maclean's short film *Kitchen Sink*.

Notes

1. Julia Kristeva (1980) *Desire in language: A semiotic approach to literature and art*. New York: Columbia University Press, p. ix.
2. John Lechte offers an account in terms of a 'trajectory': John Lechte (1990) *Julia Kristeva*. London: Routledge. Roudiez (1980) offers a shorter and more personalized story of Kristeva's life and work in his introduction to *Desire in language*: Léon Roudiez (1980) 'Introduction'. In J. Kristeva *Desire in language: A semiotic approach to literature and art*. New York: Columbia University Press. Elizabeth Grosz places much of Kristeva's earlier work in the historical context of other changes in European thought: Elizabeth Grosz (1989) *Sexual subversions: Three French feminists*. Sydney: Allen and Unwin.
3. For one example of a negative position, an example to be drawn upon in this chapter, see Nancy Fraser and Sandra Lee Bartky (Eds) (1992) *Revaluing French feminism: Critical essays on difference, agency, & culture*. Bloomington: Indiana University Press.
4. Kristeva (1980, p.3).
5. Toril Moi (1985) *Sexual/textual politics*. London: Methuen.
6. Cited by Roudiez (1980, p.1).
7. Ibid., p.12.
8. Cited in Toril Moi (Ed.) (1986) *The Kristeva reader*. Oxford: Basil Blackwell, p.150.
9. Moi (1985, p.151).
10. Kristeva (1980, p.223).
11. Fraser and Lee Bartky (1992, p.189).
12. Kristeva's major reference is to Freud's 1919 essay on 'The Uncanny' (*Das Unheimliche*). Sigmund Freud (1964) 'The uncanny'. In J. Strachey (Ed.) *The Standard edition of the complete psychological works of Sigmund Freud*, vol. 18. London: Hogarth Press. See Julia Kristeva (1991a) *Strangers to ourselves*. New York: Columbia University Press, pp.182–195.
13. For an historical analysis of art that emphasizes changes in the social order, see, for example, Arnold Hauser (1982) *The sociology of art*. London: Routledge & Kegan Paul. Translated by Kenneth J. Northcott. For an example from film analysis, see Robin Wood's linking of the emergence of representations which emphasize the other as 'aliens' with

the extent to which societies engage in a degree of repression beyond what is needed to enable us to live with others: Robin Wood (1985) 'An introduction to the American horror film'. In B. Nichols (Ed.) *Movies and methods*, vol. 2. Berkeley: University of California Press.
14. Fraser and Lee Bartky (1992, p.177 and p.179).
15. bid., p.189.
16. Moi (1985, p.171).
17. Grosz (1989, p.54).
18. The dichotomies noted as of interest to Cixous are cited by Moi (1985, p.104). For Rosaldo's argument, see Michelle Rosaldo (1974) 'Women, culture and society: A theoretical overview'. In M.Z. Rosaldo and L. Lamphere (Eds.) *Women, culture and society*. Stanford: Stanford University Press.
19. Moi points to the related argument by Derrida that no term has meaning in itself. The term 'feminine', for instance, receives its meaning from its opposite, 'masculine'. More generally, 'meaning is never truly present, but is only constructed through the potentially endless process of referring to other, absent signifiers' (Derrida's concept of *differance*) (Moi, 1986, p.106).
20. For a general discussion of assumptions exemplified by '*cogito ergo sum*', see especially Grosz (1989). Grosz adds further comparisons between Kristeva and Lacan in Elizabeth Grosz (1990) *Jacques Lacan: A feminist introduction*. Sydney: Allen and Unwin.
21. The term 'semiotic' may benefit from a brief note. Where Lacan uses the 'imaginary' as an opposition to the 'symbolic', Kristeva uses the term 'semiotic'. Terry Eagleton's description is the most helpful:

   She means by this a pattern or play of forces that we can detect inside language ... [T]he child ... does not yet have access to language ... but we can imagine its body as criss-crossed by a flow of 'pulsions' or drives which are at this point relatively unorganized. This rhythmic pattern can be seen as a form of language, although it is not yet meaningful. For language as such to happen, this heterogeneous flow must be as it were chopped up, articulated into stable terms, so as that in entering the symbolic order this 'semiotic' process is repressed. The repression, however, is not total; for the semiotic can still be discerned as a kind of pulsional pressure within language itself, in tone, rhythm, the bodily or material qualities of language, but also in contradiction, meaninglessness, disruption, silence and absence. The semiotic is the 'other' of language which is nonetheless intimately entwined with it. Terry Eagleton (1983) *Literary theory*. Oxford: Blackwell, p.188.
22. Grosz (1989, p.42).
23. Kristeva (1980, p.24)
24. Ibid., p.24, final emphasis added.
25. Ibid., p.1.
26. Ibid., p.viii, emphasis in original.
27. The quotation is from Kristeva's essay, 'System and the speaking subject', reprinted in Thomas Sebeok (Ed.) (1975) *The tell-tale sign: A survey of semiotics*. Lisse, Netherlands: The Peter de Ridder Press, p.55.
28. Fraser and Lee Bartky (1992, p.156).
29. This argument is an essential part of Julia Kristeva's (1984) *Revolution in poetic language* (New York: Columbia University Press), and of *Desire in language* (Kristeva, 1980).
30. See, for instance, Julia Kristeva (1987b) *Tales of love*. New York: Columbia University Press, p.227, or Julia Kristeva (1993) *Nations without nationalism*. New York: Columbia University Press, p.35.
31. I do not wish to imply that the potential variety of emotions in the face of destabilization is the only possible source of Kristeva's interest in 'affect'. Jacqueline Rose suggests some further factors (Jacqueline Rose (1986) *Sexuality in the field of vision*. London: Verso). One is Kristeva's interest in questions of identity: an interest Rose sees as prompting the turn to psychoanalysis (p.150). The other is the particular influence of the school of

psychoanalysis with which Kristeva trained. This school, one that broke from Lacan in 1964, included Alan Green, who placed a strong emphasis on the concept of 'affect', in opposition to Lacan's emphasis on representation and linguistic signs (p.152).
32. The phrase 'text of society and history' is from the essay on 'The bounded text' in *Desire in language* (Kristeva, 1980, p.37).
33. 'Word, dialogue, and novel' in *Desire in language* (Kristeva, 1980, pp.64–65, emphasis in original).
34. Ibid., p.65.
35. Ibid., p.66, emphasis in original.
36. Bakhtin cited in: Robert Stam, Robert Burgoyne, and Sandy Flitterman-Lewis (1992) *New vocabularies in film semiotics: Structuralism, post-structuralism and beyond.* London: Routledge, p.205.
37. Stam et al. (1992, p.204).
38. Ibid., pp.205–206.
39. Ibid., p.204.
40. Kristeva (1980, p.vii).
41. Moi (1985, p.155).
42. Ibid., p.155, emphasis in original.
43. Kristeva (1980, p.36, emphasis in original).
44. Kristeva (1980, p.76).
45. Ibid., p.86.
46. Ibid., pp.80–81.
47. Ibid., p.83.
48. Roudiez (1980, p.15). Kristeva introduced at the same time a phrase that has fortunately not been taken up: 'the ideologeme of the sign'. For those who are curious: 'The concept of text as ideologeme determines the very procedure of a semiotics that, by studying the text as intertextuality, considers it as such within (the text of) society and history. The ideologeme of a text is the focus where knowing rationality grasps the transformation of *utterances* (to which the text is irreducible) into a totality (the text) as well as the insertions of this totality into the historical and social text' (Kristeva, 1980, p.37, emphasis in original).
49. Cited by Stam et al. (1992, p.206).
50. Kristeva (1980, p.72).
51. Ibid., p.73.
52. Ibid., p.73.
53. Ibid., p.73.
54. This is one point of distinction between Kristeva and Bakhtin. For Kristeva (1980, p.74), the notion of univocity ... or of the denotative object-oriented word, cannot withstand psychoanalytic or semantic analysis of language .... Not withstanding Bakhtin and Benveniste, dialogism appears on the level of the Bakhtinian denotative word ... as well as on the level of the 'story' in Benveniste. ... [It is] a principle of every enunciation .... By the very act of narrating, the subject of narration addresses an other; narration is structured in relation to this other[.]
55. Kristeva (1980, p.73).
56. Ibid., p.86.
57. Ibid., pp.82–83.
58. Ibid., p.83.
59. Ibid., pp.82–83.
60. Ibid., pp.84–85.
61. Ibid., p.86.
62. Rosalind Coward and John Ellis (1977) *Language and materialism.* London: Routledge & Kegan Paul, p.27. The reference to myth is to the work of Barthes and his view of myths as 'forms of representation that naturalise certain meanings, externalise the present state of the world, in the interests of the bourgeois class' (ibid., p.26).

63. Ibid., p.274, emphasis in original.
64. Ibid., p.275.
65. Ibid., p.274.
66. Ibid., pp.274–275, emphasis in original.
67. Ibid., p.339.
68. Kristeva (1980, p.74).
69. Kristeva (1989, p.310).
70. 'Giotto's joy', in Kristeva (1980, p.223).
71. Kristeva (1980, p.87).
72. Matisse, cited in 'Giotto's joy' (Kristeva, 1980, p.221, emphasis in original). In this essay, Kristeva refers also to Marcellin Pleynet's analysis of Matisse (Pleynet was one of the group to visit China in 1974 – along with Barthes, Kristeva, and Sollers): an analysis that links the use of colour to infantile eroticism and is related to Kristeva's argument that colour 'escapes censorship' (ibid., p.219).
73. Ibid., p.233.
74. In, for example, her study of Giotto's Joy, Kristeva is not indifferent to the role of economic/materialist aspects but considers them less interesting: 'this sociological aspect, however important it may be to the history of painting, shall not concern me here' (ibid., p.211).
75. Coward and Ellis (1977, p.152).
76. Kristeva (1980, p.85).
77. E.g. John Ellis (1982) *Visible fictions: Cinema, television, video*. London: Routledge & Kegan Paul, or Tania Modleski (1982) *Loving with a vengeance*. New York: Methuen, for the industry; Christine Gledhill (1988) 'Pleasurable negotiations'. In E.D. Pribram (Ed.) *Female spectators: Looking at film and television*. London: Verso, or Stephen (1985) for the latter.

Chapter 2

HORROR – BASIC CONCEPTS: THE ABJECT AND ITS VARIETIES

In essence, Kristeva offers a two-part argument. The first is that horror resides in threats to the boundaries that ordinarily regulate the social order: boundaries, for instance, between the living and the dead, human and animal, human and alien, male and female. The experience of these threats is the heart of our encounters with 'the abject': with that which 'disturbs identity, system, order ... does not respect borders, positions, rules'.[1]

The second part of the argument is that all threats to boundaries cannot result in an equal sense of horror. That leads to the proposal that there are varieties of the abject, differing in the way and in the degree to which they evoke horror. The distinctions have to do with the abject without as against within the body, with the abject that is recognizable as against the abject which presents with a clean, false face, and with the abject in the form both of the collapse of differences between male and female and of reminders of some particular differences between them. A final special form of the abject has to do with the association with motherhood.

The general concept of the abject, and the distinctions among its varieties, provide a base for asking how horror films come to evoke the feelings that they do. As a particular example, I shall take a short film, Alison Maclean's *Kitchen Sink*: the first selection from the New Zealand set. A brief introduction to the film will open the chapter, to be followed by analyses of the abject and its varieties that interweave Kristeva's proposals with aspects of the film. In effect, the film acts as a base for concretizing and explicating Kristeva's proposals. In turn, Kristeva's proposals serve as a base for understanding what it is about this film that has earned it the reputation of being particularly 'horrific'.

Introducing *Kitchen Sink*

Kitchen Sink was produced in 1989 and is Alison Maclean's fourth short film. The producer was Bridget Ikin, with funding from the New Zealand

Film Commission. The film premiered in competition at Cannes in 1989, and has won awards at film festivals worldwide. In a phrase that conveys some sense of its style and place in history, the *Village Voice* described it as 'a horror fantasy worthy of Mary Shelley'.[2]

Kitchen Sink has become a cult film amongst aficionados of horror. It is not likely, however, to be familiar to a wide audience, and a brief summary will be in order. The fourteen-minute story begins with a woman washing the dishes in her suburban kitchen sink. With all else clean, she notices a hair-like thread extending from the drain and proceeds to remove it. As she continues to pull, the thread becomes thicker and eventually a mass appears: slimy, hair-covered, possibly foetus-like. Without much expression – perhaps a slight disgust – she places it in a plastic bag and puts it in the rubbish bin.

Seemingly regretting her action, she subsequently removes the thing from the bin, places it in her bathtub and turns on the tap. She turns away to answer the telephone. On her return to the bathroom, she finds that the tub is about to overflow and that the being has grown to the size and shape of a full-grown man. She drags this male shape to her bedroom and begins to groom it, shaving off the hair that covers it completely. She then places the dead or sleeping being – now with a surface of visible skin – in her bed.

After a night spent next to the immobile 'monster', she again places it in a disposal bag. The being then wakes up (or comes to life) and begins to choke. The woman, after a slight hesitation, slices open the bag and lets the being out. A scene of aggression and reconciliation is then played out with the two finally embracing. During the embrace, the woman discovers a hair protruding from the being's back, which she begins to pull. The being recoils with a scream, its facial features seemingly being drawn tight. The spectator is left with a final image of the hair being drawn endlessly up through the skin.

The film is presented in black and white, in a style that has some of the apparent roughness of a low-budget documentary or a 'home movie'. It is also largely silent. The woman speaks to a child at the door and to some adult when she answers the phone, but she never speaks to the creature. Apart from the time when it makes choking sounds, the creature is also silent, and without expression, except for the Munch-like scream at the end. The woman also varies relatively little in her facial expression, contributing to a pervasive quality of emotional flatness or ordinariness that makes the film all the more eerie.

The abject, borders, and images of pollution

What concepts does Kristeva offer that may help account for the impact of films such as *Kitchen Sink*? I shall start with the concept of the abject.

To be noted first is that the concept of the abject draws upon Kristeva's distinction between two worlds, states of being, or forms of experience. One of these is fluid, suffused with feeling, and attuned to the physical, to music, and – to the extent that it is not wordless – to the rhythm of speech and the ambiguities of poetry. The other (the symbolic rather than the semiotic) is more conventionally ordered. Entered through language (through its syntax rather than its rhythm) the 'symbolic order' is where the individual learns 'a system of signs ... organized into logico-syntactic structures whose aim is to accredit social communication as exchange purified of pleasure'. Acquired also is a way of speaking and thinking which 'involves an increasingly logical, positive, and "scientific" form of communication that is stripped of all stylistic, rhythmic and poetic ambiguities'.[3]

In the course of human life, the semiotic precedes the symbolic, but is never completely overridden by it. Its being completely superseded would, in fact, face the individual with a world of unrelieved logic, control, system, and technocracy. Like Lacan in his distinction between the imaginary and the symbolic,[4] Kristeva thinks in terms of a progression. Unlike Lacan, however, she insists upon the continued life and value of the semiotic.

For Kristeva, the progression to the symbolic order and the need for maintained contact with the semiotic contribute to the inherent instability of the imposed symbolic, paternal order. 'Language, and thus sociality, are defined by boundaries admitting of upheaval, dissolution, and transformation'.[5] Life becomes like 'dancing on a volcano':[6] a state where the carefully constructed borders between the meanings of male and female, human and animal, living and dead, clean and unclean, self and other, are continually liable to collapse.

What Kristeva terms 'abject' is, then, first of all that which threatens boundaries. The abject 'is neither subject nor object'.[7] It 'draws me towards the place where meaning collapses'.[8] 'The abject ... confronts us ... with those fragile states wherein man strays on the territories of *animal*.'[9] In short, the abject is everything that threatens the collapse of order by threatening the collapse of meaning and the annihilation of the self. Corpses provide one specific example:

> In that compelling, raw, insolent thing in the morgue's full sunlight, in that thing that no longer matches and therefore no longer signifies anything, I behold the breaking down of a world that has erased its borders .... The corpse, seen without God and outside of science, is the utmost of abjection. It is death infecting life. Abject.[10]

How do these first proposals apply to *Kitchen Sink?* They prompt us, I propose, to go back to the film to locate the unstable borders, the areas of ambiguity. Interestingly, they turn out to be of four kinds: the borders between living and dead, human and nonhuman, clean and unclean, love and destruction. Part of the horror, then, stems from the combined presence of all four types of threat.

To start with, the monster seems to waver between life and death. It seems to be alive at the moment of its 'birth' up through the suburban kitchen sink. At this point, it hops, and quivers. Later, however, it seems to be lifeless. The woman in fact seems so assured of its stillborn status that she discards it into the rubbish bin. Its rapid change in the bath from a foetus to the size of a full-grown man, however, leaves one unsure of its state.

The spectator's state of wary anticipation is added to by a second ambiguity. The monster in *Kitchen Sink* is not clearly human or nonhuman. Once it is full-size and cleaned up, it has the general appearance of a human (it is at least now totally without hair). However, its place of birth, manner of growth and initial appearance (it seems either very premature or disabled: the eyes bulge, the legs are abnormally long and scrawny) leave room for question. The uncertainty is all the more marked because the woman treats it both as a human that may be loved or desired, and as an object that may be discarded at will.

The border between clean and unclean is the third to be transgressed, initially by the emergence of 'filth' from a presumably sterile site – a suburban, newly cleansed, kitchen sink. This border is further transgressed in the bath, another clean site. Here also, horror comes from the image of the woman having to put her 'clean' and vulnerable arm into the dirtied bath water to pull the plug, as the bath has begun to overflow. Finally, the monster, once it has become clean, i.e. groomed and shaven, does not keep its clean image. Its internal filth is revealed at the end with the discovery of the hair on its back and the implication that, within it, only filth is to be found.

The fourth and last border to be noted for *Kitchen Sink* is that between caring (or loving) and destroying. The woman vacillates between the two. The man also shifts ground: his embrace is at one time loving and at another life-threatening. For most of the film, the greater power is in the woman's hands. The use that either party will make of their closeness to the other, however, is a major source of uncertainty and threat, especially since one of the major barriers to destruction (the sense that this is a creature like oneself) is absent: certainly so for the woman, and possibly so for the man.

In effect, *Kitchen Sink* brings out the way in which the accumulated transgression of several kinds of border is related to the spectator's sense of horror. Any horror film, Barbara Creed points out, involves a violation of borders:

> [T]he concept of a border is central to the construction of the monstrous in the horror film .... Although the specific nature of the border changes from film to film, the function of the monstrous remains the same – to bring about an

encounter between the symbolic order and that which threatens its stability. In some horror films the monstrous is produced at the border between human and inhuman, man and beast (*Dr. Jekyll and Mr. Hyde*, *Creature from the Black Lagoon*, *King Kong*); in others, the border is between the normal and the supernatural, good and evil (*Carrie*, *The Exorcist*, *The Omen*, *Rosemary's Baby*); or the monstrous is produced at the border which separates those who take up their proper gender roles from those who do not (*Psycho*, *Dressed to Kill*, *Reflection of Fear*); or the border is between normal and abnormal sexual desire (*Cruising*, *The Hunger*, *Cat People*).[11]

The concept of a border applies also to the appearance of living corpses (zombies), vampires (bodies without souls), or werewolves (both human and animal). Each is a figure that threatens or signifies a collapse of boundaries, or that reminds us of the fragility of the boundaries which regulate social life and our sense of meaning or identity. What is distinctive to *Kitchen Sink*, however, is the way in which one transgression to the usual separation of opposites, one ambiguity, is laid upon another.

Images of pollution

Reminders of borders and their fragility are certainly powerful sources of horror. By themselves, however, they provide an insufficient account. In Kristeva's analysis, the abject covers as well all images of pollution. Kristeva's opening discussion of abjection has in fact the heading 'the improper/unclean', using the French term *propre* to refer to both what is 'clean' and what is 'proper' or 'correct'.[12] *Kitchen Sink* neatly illustrates Kristeva's argument. The slime, the dirt, the implication of rotting filth in the depths of the drain, together with the extreme hair covering on something which should be innocent, a newborn, are all images of pollution contributing to the spectator's sense of horror.

Once again, this type of point need not be restricted to *Kitchen Sink*. Horror films in general involve images of pollution. To take some specific examples where images of pollution are especially salient, and to illustrate the variety of forms that these images (not present in *Kitchen Sink*) may take, the monsters in the *Aliens* series[13] shower with slime the surfaces that humans touch. The monsters' deaths involve a liberal scattering of blood and flesh. Their 'blood' is a corrosive acid that blinds; the cocoons in which they wrap their captured humans (*Aliens*) are webby secretions, dirty grey rather than the innocent white of silk. Worse still, pollution in horror films may reach into places where it should not occur. The act of love leaves disease in its wake (*Dressed to Kill*). Blood bursts forth or, worse still, is sucked out of one body into another (the hero in *Dance of the Vampire*, for instance, is sucked completely dry by the person whom he loves). Flesh contaminates by touch or – still more horrifying – by taking the other's flesh into one's own body, as the cannibalistic neighbours do in *Night of the Living Dead*. In short, to take a second comment from Creed:

> The horror film abounds in images of abjection, foremost of which is the corpse, whole or mutilated, followed by an army of bodily wastes such as blood, vomit, saliva, sweat, tears and putrefying flesh.[14]

In comparison with such images, the suggestions of pollution in *Kitchen Sink* are subtle. All the more reason then to turn to a further part of what Kristeva proposes in order to understand why the film is disturbing.

Varieties of the abject

I began by saying that the abject has been defined as that which 'disturbs identity, system, order', which 'does not respect borders, positions, rules'.[15] That statement might be made, however, with reference to many forms of satire or comedy. It also does not enable us to say whether the emotion that results will be one of horror or one of panic, suspicion, aggression, amazement, or amusement.

The concept of accompanying images of pollution is a first, and a major step, towards such specification. A second step is taken with Kristeva's proposal that there are several varieties of the abject, that what is abject may take many forms. From Kristeva's discussion, I shall abstract several distinctions among the phenomena that fall within the category of abject. These distinctions serve two purposes. They provide a first step towards differentiation (the concept is otherwise too general to be fully useful). They also bring out additional features of horror films, adding to our understanding of their impact and of what they share with one another. Again, *Kitchen Sink* will serve as a primary base, supplemented where needed by references to some other horror films.

A first distinction: The abject without and within

Kristeva's first distinction is between the abject that is within the body and the abject that is outside it:

> Excrement and its equivalents (decay, infection, disease, corpse etc.) stand for the danger to identity that comes from without: the ego threatened by the non-ego, society threatened by its outside, life by death.[16]

In contrast, cancerous growths and – in some circumstances – pregnancy, represent danger within. In pregnancy, for example:

Cells fuse, split, and proliferate; volumes grow, tissues stretch, and body fluids change rhythm, speeding up or slowing down. Within the body, growing as a graft, indomitable, there is an other. And no one is present, within that simultaneously dual and alien space, to signify what is going on.[17]

Two points in Kristeva's comments on this first distinction are especially relevant to horror films: (a) the abject within is the more horrifying, and (b) images of skin have a particular significance.

The reasons for the special horror of the abject within are twofold. One is that the abject within is less viewable and so less easy to cope with. The other is the threatening possibility that one's sense of identity will be lost. Then 'the abject permeates me: "I" become abject', subject to a 'structure within the body, a nonassimilable alien, a monster, a tumour, a cancer'.[18] Special horror will then be attached to reminders that the body may contain internal, monstrous growths, unknown to oneself until they take over and produce death.

The horror of the abject within, Kristeva argues, gives a special status to images of skin. The reasons are again twofold. The state of the skin provides a marker for the nonviewable internal state. And skin provides a border, makes a container for one's blood and guts, provides a wholeness to one's sense of self. Breaks, tears, or cuts in the skin, that 'container' of one's self, confront us then with 'the collapse of the border between inside and outside' the body:

> It is as if the skin, a fragile container, no longer guaranteed the integrity of one's 'own and clean self' but, scraped or transparent, invisible or taut, gave way.[19]

It is not surprising then, Kristeva argues, that the Old Testament forbids approach to the Temple to anyone whose body or whose body surface departs from what is 'proper':

> For whatsoever man he be that hath a blemish, he shall not approach: a blind man, or a lame, or he that hath a flat nose, or anything superfluous. Or a man that is brokenfooted, or brokenhanded ... he shall not come nigh to offer the bread of his God.[20]

How do these proposals apply to the sources of horror in film? To start again with *Kitchen Sink*, the first source of horror – the non-viewable abject within – is prominent. The internal state of the creature cannot be known from the outside. It's internal state, however, is suspect, both because the internal state of any nonhuman creature is suspect to us, and because of this creature's ambiguous quality. It has started from an oddly hairy umbilicus. Moreover, its ability to inflate, and its subsequent deflation, leave the spectator unsure of what it possesses: unsure that it has a brain to think and live with, or a heart to love with. Its questionable state is all the more important because one of the film's themes revolves around the possibility of love. For this possibility to exist, the being must not appear to be nonhuman. Its difference within should not be brought into question, but that question consistently intrudes.

Within *Kitchen Sink* also, the creature is far from presenting the clean, clear skin that goes with purity and innocence within. As a newborn, it is covered with thick hair. The woman shaves this off, until the body has a clean and smooth surface. It is at this moment, at this sign of possible innocence or humanness, that the woman begins to feel a sense of empathy or sympathy for the being. She places it in her bed, allows it to spend the night by her side, and begins to feel some stirrings of desire. The return of hair, this time on the creature's back, signals a return of horror, of monstrosity. The moment is one of reconciliation – the monster has begun to move and after an initial struggle is now in an embrace with the woman. In a loving gesture, she passes her hand over his back, discovers the hair, hesitates, pulls it and causes his deflation. The 'unclean surface', now reappearing, functions as a reminder that its internal state may be less 'proper' than it should be.

In addition to the aspects of skin that signal an internally monstrous state, *Kitchen Sink* derives a further part of its horror from threats to the integrity of skin. In the shaving scene, the woman's choice of implement – an old-fashioned razor of the kind once used by barbers – immediately suggests the threat of a slash, a severing of the skin. The close-up shots of the blade on the skin's surface, combined with the overemphasized sound effects of grating and tearing, heighten the spectator's sense that a slice through the skin may occur at any moment. A further image of severance comes when the full-grown being has been consigned to a large plastic rubbish bag. It apparently wakes up, and can be heard making the sounds of someone choking. The woman is faced with a choice. Will she let it die, leave the being 'under wraps'? Or will she slash through the bag and let out the possible horror within? She decides to do the latter but again the spectator is confronted with the visual image of a slash and the tearing sound of a surface sliced from top to bottom.

Kitchen Sink, in its short fourteen minutes, cannot offer all the examples of the varieties of the abject that one needs in order to bring out the way this concept illuminates the sources of a sense of horror. I turn then to a few other films to bring out more fully the special horror of the abject within, and the significance of images of skin.

To start with, one needs to go beyond *Kitchen Sink* to find a strong illustration of Kristeva's proposal that one reason for the special horror of the abject within is that it can involve a slow, unrecognized loss of one's identity, a hidden metamorphosis. The relevance of that proposal is well brought out, however, by a film with overtones of *Kitchen Sink*. This is David Cronenberg's 1986 remake of *The Fly*. In the original 1958 version, the scientist emerges from his matter-transfer experiment with a very visible change – the head of a fly. In the remake, the scientist's head remains relatively normal until close to the end of the film. The presence of a foreign element is signalled at first only by his increased appetite for sugar, his hyperactivity and jerky locomotion, and then by small changes to the body itself. The wiry hairs on his back, when taken by his girlfriend to be analysed, turn out to be nonhuman.

The Fly illustrates as well the way in which the abject within may give rise to a final loss of identity: death. In both the original and the remake of *The Fly*, the growth of the abject within results in the death of its host. Death for the person taken over is also the case in *Alien*; a quick, violent death in which the body is explosively torn apart as the monster, growing within unknown to the host, bursts forth. This is the fate of Kane; this is Ripley's nightmare; and this, in *Aliens 3*, is her own fate. Death to the host, however, need not be the only way in which identity and a sense of self are lost. The abject within may surface and take over sporadically and unpredictably, causing the death of others. *Cat People, American Werewolf in Paris, A Company of Wolves, Dr. Jekyll and Mr. Hyde* (and certain Michael Jackson videos – *Thriller* and *Black and White*) all display this theme. The abject takes over only temporarily and it remains unclear whether 'it' is a completely foreign being or is an extension of self, of repressed sexuality or animality. The horror nonetheless remains in the loss of the 'I' at the hands of something that resides within one's own body, an internal 'indominatible ... other'.[21]

Finally, the significance of images of skin emerges in several horror films. It is no coincidence that monsters are often given scaly, warty bodies: markers of the evil within. In related fashion, Kristeva's proposals lead one now to look with new interest at the way in which a change in the state of the skin signals a change in internal state. The growths that begin to emerge on the skin of the character played by the rock star Sting in *Dune* provide one example, implying disease and decay within as the result of sexual activity. That implication is even stronger in David Lynch's *Eraserhead*. Harry Spencer's fantasy about a woman in his gas heater begins with her dancing seductively. That dance turns horrific, however, as bulging tumours begin to emerge on her face: a transformation supporting the film's general thesis of sexual contact, women, and fertility as loathsome.

The optimal example of the significance of skin, however, is *Silence of the Lambs*. Both the hunted monster (Buffalo Bill also known as James Gumb) and Dr Hanibal Lecter steal the skin of others to create new identities for themselves. Dr Hanibal steals the skin of others to create a new face. Gumb steals skin in order to create a complete new image. Dissatisfied with the physical image of himself in the mirror, he captures pure young women and skins them, after a period of starving them in order to make the skinning easier (a sacrificial preparation that maintains the spectator's horror and gives a gruesome twist to Gumb's interest in the women's size). Gumb then cobbles the skin pieces together to create a completely new container for himself.

In short, Kristeva directs our attention, when we consider *Kitchen Sink* or other horror films, to a first set of questions about the location of what is horrific – within or without? – and to the use of images of skin (its state, its integrity) as reminders that what we cannot see may be foul and that what is currently safely contained may at any time lose its containing envelope. What more does her analysis of varieties of the abject prompt us to consider?

The recognizable abject and the abject with a clean, false face

Monsters covered with warts and scaly skin are readily identifiable as loathsome. One is then forewarned and may take evasive or protective measures. In films in which the abject presents with a clean, false face, however, the horror is hidden, not behind the surface of the body as some internal growth may be, but behind a benevolent disguise.

This second distinction among varieties of the abject is part of Kristeva's analysis of duplicity and disguise in relation to horror. Her analysis is again two-pronged. One prong is her interest in what she terms 'the composite'. The other is her attention to deliberate duplicity under the surface of what is lawful or good.

The concept of the composite. The notion of a 'composite', like many other terms that Kristeva uses, is never precisely defined. Its meaning, however, emerges from a comment on Auschwitz:

> In the dark halls of the museum that is now what remains of Auschwitz, I see a heap of children's shoes, or something like that, *something I have already seen elsewhere*, under a Christmas tree, dolls I believe: the abjection of Nazi crime reaches its apex when death ... interferes with what, in my living universe, is supposed to save me from death: childhood, science, among other things.[22]

Among the composites within *Kitchen Sink*, several involve placing the dirty and the clean together. The washing of dishes, the wiping of the sink and ultimately the clearing of the drain of a few unwanted hairs lead to the appearance of the monster. The placing of the filthy, slime-covered, newborn in the clean bath provides a further example. Composite also is the siting of this domestic horror in suburbia, an area that usually signals a safe, uneventful haven. Horror is no longer in some separate, far away, science-fiction setting, but is now close to home: a 'homeliness' emphasized still further by the rough quality of the black and white filming and the woman's lack of glamour.

Again, to bring out the concept and its uses, we may go beyond *Kitchen Sink*. Within *Alien*, for instance, the notion of the composite helps account for the particular horror of Kane's death. The scene is set, like the Christmas scene Kristeva recalls, or like a Last Supper, for a relaxed 'family time' together. Kane has returned to consciousness, the alien organism that was attached to his face is dead, and the danger seems to have passed. The crew decides to enjoy a meal together before returning to their pods for a long sleep on the return to Earth. They joke together. Kane laughs. In the midst of an enjoyed mouthful, however, he begins to gag and to heave, and blood spurts out of his chest. The alien newborn bursts forth, glares at the crew with its bloodied snake head, bares its teeth, and – at this point the size and shape of a large snake with a massive head – exits through the door of what was once a pleasant dining area. The scene provides a truly 'composite' image, all the more disturbing for the violence taking place not in a dim, dank place but in the bright light of an area associated with pleasure, family relaxation, and togetherness.

David Lynch's films supply further examples. In *Eraserhead*, for instance, in a scene comparable to Kane's last meal, Spencer takes his first meal with his parents-in-law. On the surface, the setting is one of warmth and life. As Spencer begins to carve the headless bird placed before him, however, it moves and slowly begins to spout blood. Later in the film a normally caring act – changing a baby – is converted into one of violence. For most of the film, the body of the baby is wrapped in cloth. Towards the end, however, Spencer cuts through the cloth with scissors and the infant dies: its claims to the status of 'baby' undercut by the sight of the infant's few internal organs, and by the spectator's awareness that what the child has worn is some strange cloth-skin. Innocence and violence appear side-by-side.

Blue Velvet uses the same kind of device. The apparently safe and friendly town is revealed as containing activities antithetical to its surface: even the grass reveals an underlife and body parts. So also does *Wild at Heart*. A cruise along the highway, for instance, leads to a bloody collision. A dying woman clutches her lipstick and her handbag: beauty items that are as misplaced within the violence of the scene as the shoes in Auschwitz.

The impact of deliberate duplicity. The second form in which the abject with a false face emerges is indicated by several passages in Kristeva's *Powers of Horror*. All of these deal with deliberate duplicity. One such passage deals with the use of rules and prohibitions in order to achieve a subversion of the law:

> [T]he abject is perverse because it never gives up nor assumes a prohibition, a rule, or a law: but turns them aside, misleads, corrupts, uses them, takes advantage of them, the better to deny them. It kills in the name of life – a progressive despot; it lives at the behest of death – an operator in genetic experimentations; it curbs the other's suffering for its own profit .... Corruption is its most common, most obvious appearance. That is the socialized form of the abject.[23]

A second passage compares two characters in Dostoevsky's *The Possessed*:

> Verkhovensky is abject because of his clammy, cunning appeal to ideals that no longer exist .... Stavragin is perhaps less so, for his immoral admits of laughter

and refusal, something artistic, a cynical and gratuitous expenditure that ... does not serve an arbitrary, exterminating power. It is possible to be cynical without being irremediably abject; abjection on the other hand, is always brought about by that which attempts to get along with trampled-down law.[24]

A third passage contains a particular reference to treachery:

It is ... not lack of cleanliness or health that causes abjection but what disturbs identity, system, order. What does not respect borders, positions, rules. The in-between, the ambiguous, the composite. The traitor, the liar, the criminal with a good conscience, the killer who claims he is a saviour .... Any crime, because it draws attention to the fragility of the law, is abject, but premeditated crime, cunning murder, hypocritical revenge are even more so because they heighten the display of such fragility. He who denies morality is not abject; there can be grandeur in amorality and even in crime that flaunts its disrespect for the law. Abjection, on the other hand, is immoral, sinister, scheming and shady; a terror that dissembles, a hatred that smiles, a passion that uses the body for barter instead of inflaming it, a debtor who sells you up, a friend who stabs you.[25]

To turn again to *Kitchen Sink*, treachery and duplicity occur on both sides in the course of the power struggle between the two main characters. It is unclear whether the monster is good or evil, whether it will appreciate the woman's gift of life or turn against her. In fact, when it does wake up, it oscillates without warning between caressing and attacking the woman. The woman is also not to be trusted. With no clear clues to the way she feels or what she might do (her actions seem at times to stem from motives no stronger than a relatively idle curiosity), she moves from rejection, and disposal, to interest and desire and then back to rejection and eventually the murderous act of deflation.

To provide a full sense of the way Kristeva's analysis of treachery and duplicity illuminates the nature of horror in films, however, I shall again look outside *Kitchen Sink*. To start with, Kristeva's insistence on the special horror of the clean, false face helps bring out why Gothic films are often disturbing: especially those where smiling husbands – appearing at the outset to have only the best intentions towards their wives – are in reality planning to destroy or replace them (*Gaslight*, *Sleep My Love*, the original *Stepford Wives*).

The films worth particular note are those in which the presence of a clean, false face creates two layers of monster, doubling the sense of horror. *Aliens* provides a first example. To use Kristeva's phrase, the character Burke 'lives at the behest of death'.[26] His loyalties are given to 'the Company', especially the Weapons Division and its interest in taking advantage of the alien's/s' special strengths. ('The Company', one may note, is a term well-known in many U.S. circles to refer to the C.I.A. and the use of this label to refer, in *Aliens*, to an organization that operates by rules of its own seems likely to be deliberate.)

The approach Burke makes to Ripley, however, is phrased in terms that are far from revealing an interest in power or a readiness to break the law. He wishes to persuade her to return to the monster's site. His first approach is phrased in terms of Ripley's own interests. He offers her the inducement of regaining her flight status; she is at the time working as a dock loader. When this inducement does not work, he appeals in terms of the good of others. He points out that she may be able to help some of the families of colonists who have been settled on the site. 'Families?', Ripley asks, and agrees. This is the same Burke who proposes to Ripley that they slip some small forms of the alien organisms past quarantine – 'We'll make millions' – and then tries to arrange events so that Ripley and Newt become impregnated, in the hope that he may in this way evade the law he is supposed to uphold. He is truly a character who, in Kristeva's phrase, 'does not respect borders, positions, rules ... a terror that dissembles'.[27]

Dr Hanibal Lecter in *Silence of the Lambs* is a further case in point. He is a monster, an acknowledged cannibal. He appears nonetheless in the guise of an intelligent, almost fatherly doctor, highly civilized and widely read. Even his final line – 'I am having a friend for dinner' – is on the surface urbane.

In short, a special horror is likely to lie in events where what is evil presents with a clean, false face as well as with a surface that readily signals evil. The spectator is then presented with two versions of the monstrous: one explicitly dubbed monstrous from the start and one emerging only from a façade that originally belies monstrosity. The double presentation is destabilizing for the viewer: who is the monster here? The doubling also adds to the viewer's sense of threat. Danger now may lurk not only in every recognizable threatening situation or form of life, but also behind every closed door and every smiling face.

The abject in the form of reminders of sexual sameness and difference

The third variety of the abject to be abstracted from Kristeva's discussion has to do with males and females. Horror may reside in reminders of the difference between males and females. This is, Kristeva argues, part of the horror that menstrual blood may provoke.[28] Horror may also reside, however, in reminders of the similarity between males and females or in the collapse of the male/female boundaries contained in the social and symbolic order.

At first sight, these two proposals appear to contradict one another. To see how both may exist within a single theoretical position, one needs to go back to the narratives of origin contained within psychoanalytic theory: both classical Freudian theory and the Lacanian-style theory from which Kristeva starts.

In both types of theory, the original state is assumed to be undifferentiated by gender. Male and female do not matter. What exists is a child united with, and part of, its mother. Gender identity (along with a gender hierarchy with males dominant) arises only at a later point.

In classical psychoanalytic theory, this point occurs when the child encounters the demand to identify with the father, repudiating the mother and denying her importance. In Lacanian-style theory, it occurs when the child encounters the imposition of paternal law and symbolic order, placing the authority of the mother outside the realm of system and order.[29]

In the process, it is argued, all forms of 'the feminine' are downgraded. The enforced distinction by gender, however, is also likely to be accompanied by feelings of loss and by associations with violence, with the latter stemming either from reminders of the 'immemorial violence with which the body becomes separated from another body in order to be',[30] or from the suspicion that the difference between males and females rests on mutilation.

Women, according to this suspicion, are castrated males: frightful in themselves and as reminders of what could happen to men. Their genitals then become too horrific for direct viewing. At least for men (the position of women is debatable), looking becomes possible only indirectly (Perseus looks at the Medusa's head, for instance, only in a mirror) or by substituting some other body part or some other object for fetishistic, obsessive viewing. As a further aspect of separation, the violence of the process will be repressed or denied. For both men and women, for example, the violence of birth becomes sanitized in most representations of birth, with birth occurring either off-stage or with a minimum of blood.

It is this type of history that then gives rise to the possibility that both the underlining and the wiping out of gender differences may be horrific. How does this double possibility apply to film?

Blood and filth as reminders of the difference. Blood as a sign of women's difference from men is not a prominent part of *Kitchen Sink*, at least in comparison with a film such as *Carrie*. Within *Carrie*, in the midst of a scene of cleanliness (a shower at the school gym), blood begins to seep down the inside of Carrie's thighs and, as she searches for the apparent wound, spreads to her fingers, resulting in her complete panic. On a later occasion when a bucket of pig's blood is tipped over Carrie to shatter her belief that she is the 'belle of the ball', blood is also a sign of Carrie's new power, her ability to use anger in order to destroy by fire those who have fouled her. She is now not only a sexually mature young woman physically, but a violent female force.

Filth in association with birth, however, is certainly present as a source of horror in *Kitchen Sink*. The hair that the woman pulls turns thicker and is covered with a sticky substance that clings to the woman's hands. The head crowns from the sink, dropping back between each pull in a gruesome parallel to the birth process. Here, however, birth has not been sanitized. Birth – an intensely female phenomenon – is presented as clearly unclean.[31]

Wiping out differences. Within *Kitchen Sink*, the loss of male/female differences occurs by way of the male creature being assigned a passive state normally assigned to women. He is completely under her control, 'feminized' and with his life and death at the mercy of her vacillating mood. Why should this type of narrative be disturbing? To answer that question, one needs to take account of the several ways in which the usual male/female differences may be wiped out.

To be noted first is the fact that horror is not always the emotion that is produced. The wiping out of gender differences need not be horrific if it is part of a gentle, nostalgic return to the original state, either in the womb or during early infancy. As Vivian Sobchack in particular points out, many science-fiction films are built upon such circumstances. They represent a journey toward origins and a return to infantile experience, even though the surface text is one of advanced technology.[32] Spaceships are enclosed, womb-like spaces: computers take care of many daily tasks, and the characters have a general air of technical asexual competence with machinery rather than with close relationships.

What happens then in a second set of circumstances: in films in which men dress as women? Here again, the wiping out of a sexual difference does not necessarily bring a sense of horror. The motive for the masquerade, for the wiping out of differences, is clearly important. Michael Caine's character, for instance, in Brian de Palma's *Dressed to Kill*, involves the spectator in instances of horror because he poses as a woman with pleasure and with the intent to kill. In contrast, *Tootsie* creates no horror in the spectator because the motive behind the masquerade is work-related and because Tootsie makes it clear that he never loses his preference for masculinity or his discomfort in drag.

Clearly, more needs to be considered than the simple disappearance of differences or even the reminder of the loss of identity that may accompany a return to an early state of oneness with the mother. The specific motives attached to the loss, and the quality of the pleasure attached to the breaking down of barriers, must also be taken into account.

There is also – and this appears to be essential – the issue of who is losing a sexual identity. *Kitchen Sink* places the man in a vulnerable, instantly threatened position, continually at the mercy of a woman who from moment to moment may not care whether he lives or dies. This set of circumstances applies in some other films. In *Alien/Aliens*, for instance, both men and women may be used as gestation sites for the monsters. Kane – that coolly competent male officer – seems a particularly disturbing choice as a demonstration that even strong men may become hosts to a monstrous unborn and die violently in the course of its birth. A female-like vulnerability (this time to violence short of death) is also the implication of images of raped males (Harry Dean Stanton's character, for instance, in *Wild at Heart* and, metaphorically, Ren in *Videodrome*).

The cases I have cited all have to do with the 'feminization' of males and their accompanying vulnerability. When differences are wiped out by women becoming men or becoming like men, one might well expect that the same reaction of horror will not occur, or that it may not occur equally among both men and women.

The maternal as a specific variety of the abject

This is the fourth and last distinction among varieties of the abject that I shall abstract from Kristeva's account. It has to do with images of the mother. As mentioned earlier, the feminine body is felt to be abject on at least two grounds. One is the presence of menstrual blood, suggesting the presence of some internal damage or wounding. The other is its capacity to remind the viewer of loss, separation, lack. In classic psychoanalytic terms, the feminine body has no penis and is a reminder that the body's hold on its parts – for males, the penis especially – is fragile or vulnerable.

In Kristeva's analysis, mothers may be more abject, and hence more provocative of horror and more subject to oppression, than women in general. One reason for this is that birth is often associated with expelled bodily waste. A second reason is that the mother differs from the feminine in her possession of authority. This authority stems from two sources. One is the mother's power to reproduce: a constant threat to conventional order and control. As Kristeva notes, 'fear of the archaic mother is essentially fear of her generative power'.[33] The other is the authority the mother held before 'the law of the father' took hold. This is an authority that does not always coexist comfortably with conventional/patriarchal law and order. The image of the mother then becomes a reminder of the child's break from the mother: a break which is often violent and a threat to the borders of identity. In Kristeva's phrase, the separation from the mother is often 'a violent, clumsy breaking away, with the constant risk of falling back under the sway of a power as securing as it is stifling'.[34]

In effect, images of birth are abject only when they are accompanied by violence, or implications of violence, and when the violence is explicitly shown rather than birth being sanitized, converted to an off-screen event, or presented with an emphasis only on its beatific aspects. And images of mothers are abject only when they bring up associations with unclean birth, with other violent separations, or with an authority that lies outside and existed before the authority of conventional law and order.

How do these proposals fit with images in *Kitchen Sink*? To start with, the implied birth is distinctly unclean. In addition, the woman's authority is pervasive. She has the authority to decide whether to nurture the being, groom it, and take it into her bed, or to have some ignominious death be its fate: death by way of a plastic binbag or by being pulled apart. The fearful authority of mothers is suggested also through the kitchen drain being the site from which the monster emerges. If the being is human or at least a cross between human and alien, it would appear that a mother in some other place – in the course of some 'kitchen abortion' – has also acted with authority, ending a life by flushing this being into the sewer or water system.

Mothers, we are reminded, are beings upon whom we must rely but also cannot rely. The film violates our expectation that women will nurture the creatures to whom they give life. Worse, it plays with that expectation – perhaps the woman will, perhaps she will not – reviving continually the lurking fear that the ultimate use of a woman's power will be a relatively unconcerned, almost out-of-curiosity-alone consignment of the other to nonexistence.

Summary comment

This chapter has outlined Kristeva's concept of the abject and raised the question: when are particular images likely to be abject, to be sources of horror? It is not enough to say, for instance, that everything that is ambiguous or everything that reminds us of the instability of borders is likely to evoke a sense of horror. Many a comedy, as I noted earlier, could qualify as ambiguous or as unsettling boundaries, but not as abject.

As a first step towards making the concept of the abject more specific, and more useful for the analysis of particular films, I have turned in this chapter to Kristeva's proposals about varieties of the abject. This material yields a number of particular circumstances – a number of additional features – that need to apply in order for a shaking of boundaries to be a source of horror. Two further circumstances that can be abstracted from Kristeva's account of horror provide the focus of the next chapter.

Notes

1. Julia Kristeva (1982) *Powers of horror: An essay on abjection*. Translated by Leon S. Roudiez. New York: Columbia University Press, p.4.
2. *Village Voice* (New York) as cited in press release for *Crush*, p.3.
3. Julia Kristeva (1986a) 'About Chinese women'. In T. Moi (Ed.) *The Kristeva reader*. Oxford: Basil Blackwell, p.151.
4. See Jacques Lacan (1977) *Écrits*. London: Travistock, p.255ff.
5. Julia Kristeva, *Revolution in poetic language*. In T. Moi (Ed.) (1986) *The Kristeva reader*. Oxford: Basil Blackwell, p.113.
6. Kristeva (1982, p.210).
7. Ibid., p.1.
8. Ibid., p.2.
9. Ibid., p.12, emphasis in the original.

10. Ibid., p.4.
11. Barbara Creed (1993) *The monstrous-feminine: Film, feminism, psychoanalysis*. London: Routledge, pp.10–11.
12. *Powers of horror* (Kristeva, 1982). The comment on the difficulties of translating *propre* is a translator's note, p.viii.
13. *Alien, Aliens, Aliens 3*.
14. Creed (1993, p.10).
15. Kristeva (1982, p.4).
16. Ibid., p.71.
17. Ibid., p.237.
18. Ibid., p.11.
19. Ibid., p.53.
20. Ibid., p.103: Leviticus, cited by Kristeva.
21. Ibid., p.xxi.
22. Ibid., p.4, emphasis in original.
23. Ibid., pp.15–16.
24. Ibid., p.19.
25. Ibid., p.4.
26. Ibid., p.15.
27. Kristeva (1982, p.4). The same kind of scene is played out again in *Aliens 3* where one of the rescue team (a man who looks like the good android Bishop of *Aliens* and who claims to have invented and programmed Bishop) first tries to entice Ripley to the rescue ship on the grounds of her own safety (a surgical team will remove the monster growing within her) and then, when Ripley resists, insisting that she cannot believe in her survival ('I'm dead anyway') tries a different method of persuasion: 'We have so much to learn'.
28. Ibid., p.171.
29. See, for instance, Lacan (1977, p.255ff).
30. Kristeva (1982, p.10).
31. In similar fashion, horror stems from the way that birth and pregnancy are stripped of their usual sanitation in the trio of *Aliens* films. Kane dies after being burst asunder. A woman pleads to be destroyed – and is – before a similar fate can occur. Birth, in fact, is so horrific in *Alien/Aliens* that Ripley is presented only as a de facto adopting mother (Newt calls her 'Mummy' after Ripley rescues her from the Alien Mother), leaving biological motherhood to be the province only of the alien monster. Only in *Aliens 3* does Ripley become pregnant. It is, however, to an alien, and leads to Ripley's destruction. In a poignant gesture, she clutches the monster emerging from her shattered chest as if it were a loved newborn. The gesture, however, is designed only to take the monster with her to death in the furnace of poured iron. Motherhood's unpleasant connotations remain unchanged.
32. Vivian Sobchack (1990) 'The virginity of astronauts: Sex and the science fiction film'. In A. Kuhn (Ed.) *Alien zone: Cultural theory and contemporary science fiction cinema*. London: Verso, pp.103–115.
33. Kristeva (1982, p.77).
34. Ibid., p.13.

Chapter 3

HORROR – SPECIFYING THE CIRCUMSTANCES

When do particular images evoke horror? What are the specific circumstances under which an image evokes a strong or weak sense of horror or is accepted with relative calm? All occasions on which boundaries are shaken – all violations of an expected order – do not evoke horror. What then needs to be added in order to pin down the bases to a sense of horror and its varying degrees? Why, to refer again to our major test case, is *Kitchen Sink* so particularly revolting, and at the same time so acclaimed?

To begin answering that question, I turned in the previous chapter to Kristeva's proposal that there are varieties of the abject. Degrees of horror, the argument runs, may vary depending upon whether the abject is within or without, presents with a clean, false face rather than with visible signs of evil or pollution, contains reminders of old losses, injuries and vulnerabilities (especially those incurred in the course of acquiring a sense of gender), or brings reminders of a maternal authority, power, and drive that are outside the reaches of conventional law and order and seem uncontrollable by any other force. *Kitchen Sink*, it turns out, piles one variety of the abject upon another, compounding the horror.

The argument so far, however, seems to take little or no account of Kristeva's insistence that subjects are situated in a society and a history and that the impact of any new text reflects the nature of the connection between the new text and the texts that constitute the society and history of the narrator or the 'addressee'. There is nothing in the material so far, for instance, that incorporates the kind of concern with historical circumstances that anthropologist Mary Douglas highlights in her analysis of purity and danger.[1] (The association of 'filth' or 'pollution' with sex, Douglas argues, is likely to be especially strong when sex roles are in transition rather than being firmly fixed by tradition.) Nor has there been attention so far to how it is that a new or different text comes to emerge. We need a clearer sense of how a new text comes to be inserted into a society's storehouse: comes to emerge in a particular shape, comes to be received in one way rather than another – to be greeted, for instance, with alarm or to be taken over by the mainstream as acceptably daring.

In addition, the arguments so far contain little attention to circumstances that others have seen as central to horror. There is, for instance, nothing so far that incorporates the assumption of a gendered spectator, an assumption that prompts several analysts of horror films to ask: Whose horror is this? Whose carcasses litter the field?[2] In short, we are in need of expansions that will help us answer the questions: Is the experience of horror timeless or does it vary from one occasion to another? Is the experience universal or does it vary from one person to another? How does any new representation of the horrific come to emerge?

To take up those questions, I shall first consider Kristeva's concept of 'rituals of defilement'. In the later part of the chapter, I shall then consider questions about the impact of differences among spectators – among the participants in ritualized encounters with horror.

The nature of rituals of defilement

Kristeva takes from Douglas (in particular Douglas's material on *Purity and Danger*[3]) the proposal that what each society calls 'filth' is that which threatens a social or moral order. The proposal fits especially neatly with the way the French term *propre* refers both to what is 'clean' and to what is 'proper' or 'correct', calling for the double English heading noted in the previous chapter – the improper/unclean – for Kristeva's opening discussion of abjection. From Douglas, Kristeva takes also the notion that all societies develop rituals or ceremonial forms that help avoid contact with 'filth' or – where contact is unavoidable – help to keep its impact within limits or to decontaminate the people and the places that may now be sources of danger. Every culture, Douglas argues, develops purification ceremonies to erase the effects of possible contamination. The nature of the ceremony, and the occasions when it is seen necessary, reveal what is feared and where safety is felt to lie.

Such proposals immediately prompt one to ask: what are the rituals expected to apply in contemporary times? Purification ceremonies have certainly not disappeared. Some religious groups, for instance, still use 'churching' ceremonies for women who have given birth. For examples in film, one may turn towards *Silkwood*: a modern horror film where radiation is the unseen contaminating agent that clings to the body, enforces isolation and painful treatment, and serves as a possible murder weapon. Or towards *The Virgin Spring*, where the avenging father first purifies his body by sauna and ice before slaughtering the physically and spiritually 'filthy' trio who have raped and murdered his daughter.

The rituals to which I draw special attention are those that have to do with the ways in which the dead – or the possible dead – should be treated. Given Kristeva's insistence that the corpse is one pinnacle of abjection, and given the significance of life/death and the disposal of bodies in *Kitchen Sink*, these rituals deserve a special note.

Our current and past rituals, I suggest, contain three components. The first consists of actions that people are supposed to take when death is suspected. The method may vary: a search for the pulse, a mirror at the mouth to detect any sign of breath, a CAT scan to determine 'brain death'. And the certification needed may vary: from one lay person's decision to judgement by a recognized authority (shaman, chief, midwife, physician). Some steps are usual, however, to ensure against being buried alive or making the terrible error of burying someone else alive (Edgar Allen Poe's *Fall of the House of Usher* is perhaps the prototypical horror story for the consequences of this error). In reverse fashion, some special steps may be needed to make sure that the apparently dead remain dead and are not restored to life. Vampires, for instance, require silver bullets, or burials at the crossroads with a stake through the heart.

The second component of rituals for dealing with the dead or apparently dead consists, wherever possible, of actions that involve preparations for the body's next place. The body may be washed and wrapped in clean linen; it may be 'laid out' with arms folded and pennies on its eyes to keep them closed. It may be embalmed, painted, jewelled, surrounded by whatever may seem needed for future sustenance or company. It may be wailed over, prayed over, watched over, set out for private or public viewing. Again, the specific form may vary but some preparation, some acknowledgment that this was a life rather than a shovelful of dirt, a bag of bones, will be made.

The third component consists of actions that involve the choice of a site for the dead. These again may be varied: a funeral pyre, a tree, a box in the ground, the depths of the sea. With each social group, however, there will be some sense of a 'proper' place. The dead do not remain in the presence of the living. Even their presence in incomplete form – as ashes in a funeral urn, for instance – may appear 'odd' and be a source for uneasy, ribald comment.

These three components then make up the rituals with which we surround encounters with the dead or the apparently dead. I have spelled them out because Kristeva provides more material on the functions of rituals of defilement than on their nature. A sense of their nature, however, is a critical step towards understanding those functions. It is also a critical step towards understanding the ways in which the use or the violation of rituals (*Kitchen Sink* violates all three of those I have outlined for the treatment of death) is related to the experience of horror.

The functions of rituals of defilement

In essence, Kristeva describes two functions. One of these has to do with the way rituals of defilement allow safe, controlled contact with what is abject but nonetheless attractive (attractive in large part because it is abject). This is the function that Modleski and Creed pick up in their argument that horror films are rituals of defilement.[4] The second function has to do with the use of rituals of defilement as a basis for departing from an existing order. By defiance of the rituals, or by insisting upon change within them, a new identity or a new order is signalled. This function is a critical part of Kristeva's interest in subversion, and is the function to which I shall give particular space.

A first function: Safe encounters with the abject

To be safe, we might well order our lives in such a way that we completely avoid any encounters with the unclean or the improper. That way of proceeding, however, is unlikely on two counts. First, it would be 'sterile', in both senses of the word: free of germs but also lacking in 'life'. Second, it would not be possible. We are, ourselves, sources of pain, carriers of rot or plague, producers of body wastes, gases, and odours.

The next best thing is to seek reassurance that what is impure or abject is within 'normal limits'. One checks the coating of one's tongue, the colour of urine, the consistency of stools. A major part of such reassurance, however, requires that the potential threat be viewable, be 'out there'. Kristeva makes the point in vivid prose, describing

> the spasms and vomiting which protect me. The repugnance, the retching that thrusts me to the side and turns me away from defilement, savage and muck.[5]

> [The] gagging ... spasm in the stomach, the belly ... sight-clouding dizziness, *nausea* ... 'I' want none of that element ... 'I' do not want to listen, 'I' do not assimilate it, 'I' expel it.[6]

> A wound with blood and pus, or the sickly, acrid smell of sweat, of decay ... without makeup or masks, refuse and corpses *show me* what I permanently thrust aside to live. These body fluids, this defilement, this shit are what life withstands .... Such wastes drop, so that I might live.[7]

The sight of bodily waste, in effect, is not only a reminder of the 'unclean' that is within us but also a reassurance that it is being safely ejected from the body; cast out, exiled, consigned to a 'safer' place, deprived of its strength or transformed into some inert and harmless state.

How does this first function apply to horror films? Film in itself provides evidence that the polluting abject is 'out there': viewable. In addition, as Creed points out, it offers under controlled conditions the thrill of contact with the forbidden and the impure.[8] The controlled conditions are needed in order that the emotion generated will be tolerable, will not flood one's being, overcome one's usual rationality, break down one's usual control. The spectator of horror films may come close to nausea or to total terror, but has always the assurance that what is being watched is a film, that the people are acting and do not really die, that there is a time limit to the event, and that one may always look away or leave. The individual is allowed to come close to what is abject, and is permitted the thrill of doing so, but is at the same time protected.

Creed's point is a general one, applicable to any horror production and helpful towards answering the question: Why do people watch horror productions – in fact, pay to do so? To move beyond the general points, however, one needs to ask: how is it that some films provide more assurance of safety than others? What are the 'safety procedures' that the spectator calls upon? What happens when the usual 'safety procedures' are ripped apart or in some way denied to us? And why would anyone deny us these?

For the nature of assurances of safety, one may note the variety of ways in which horror films often allow some distancing from what is seen. There is first of all evidence that what is being encountered is a film: a picture of blood, for instance, rather than real blood. In addition, events often take place in the past or the future, or in some distant place – a medieval castle, outer space. They often involve people unlike oneself; in short, they often carry the marks of fantasy. *Kitchen Sink* offers no such protective frames, no such seatbelts. Nor is there the assurance provided by a title that signals what kind of horror may be expected (*Aliens* as a sequel to *Alien*, *Jaws II* as a sequel to *Jaws*).

For the other questions given above, one needs to turn to the second function that Kristeva offers for rituals of defilement.

A second function: Challenges to the existing order

For a nicely concrete example, I shall go back to Kristeva's account of the emergence of Christianity and its points of contrast with Judaism. Kristeva begins with Old Testament injunctions against 'abominations'. These injunctions, she proposes, represent a concern with the threat of defilement from without and a major reliance on one particular way of coping. This coping is by a series of rules and prohibitions that concentrate on 'separating, with constituting strict identities without intermixture'.[9] Food shall be unleavened (no mixture of grain with yeast); what touches meat shall not be in contact with what touches milk (the Kosher kitchen); 'thou shalt not let thy cattle gender with a diverse kind; thou shalt not sow thy field with mingled seed; neither shall a garment mingled of linen and woollen come upon thee'.[10]

For Kristeva, these ways of dealing with the abject were also the ways by which Judaism struggled 'to constitute itself', to distance itself from 'paganism and its material cults'.[11] In turn, Christianity used changes in ritual as a way of establishing its separate identity, its challenge to the Judaic order. One part of the Christian challenge was 'through abolishment of dietary taboos, partaking of food with pagans, verbal and gestural contact with lepers'.[12] A second was through an 'interiorization of impurity'.[13] Where in Judaism, defilement came from without – from what was taken in, and so needed to be avoided – now defilement came from within: from the presence of sin, with some of that original sin becoming an inherent rather than an acquired part of human nature. Sin, in Kristeva's phrase, is 'subjectified abjection'.[14] Confession now becomes a way of 'ejecting the abject'. The granting of absolution, upon confession and repentance, converts the internal state of sin to an internal state of grace.

In short, Judaic rituals were a challenge to those followed by the 'pagans' around them, and Christian rituals were an equally radical change from what Judaism regarded as essential. In their turn, what are now termed 'Satanic' rituals may be regarded not as ignoring the Christian ceremonies they seek to replace, but as presenting an opposite within a similar surface form: real flesh instead of symbolic flesh, the body of a woman as an altar instead of a chaste cloth. The essential point is that a departure from the established order takes the form, not of investigating a completely new ritual, but by taking the old as an expected base and then tearing it apart, inverting it, or debasing it in a way that shakes expectations.

How do these further proposals apply to horror films? With Kristeva's proposals in mind, we can now observe that in *Kitchen Sink*, none of the expected ritual ways of dealing with the dead or the apparently dead is respected. The creature shows some signs of life in its initial quiver and hop from the sink to the floor. The next we know of it comes by way of its absence from the floor and the woman placing a plastic bag in the rubbish bin. She has simply bypassed any attempt to determine life versus death, any preparation, any special handling, any notification, any drama. It is as if all authority were in her hands alone. It is also – given her deadpan manner – as if the event required none of the actions or emotions that a new form of life or a transition to death might be expected to give rise to.

In addition, these violations are repeated. Perhaps because of curiosity (one keeps imputing motives to a woman who performs outlandish actions in a flat, everyday way) the woman takes the creature out of the bag and places it into the bathtub. Still no turning to anyone else, even when the creature inflates and begins to look human. Still no drama, no preparation for death, no selection of a death site other than a plastic disposal bag. Moreover, in these repeated violations of expected ritual order, the rest of the world has not ceased to exist or to be attended to. The woman matter-of-factly answers the phone and the doorbell. She simply acts as if all decisions with regard to the creature were hers alone, as if nothing extraordinary – nothing that would call for considering anything but her decisions and moods alone – were occurring. A society's established ways of dealing with new forms of life or with the apparently dead are simply treated as if they did not exist.

Let me underline that way of proceeding by contrast with *Alien*. Some of the crew are returning to the spaceship with a new form of life. It is attached to Kane. There is here no scarcity of emotion or of concern with procedures. Ripley reacts with alarm, caution, and a swift reference to quarantine procedures. Her argument is that neither Kane nor the new form should enter the ship. The Science Officer, Burke, argues for suspending the usual procedures, allowing them to study the creature and possibly to save Kane. The positions taken vary, but no one is uninvolved, no one pretends that there are no procedures to be considered, and the possibility that one person's mood or whim could be the deciding factor never emerges. In *Kitchen Sink*, that possibility is all that emerges. In a quiet, almost prosaic fashion – without any recourse to lashings of blood and gore, to prehistoric monsters, extraterrestrrials, or psychotic killers – it gets under the spectator's guard and succeeds in being truly horrible. In fact, it proceeds as if the producer were well aware of where the fears and the defences are, well aware of the expected rules of play, and proceeded to use that knowledge in order to rewrite the rules, to pop up inside the defence walls.

Questions about rituals

I have argued, as Kristeva does, that the degree to which a sense of horror is aroused by an image or text stems in part from the presence, absence, or deliberate degrading of protective ritual formulas. The argument enhances one's understanding of how a film such as *Kitchen Sink* comes to have the impact that it does. Once again, however, it prompts several questions.

One of these has to do with the further functions that rituals may serve (beyond offering safe contact and providing a route for challenge). Within films and within written texts, following a ritual or expected line is one way of establishing a mood or a set of expectations. A shared shorthand gets the listener or the spectator quickly into the story, sets the stage for what may happen. The narrator may then violate those expectations, leaving the other to face the realization: 'Oh, this is not that kind of story after all'. The shared meaning nonetheless rests upon the presence of some recognized actions, some known signal posts.

This kind of function to rituals within texts is certainly not alien to Kristeva. Her discussion of 'the bounded text' is in fact an account of the way in which the opening sections of a text – a novel, for instance – set the 'trajectory' for what is expected to unfold.[15] The several parts of the text will be expected to interconnect in particular ways; the nature of the characters and the quality of their actions are expected to conform to the 'bounds' set by the opening. The argument is one that fits well with the impact of opening lines ('Once upon a time', for example) and, in film, opening scenes that define their genre.

The second point is a larger one. To say that rituals or changes in rituals serve protective or challenging functions bypasses an important question:

what is needed for rituals or their violations to be effective, to have an impact? For this to happen, the ritual actions need to have meaning for all participants. Some of that meaning will derive from experience that is common to all or most people: the experience, for instance, of loss and implied violence that goes with separation from the mother and the imposition of patriarchal control. A further part of meaning comes with the acquisition of a particular culture. Biblical stories of prodigal sons, Christian tales of exorcisms and deathbed confessions: for people in Western societies these are shared sources for examples of the abject. They are part of our cultural past, our store of knowledge.

Does such a past matter? From Kristeva's analysis, one may abstract two ways in which this cultural store of knowledge – this 'text of society and history' – matters. It matters to the producer of images: the writers of horror stories, the designers of rituals, and the selectors of particular violations. The store of past images and past meanings is what the deliberate producer of horror works with and changes in order to tell a new story, produce a new variant or level of horror. It matters also to the spectator. To all images, we bring a history and a set of standard images that we use to see or read. We bring a knowledge of past tales of sin and forgiveness, past stories of love, past silences about what is unnameable, past veils over what may not be seen. Moreover, that knowledge may vary among spectators, offering a possible way of distinguishing between one spectator and another. To use for the last time an example from the Judaic/Christian contrast, consider the position of two Christians. One is a convert from Judaism in the early days of Christianity. The other was born into Christianity and has little or no knowledge of Judaic taboos. For these two people the sight of milk products mixed with meat products, or of people eating pork, will have quite different meanings. For the latter, there is no knowledge of a past taboo. For the former, there is a clear knowledge that what is being seen or done has long been regarded as an insult to the old God, and dangerous.

Clearly, it is easy to indicate that the cultural store of narratives and images is part of the making and the reception of any text. Less easy to answer is the question: how are we to describe and conceptualize the nature of this cultural store and its use? This question is the one I took up in general terms in Chapter 1, in the description of Kristeva's concept, 'the text of society and history'. I now wish to see what form such knowledge and its use takes when it comes to films such as *Kitchen Sink*.

The knowledge that rituals imply

In themselves, written texts provide ritualized encounters with what is new, disturbing, or horrifying. The effectiveness of the ritual form as a protective device, and the effectiveness of an ignored or altered ritual as a form of challenge or a source of disturbance, however, depend upon the shared knowledge of all who are involved in the ritual: its orchestrators and its participants or viewers.

Where films are the text, what is the nature of this knowledge? Some of it is knowledge that all are likely to share and to bring to any text. The knowledge of skin as a sign of the body's integrity – its wholeness as a container, and its wholesomeness – is an example of such general knowledge. What forms of knowledge, we need to ask, go beyond these universal associations?

I shall argue for two forms of relevant knowledge and illustrate both by reference to *Kitchen Sink*. The first has to do with everyday contemporary knowledge. Part of that knowledge consists of the awareness that 'kitchens' and 'abortions' do at times go together, even though the knowledge is not dwelt upon. Kitchens are the sites where women at least may encounter the production of beings who are incomplete, arrive in a bloodied form, and raise issues of the lines between life and death. Part of that everyday knowledge also has to do with a knowledge – again not easily dwelt upon and seldom referred to explicitly – that the means by which a foetus meets its end do not always conform with what is supposed to be part of 'respect for the dead'. This creature, or this mass of tissue depending upon definitions that are often felt to be shaky or arguable, may well end, one fears, in a bucket or a rubbish bag. Part of the claims made against abortion clinics, one of the ways in which their antagonists raise alarm, is by calling upon the fear that this is the way a once-living piece of a body, a potential human being, is 'disposed of'. The precise nature of the ending – respectful burial, disposal along with other unwanted parts of bodies, research use as foetal tissue – is seldom an explicit topic for everyday discussion. An uneasy knowledge that 'disposal' is one possible scenario, however, is certainly widespread.[16] What *Kitchen Sink* does is to play upon that uneasy knowledge, presenting us with an explicit view of disposal, as kitchen waste, of a creature whose state is questionable, by a woman. The possibility that many would rather not think about is not only in full view; it is also presented as a matter-of-fact, everyday event.

The second form of relevant knowledge is media-specific. It takes several forms and calls for some special consideration.

Media-specific knowledge

Most church-goers know that the form of a religious service is likely to vary with the site and the time of day. Cathedrals are likely to proceed with more formality than village churches. Anglican services leave less space for the participants to give voice than do Pentecostal services. Vespers or benedictions are different from an early morning mass or High Mass.

Experienced cinema-goers and television viewers have a similar knowledge of what to expect from the time of a viewing (one would not expect to see *Kitchen Sink* during television prime time or 'family time'). *Kitchen Sink* seen at a horror or fantasy festival would be expected to be horrific: more so than if it were presented without the 'horror' label in a collection of films entered for competition as a film with a particular 'personal vision' (the Cannes selection of *Kitchen Sink* was for films in this category, '*Un Certain Regard*'). Experienced spectators know also that a film seen at an 'art-house' cinema is likely to have a different style from one shown at the local multiplex. A film that is seldom shown but that comes to be known through the existence of many pirate copies (Bridget Ikin has commented that she met many people in Hollywood who had seen *Kitchen Sink* by this route)[17] is even more likely to be known in advance as 'bound to be different'.

More finely, media-specific knowledge has to do with overlapping films.[18] At the level of the general story, *Kitchen Sink* would not be the first time that film-goers have encountered the message: people who create new forms of life or tamper with nature do so at their peril (a message that is of course not confined to films). *Frankenstein* is part of that knowledge (the *Village Voice*, it will be recalled, described *Kitchen Sink* as 'worthy of Mary Shelley' (see Chapter 2)). So also are *The Fly*, *Jurassic Park*, and *Pygmalion* (*Pygmalion* is a gentler version of the usual narrative but again the story is about a created being who turns out to have a mind and an agenda of its own). At the level of particular scenes, this will not be the first time that film-goers have seen tension built up around the act of being shaved. Films such as *The Color Purple*, musicals such as *Sweeney Todd*, contain sharp razor blades, especially of the barbershop variety, and throats that are obligingly presented for slaughter. Barbers start with a soothing beginning: lather on the face, hot towels. The woman in *Kitchen Sink* also begins with a gentle stroke: her stroke with the blade on the creature's leg has some of the elements of a caress. The spectator may well be forgiven for feeling that dismemberment is a possible next step.

The viewer of *Kitchen Sink* also knows, from other films, the implications of particular sounds and particular camera shots. The shaving scene in *Kitchen Sink* is accompanied by a harsh, scraping, tearing sound that underlines still further the possibility that the skin will be broken through, revealing what one would rather not see, or that the creature will end in chopped pieces. Several scenes use camera shots that play upon the expectation of threat and upon the vulnerability that accompanies incomplete knowledge. Horror films in general often use slow tracking shots that follow one of the characters or that come from behind a character, signalling the approach of something or someone. The point of view belongs to that unseen something or someone, rather than to the visible character or to the spectator, both of whom are left without knowledge of what or who approaches. *Kitchen Sink* makes a clear use of such techniques. Twice, the point of view shifts from the main character to a viewpoint behind her. The spectator now has knowledge that the woman does not: knowledge that something is approaching. The first time is a false alarm, raising tension and then releasing it. The woman is seated at the table; the full-size being is in its second bag. The camera shot, and the accompanying sound, suggest that it may have broken loose and be approaching, but in fact nothing happens. On the second occasion, the woman is again seated at the table; the being is supposedly sleeping. On this occasion, the point of view signals the actual approach of the being after it wakes: a signal that comes well before the woman or the spectator can know what form it will take or what its actions will be.

Does media-specific knowledge matter? It matters for three reasons. The first is that this type of specific knowledge offers a way of moving from Kristeva's general proposals to the specifics of film analysis. The second is that media-specific knowledge suggests a different view of the way knowledge is built up from the picture that Kristeva usually presents. Kristeva takes a long sweep through history. The accumulation of textual knowledge occurs over centuries. In contrast, attention to media-specific knowledge suggests that at least some forms of knowledge may be built up over a relatively short period of time. Modleski's analysis of Hitchcock films offers an example. At first, Modleski notes, the theme of the mother as responsible for the disturbed nature of her son is made explicitly. The mother needs to appear and to be shown as overprotective and dominating (*Psycho*). Further along in the series – by the time the film *Frenzy* is reached, for instance – all that needs to be presented is a large picture of a mother on the wall of her son's house. The prominence of the image is all that is needed to imply that here is an overdependent son, likely to be twisted and unpredictably violent. In short, another Norman.[19] Such a short-term build-up may be particularly likely to be the case for media-specific knowledge, but its sheer existence means that one would wish to add short-term history to Kristeva's centuries-long sweep.

In fact, the build-up may even take place within a film. In Chapter 1, for instance, as an example of intertextuality by transposition I took the three scenes in *Vigil* that involve an offering to God. The first two are respectful offerings. These set the stage for the contrast of the third, derisive offering ('Beans to God'). *Kitchen Sink* provides a further example of the use of repetition: this time a repetition of disposals. Early in the action the woman has looked at the creature – fresh from the sink – and consigned it to death in a plastic rubbish bag. She takes it out and shaves it, but again, after overnight inspection, consigns it to the rubbish. At the end, she begins to pull upon a loose hair, to the creature's agony. The implication is that this unravelling will be the creature's end. The earlier disposals suggest at the least that mercy will not be shown in the third round of this cat-and-mouse game.

The third reason for pointing to media-specific knowledge is that its nature and its utilization offer a step towards a further form of specification: a specification of the people involved in the production or reception of a text and of the way their interests, intentions, background, and circumstances exert an influence.

Differences among spectators

This section will bring with it a distinction between two groups of people as well as within each of these groups. The two large groups are those usually referred to as 'spectators' and those usually referred to as 'filmmakers'. I shall begin with that distinction but with the proviso at the start that the two are by no means totally separate or fixed. Scriptwriters are themselves an audience for what is written. So also are the directors, producers, editors, and funding bodies. Moreover, the maker and the viewer are engaged in a joint activity. To take a point insisted upon by Kristeva, 'by the very act of narrating, the subject of narration addresses an "other"; "productivity" is the result of their joint work'.[20]

Let me begin with the notion of 'spectators' and ask what provision there is in Kristeva's work for variations in horror as a function of the spectator's history, experience, position, or gender.[21]

That individual differences exist in what is regarded as horrible is a statement with which few would quarrel. The real challenge is to find the dimensions that most effectively differentiate among individuals. For film spectators, age is one that is frequently suggested. It is certainly enshrined in restrictions upon the ages at which certain kinds of films may be seen alone or in the company of an older person, as well as in market surveys of the age of film audiences. The dimension most often considered within film theory over the last ten to twenty years, however, is gender. Men and women, the argument runs, are unlikely to respond in the same way to scenes of love or violence, to feel the same degree of threat in, say, scenes of men or women being raped, being forced to be a pregnant host as in *Alien*, or being subject to peremptory disposal in a rubbish bag, as in *Kitchen Sink*.

Even a distinction between men and women, the argument continues, is not enough. Women are not all alike. Anneke Smelik, for example, draws attention to differences between gay or lesbian spectators and those who are heterosexual.[22] At the least, both men and women may come in different 'colours', making it likely, for instance, that 'women of colour', or black women, will respond to a film such as *The Color Purple* in a way that differs from the experience of either white women or black men.[23]

There is by now a considerable literature on the topic of the gendered spectator.[24] Rather than review its details, I shall emphasize the question: what does Kristeva suggest as a way of understanding how gender might make a difference to what is experienced as horror? The broader nature of Kristeva's general proposals about male/female differences, and of the reservations expressed with regard to these proposals, will then be taken up in Chapter 9.

Kristeva on differences between men and women

There is little comment within *Powers of Horror* on the possibility that men and women may differ in their vulnerabilities to various forms of the abject. The concern is more with universals; with the impact of corpses, torn skins, false faces, etc. upon people in general and upon the way these various features of the abject are related to defences such as being able to see the abject, to have it 'out there'. The concern is also with the historical situating of subjects: with, for example, the differentiation of various religious groups in terms of their definitions of 'abominations' and their views about appropriate ways of dealing with abominations, or with the particular literary and social order broken by a particular narrative or a particular image.

This inattention to gender differences is in strong contrast to a position such as Modleski's. Modleski's analysis of Hitchcock films is built around the way these films represent both male and female views of gender relationships, and need to be read in terms of whether the spectator is male or female.[25]

Why is there so little direct comment from Kristeva on possible male/female differences in relation to horror? One possible explanation is that she is indifferent to the issue. That explanation can be quickly dispensed with. If it were the case, she would not write about Chinese women rather than about Chinese men,[26] about the kind of representation of motherhood that the Mater Dolorosa offers to women,[27] or about 'generations' of feminism.[28]

The other explanation is that Kristeva regards male/female differences in a way that does not make paramount the gender difference per se. There is no essential, given or biological difference. What matters is the presence (a) of differences in social position (e.g. in the extent to which men or women occupy central or marginal positions in various sectors of society) and (b) of differences in the experience of separation from the mother and of submission to a rational, word-oriented order.

This second explanation is a better fit with what Kristeva has written. Kristeva is indeed wary about suggesting that male/female differences are in any sense 'essences' and 'fixed'. Instead, she regards them as constructed or constituted in the course of language and its practices.[29] She is also strongly inclined towards a Marxist view of people as varying primarily in their social position, and a psychoanalytic view of them as varying in the forms of experience they are likely to encounter or to which they are likely to have access.[30]

For the moment, let me set aside the general issue of Kristeva's attention to male/female differences and ask the more focused question: what is there in Kristeva's analysis that might be especially brought to bear upon the differential experience of horror? One argument she offers is that women, by virtue of their usual exclusion from the centre of patriarchal society (their social position), may be particularly able to note what is excluded from established forms of order: what is lost or sacrificed. Women may be especially adept at 'recognizing the unspoken in all discourse',[31] at reading the subtext.

A second Kristevan argument is that women and men may respond differentially to the destabilization of any established order. This difference (it is a point Kristeva makes in several contexts) stems from the differential costs that men and women incur in the course of entering the symbolic order.

The argument begins with a departure from Freudian theory in what is regarded as a critical moment in development. Freud, Kristeva notes, argues that 'the essential moment in the formation of any psyche, male or female, is the fear of castration'.[32] Kristeva argues for a change: for 'locating this fundamental event ... in the *process of learning the symbolic function* to which the human animal is subjected from the pre-Oedipal period onwards'.[33] This process calls for a separation from the mother, and a turning towards the father and the order he represents. In the process, both men and women may come to derogate the mother and women generally, if only because it is easier to leave what is now defined as less valuable. For men, the potential cost of doing so lies in becoming cut off from tenderness. For women, there is the potential 'price of censuring herself as a woman'.[34]

Three consequences are suggested. One is that women will be less able to cut themselves off from the response of compassion, or of derogation, when horrific events occur to women. A second is that the responses will be more variable among women than among men. The women who are especially disturbed by what is done to women may be those 'who are more bound to the mother and more tuned into their unconscious drives'.[35] A third is that men and women may respond differently to signs that an established order is collapsing, with women having 'nothing to laugh about when the symbolic order collapses'.[36]

Both sources of differences between men and women (different social positions, differential entry into the symbolic order), and the kinds of consequences suggested, are different from what one might expect from any theory based only on a concept such as identification. There clearly still remains a large gap between Kristeva's analysis of response to the abject or participation in rituals of defilement and what many film theorists would expect to find by way of attention to the nature of the spectator and to differences among members of an audience. Nevertheless, there is within Kristeva's work a possible base for taking a novel approach to the form that these spectator differences may take.

That base, moreover, is consonant with some approaches within film theory to the way that social position alters the stance that a spectator brings to a film. As an example, I shall take Jacqueline Bobo's analysis of responses to *The Color Purple*: in particular, the responses of African American males and females. Adopting a position she attributes to Stuart Hall and Frank Larkin, Bobo proposes that past experience with representations and in everyday life lead to a spectator's bringing to a film, even before it starts, a 'stance' that may be:

> dominant, negotiated or oppositional. A dominant (or preferred) reading of a text accepts the content of the cultural product without question. A negotiated reading questions part of the content of the text but does not question the dominant ideology which underlies the production of the text. An oppositional response ... is one in which the recipient of the text understands that the system that produced the text is one with which she/he is fundamentally at odds .... An audience member from a marginalized group (people of colour, women, the poor, and so on) has an oppositional stance as they participate in mainstream media ...[;] we understand that mainstream media has never rendered our segment of the population faithfully. Out of habit, we have learned to ferret out the beneficial and put up blinders against the rest.[37]

One could easily put Bobo's 'oppositional' or 'negotiated' stance together with Kristeva's argument that marginalized positions can provide a particular point of sensitivity to the unspoken in any discourse and possibly a particular readiness to critique established forms of order.

These comments by no means exhaust all that might be said about the extent to which some representations of the abject will evoke the same feelings in all members of an audience, even at one historical time. Nor do they exhaust all that might be said or asked about the ways in which a new or distinctively different text builds upon the past but departs from it, or about the ways in which known codes and formats keep us from sliding into the abyss, into the loss of meaning, stability, and identity that Kristeva sees as a constant but briefly attractive danger. There are, however, themes that will recur. Let us see then how they reappear and are added to in Kristeva's analysis of what is involved in experiences and narratives built around encounters with strangers or being a stranger.

Notes

1. Mary Douglas (1966) *Purity and danger: An analysis of concepts of pollution and taboo.* London: Routledge & Kegan Paul.
2. Tania Modleski (1988) *The women who knew too much: Hitchcock and feminist theory.* New York: Methuen, p.114. On gender and horror see also the essays in Carol J. Clover (1992) *Men, women and chain saws: Gender in the modern horror film.* Princeton: Princeton University Press; and Barry Keith Grant (Ed.) (1996) *The dread of difference: Gender and the horror film.* Austin: University of Texas Press, on the slasher film.
3. Douglas (1966).

4. Barbara Creed (1985) 'Horror and the monstrous-feminine: An imaginary abjection'. In *Screen*, issue 27(1); Modleski (1988, p.108).
5. Julia Kristeva (1982) *Powers of horror: An essay on abjection*. Translated by Léon S. Roudiez. New York: Columbia University Press, p.23. Emphasis in original.
6. Ibid., p.2, emphasis in original.
7. Ibid., p.3, emphasis in original.
8. Creed (1985).
9. Kristeva (1982, p.93).
10. Ibid., p.93.
11. Ibid., p.94.
12. Ibid., p.113.
13. Ibid., p.122.
14. Ibid., p.128.
15. 'The bounded text', in Julia Kristeva (1980) *Desire in language: A semiotic approach to literature and art*. New York: Columbia University Press, pp.36–63.
16. For that matter, the term *disposal* is in English as polysemic as the French *propre*, if not more so: *at my disposal, disposed of, indisposed*, and *rubbish disposal* are some common English expressions.
17. Bridget Ikin in a taped interview with K. Goodnow (December, 1993).
18. For a discussion of 'insider knowledge' with regards to horror films, and in particular serial films, see, Isabel Cristina Pinedo (2004) 'Postmodern elements of contemporary horror film'. In S. Prince (Ed.) *The horror film*. New Brunswick: Rutgers University Press.
19. Modleski (1988, p.106).
20. 'Word, dialogue, and novel', in Kristeva (1980, p.74).
21. For an historical overview of feminist theory, gender and spectatorship see Michele Aaron (2007) *Spectatorship: The power of looking on*. London: Wallflower Press, Chapter 2: 'Spectatorship and difference: Gender and the rub of submission'. See also Clover (1992) on male and female spectators of slasher films.
22. Anneke Smelik (1999) 'Feminist film theory'. In P. Cook and M. Bernink (Eds) *The cinema book*. London: British Film Institute.
23. Jacqueline Bobo (1988) '*The Color Purple*: Black women as cultural readers'. In E.D. Pribram (Ed.) *Female spectators: Looking at film and television*. London: Verso.
24. See, for example, on female spectators, Jane Gaines (1984) 'Women and representation: Can we enjoy alternative pleasure?' *Jump Cut 29*; E. Ann Kaplan (1987) 'Feminist criticism and television'. In R.C. Allen (Ed.) *Channels of discourse*. London: Methuen; Modleski (1988); E. Deirdre Pribram (Ed.) (1988) *Female spectators: Looking at film and television*. London: Verso; Laura Mulvey (1989) *Visual and other pleasures*. Basingstoke: Macmillan; Gaines (1990); Jackie Stacey (1994) *Star gazing: Hollywood cinema and female spectatorship*. London: Routledge; Linda Williams (Ed.) (1994) *Viewing positions: Ways of seeing film*. New Brunswick, NJ: Rutgers University Press; or Janet Staiger (2000) *Perverse spectators: The practices of film reception*. New York: New York University Press. On male spectators see Richard Dyer (1982) 'Don't look now: The male pin-up'. In *Screen*, issue 23(3–4); Steve Neale (1993 [1983]) 'Masculinity as spectacle: Reflections on men and mainstream cinema'. In S. Cohan and I.R. Hark (Eds) *Screening the male: Exploring masculinities in Hollywood cinema*. London: Routledge; or Kenneth MacKinnon (1999) 'After Mulvey: Male erotic objectification'. In M. Aaron (Ed.) *The body's perilous pleasures: Dangerous desires and contemporary culture*. Edinburgh: Edinburgh University Press.
25. Modleski (1988).
26. Julia Kristeva (1986a) 'About Chinese women'. In T. Moi (Ed.) *The Kristeva reader*. Oxford: Basil Blackwell.
27. 'Stabat mater', in Julia Kristeva (1987b) *Tales of love*. New York: Columbia University Press. See also the essay, 'Motherhood according to Giovanni Bellini', in Kristeva (1980).

28. Julia Kristeva (1981) 'Women's time'. In *Signs*, issue 7(1).
29. See especially Julia Kristeva (1975) 'The system and the speaking subject'. In T. Sebeok (Ed.) *The tell-tale sign: A survey of semiotics*. Lisse, Netherlands: The Peter de Ridder Press.
30. In Chapter 8, I shall give more attention to the general consequences of perceiving men and women as differing predominantly in terms of their social position and their experiences in the course of entry into the symbolic order. It is the emphasis upon social position, for instance, that has led Kristeva to place together a variety of marginal groups (from women to ethnic minorities) and to elide the dimensions of gender and class ('Call it "women" or "oppressed classes of society", it is the same struggle, and never one without the other': cited by Toril Moi (1985) *Sexual/textual politics*. London: Methuen, p.164).
31. Kristeva (1986a, p.155).
32. Ibid., p.150.
33. Ibid., p.150, emphasis in original.
34. Ibid., p.151.
35. Ibid., p.156.
36. Ibid., p.151.
37. Bobo (1988, pp.95–96).

Chapter 4

STRANGERS – BASIC CONCEPTS:
STRANGERS WITHOUT AND WITHIN

I shall start the next pair of chapters with a comment about film narratives rather than with a comment that is explicitly about Kristeva's concepts. Many a film narrative is built around encounters between strangers and those already 'in place'. In most of these narratives, 'the stranger comes to town'. The form of the stranger may vary: a new sheriff, a tourist, an immigrant, or an alien strain. The basic narrative, however – the narrative that the spectator expects – is one in which the stranger prompts a variety of emotions among the locals and sets in motion a series of changes in their lives. Those changes may be poised to occur, but the stranger is the catalyst. The two films that anchor the discussion in this chapter – *Vigil* and *Crush* – fall into this general category.

In most stranger narratives also, the focus is upon the point of view of the local. As a rule, we learn little about the way the stranger, the outsider, sees or feels events, little about the ways in which the stranger is transformed. Nonetheless, there are stories – an increasing number it appears – which take the stranger's point of view: *Mississippi Masala*, *My Beautiful Launderette*, *Camille Claudel*, *Baghdad Café*, and *Lost in Translation*, to name a few. *An Angel at My Table* – the film that provides the anchor in the next chapter – belongs within this group.

Most often, however, the point of view presented is that of the 'local', the person who stands for the established order, even when he or she becomes an outsider or undergoes a change in group membership. *Dances With Wolves*, for instance, presents a U.S. soldier as changing in the course of his contact with the only 'others' who are around him (the Lokota 'Indians'), eventually becoming one of 'them'. *Thunderheart* takes another member of the U.S. government (a half-Sioux F.B.I. agent in contemporary times) back to the people he has rejected, to work, as an F.B.I. agent, on a murder case. The film then documents his change as he comes to reconstruct his past and his affiliations, again eventually leaving the old group (the F.B.I.) and, from the point-of-view of the establishment, becoming one of 'them'. Both stories work by taking a recognized contrast of cultures – government agencies and native Americans – and playing a different tune upon an expected tension.

What insights does Kristeva offer that may profitably be brought to bear upon narratives about strangers? For that question, I shall draw mainly from two sources: the books, *Strangers to Ourselves* and *Nations Without Nationalism*.[1] Both books reflect Kristeva's increasing concern with current European politics: in particular, with the rise of militant nationalism and militant ethnicity.[2] Here again are themes that have been a continuing concern for her. One example consists of her comments on the ever broadening European Union (in 2000). Here, she felt, there was a coming together of strangers on the basis of need and their usefulness to one another. Here was a union in which 'marked economic, cultural and religious differences [would] have to be reconciled'.[3] Now we need to ask: 'Which human beings set it going and which human beings benefit or suffer as a result of it'.[4] Are there ways that would help the Union 'be meaningful and not just useful'?[5]

Strangers to Ourselves is the source that prompts my recognition of two narratives and my use of that recognition to divide this pair of chapters, with the first of the pair concentrating upon encounters with strangers, the second upon being a stranger. Most of *Strangers to Ourselves* is devoted to a sweep through history on the way foreigners have been treated in the past: narratives one might class as of the type 'the stranger comes to town'. Strikingly, however, the major part of her opening chapter describes the experience of *being* a foreigner, an outsider: an 'other' by virtue of being of a different nationality, a different sex, or from a different class. It is the other's experience and feelings – their guilt, exhilaration, anger, pride, or emptiness – to which Kristeva keeps returning.

From both books, I shall take a second opening point. This is Kristeva's insistence that the meaning of *stranger* goes beyond a difference in nationality. The stranger is the person 'who does not belong to the group, who is "one of them", the other'[6] – the Moroccan living in France, the French farmer who has moved from one province to another, the intellectual who stands apart from the bourgeoisie, the woman who works in a world where men are 'us' and women are 'other'.

If the status of being foreign by nationality comes to dominate the analysis, it will be well to remember the cover to *Strangers to Ourselves*. This is a painting by Matisse in which two people (a man and a woman) face each other. They differ sharply in their positions and in their dress. Between them is a space, filled by an open window and the vista of a garden. The painting, Kristeva has commented, appeals to her because it represents men and women as strangers to one another, with a gap between them that must be bridged if love or trust is to exist.[7] It is the cover to the second book – *Nations Without Nationalism* – that highlights as foreigners those who are of a different nationality. A photograph of people marching with a banner urging equality and condemning racism, the cover picks up one meaning of the French term *étrangèrs*: a term that, as the translator points out, covers all the meanings covered by the English terms *stranger, foreigner, outsider,* and *alien*.[8]

Those introductory points may make it sound as if Kristeva has made a radical shift away from her earlier concerns and concepts, and as if we shall now need to pursue a completely different set of questions when we turn to the films chosen as a base. There *is* novelty within Kristeva's analysis of strangers, but any discontinuity is more apparent than real. Let me then begin by sketching out some points of continuity and change within Kristeva's analysis of horror, and the questions that her analysis provokes in the context of film.

Aspects of continuity and change

One of my general concerns is to bring out the coherence underlining Kristeva's proposals. This section is one step towards doing so. To start with, the method used in the two books on foreignness is much the same as in the book on horror. Kristeva again combines the analysis of literary texts and large-scale events (in this case both Biblical and political events), with insights from psychoanalysis. She adds as well insights from her own experience as a Bulgarian living in France.

Several of the conceptual concerns are also similar. There is again a strong concern with order and disturbances of order, with the way one form of order is related to another, and with the ways by which one may make contact with what is strange without being taken over or overwhelmed. The connection between order within parts of the individual and order within one's relationship to others, however, now becomes central, displacing the earlier emphasis – in books such as *Desire in Language* or *Revolution in Poetic Language* – on a connection between changes in the order of literary texts and changes in society. As the title, *Strangers to Ourselves*, implies, a major part of Kristeva's argument is that the way we feel towards foreign others reflects the way we feel about those parts of ourselves that seem strange or unlike our usual self:

> [T]o worry or to smile, such is the choice when we are assailed by the strange; our decision depends on how familiar we are with our own ghosts.[9]

> The foreigner is within us. And when we flee from or struggle against the foreigner, we are fighting against our unconscious – that 'improper' facet of our impossible 'own and proper'.[10]

Second, there is, in both the discussion of horror and of foreignness, an emphasis upon the arousal of mixed feelings, opposing trends. The abject arouses both attraction and horror. The foreigner arouses 'fascinated rejection'.[11] Some degree of contact with what is foreign – like some degree of contact with what is abject – is invigorating, life-enhancing, and essential for renewal. Too much, however, can be confusing, overwhelming, even destructive.

Third, there is again a concern with the instability of boundaries. In Kristeva's view 'the foreigner seldom arouses the terrifying anguish provoked by death or the "baleful" unbridled drive'.[12] At the same time, there are some commonalities with the way horror is experienced. To start with, there may be a common impact in the form of a lost sense of identity and order:

> Confronting the foreigner whom I reject and with whom at the same time I identify, I lose my boundaries, I no longer have a container, the memory of experiences when I had been abandoned overwhelm me. I lose my composure. I feel 'lost', 'indistinct', 'hazy'.[13]

Some of the quality of the emotion may also overlap:

> Are we nevertheless so sure that the 'political feelings' of xenophobia do not include, often unconsciously, that agony of frightened joyfulness that has been called *unheimlich*, that in English is *uncanny*, and the Greeks quite simply call *xenos*, 'foreign'?[14]

Fourth, there is again a concern with the ways in which contact with what is disturbing is kept under control. In *Powers of Horror*, Kristeva described two forms of control. One is the avoidance of contact wherever possible, combined with the construction of boundaries of several types (from linguistic distinctions to physical barriers). The other is used when contact is unavoidable or when contact is briefly sought for its novelty and excitement. This consists of 'rituals of defilement'. Where foreigners are concerned, control is exercised again by establishing boundaries. These are now, however, most often in the form of definitions (some will be called 'foreigners' while others are not) and in the form of regulatory codes (codes that specify both the way foreigners should behave and the way they should be received).

I shall pick up some other points of similarity as I proceed. Let me at this point ask instead: in Kristeva's analysis of strangers, what is particularly different from her approach to order and its disturbances that was outlined as the basis to a sense of horror?

What stands out particularly is the value Kristeva now attaches to the preservation of some forms of order, both at the national level and at the level of the individual's sense of identity. Negativity, disruption, and transgression for their own sake – or as an ethical necessity in the face of a rigid bourgeoisie – are no longer prominent. Instead, there is a concern with keeping the best of what we have, with retaining the 'assets' of a system that has its good sides as well as its shortcomings:

The critical mind of French intellectuals often excels in self-deprecation and self-hatred. When they do not take aim at themselves and proclaim their own death, their national tradition – and especially the Enlightenment – become their privileged objects of destruction .... The time has perhaps come for pursuing a critique of the national tradition without selling off its assets. Let us ask, for instance, where else one might find a theory and a policy more concerned with the respect for the other, more watchful of citizen's rights (women and foreigners included in spite of blunders and crimes), more concerned with individual strangeness, in the midst of a national mobility?[15]

The same Kristeva who describes herself as once happily chanting with others that 'DeGaulle must go', now writes a laudatory essay on the man and acknowledges a debt: 'I live in France, and am a French citizen, thanks to DeGaulle'[16] and his policy of extending French influence – and French hospitality – to the peoples of Eastern Europe.

Why this shift? The times have changed, Kristeva notes. The current text of society and history is not what it was in earlier times. Where before the problem was one of weakening the stranglehold of a rigid order (a problem that still remains in many sectors of our lives), now the political problem is the threat of a splintered country, with each faction offering no respect to the other and with no agreement on the value of some 'contractual, cultural, or symbolic' unity.[17] Now is the time of retreat to the warmth and protection of smaller groups, to a different sense of belonging, to a different assurance as to 'who I am':

> Recently, everyone has been harking back to his or her origins – you have noticed it, I suppose? Some proudly claim their French, Russian, Celtic, Slovene, Moslem, Catholic, Jewish, or American roots – and why shouldn't they? Others are sent back to and blamed for their Jewish, Moslem, Catholic, Kurdish, Baltic, Russian, Serb, Slovak, or American background – and why not?[18]

> The values crisis and the fragmentation of individuals have reached the point where we no longer know what we are and take shelter, to preserve a token of personality, under the most massive, regressive common denominators: national origins and the faith of our forbearers. *'I don't know who I am or even if I am*, but I belong with my national religious roots, there I follow *them'*.[19]

The change of times accounts also for Kristeva now emphasizing some particular values to knowledge of the past. In *Desire in Language*, the texts of the past served to demonstrate the way in which the meaning of any text depends upon the quality of its connection to past texts: connection in the form of repetition with transformation; the inclusion of several voices from past and present, contesting with one another; or the presence of a discourse that mocks or parodies the sacred cows of established forms. In *Powers of Horror*, the texts of the past serve to show how some sources of horror are historically and culturally situated, and to bring out the way that past texts offer both an assuring ritual and a base that a new voice or a new group may take as a point of departure, or a point of violation.

Within the books on foreigners, the texts of the past now have a further function. This is the function of assisting in the creation of unity and helping us to know ourselves (for Kristeva, the critical precondition of being able to live with foreigners):

> The difficulty inherent in thinking and living with *foreigners*, which I analyzed in my book *Strangers To Ourselves*, runs through the history of our civilization and it is from a historical standpoint that I take it up in my work, hoping that confronting the different solutions offered by our predecessors would make our present-day debates on immigration more lucid, more tolerant, and perhaps more effective.[20]

Kristeva is well aware that her historical emphasis may strike some people as strange:

> People will object, however, that when an overflow of immigrant workers humiliates French suburbs, when the odor of North African barbecues offends noses that are used to other festivities, and the number of young colored delinquents leads some to identify criminality with foreignness – there is no point in poring over the archives of thought and art in order to find the answers to a problem that is, when all is said and done, very practical.[21]

To this, her reply is that a knowledge of the past, especially where the topic of nations and foreigners is concerned, is essential for all our futures:

> I am convinced that contemporary French and European history, and even more so that of the rest of the world, imposes, for a long while, the necessity to think of the nation in terms of new, flexible concepts because it is within and through the nation that the economic, political, and cultural future of the coming century will be played out.[22]

> Facing the problem of the foreigner, the discourses, difficulties, or even the deadlocks of our predecessors do not only make up a history; they constitute a cultural distance that is to be preserved and developed, a distance on the basis of which one might temper and modify the simplistic attitudes of rejection and indifference.[23]

The goal is not only to avoid disaster but also to improve the richness of one's own culture: 'The vitality of culture can perhaps be measured by the skill with which it interacts with its own memory at the same time as with the memory of other civilizations.'[24]

In short, the texts of particular concern – the historical occasions that Kristeva describes in detail in *Strangers to Ourselves* and summarizes in the first part of *Nations Without Nationalism* – have now the special status of being informative lessons.

Continuity and change in the questions prompted for films

Kristeva's proposals with regard to horror prompted a series of questions about the form of a particular narrative and – an issue of particular interest – the feelings that images and occasions of horror evoke in the spectator: feelings kept within bounds by the encounter being contained within a ritualized format to which the spectator brings some knowledge of what is likely to happen as well as an awareness that what is being watched is film.

Kristeva's proposals about strangers also prompt questions about the feelings and the expectations of the spectator, especially if that spectator belongs to a group that is likely to find particular kinds of strangers unsettling rather than interestingly exotic. Prompted also, however, are questions about the way a film represents the feelings of the characters who are part of the narrative. Kristeva emphasizes, for instance, that the stranger's impact is a function of the feelings and the needs of those who are already in place. That emphasis leads one to ask: how are these feelings or needs represented? Which feelings are underlined? Why these rather than others? Who displays the fascination? Who displays the rejection or the ambivalence? One is also led to ask: what is it about the current position of those who are in place that makes it easy for the stranger to set new events in motion and makes it likely that these events will take one direction rather than another?

Kristeva's proposals about strangers prompt as well questions about the ways in which a film represents control or lack of control over the feelings that strangers evoke. Is there, for instance, some direct representation of the tension that Kristeva emphasizes between an ethic of universalism (e.g. 'love thy neighbour as thyself') and an ethic of particularism (e.g. 'look after your own')? Or is some other form of tension between codes being brought out?

This is not to say that the feelings and expectations of the spectator are to be ignored within the chapters on strangers and stranger narratives. That concern continues. I shall move, however, to a stronger interest in questions about the nature of the narrative, reflecting in part Kristeva's own interest in bringing to our attention the form taken by several stories that may be drawn from history. A number of further questions will arise as I proceed through the particular films chosen as a base: films that now need a brief introduction.

Introducing two films: *Vigil* and *Crush*

Two films will serve as an illustrative base in this chapter – *Vigil* and *Crush*. A brief general description is in order. *Vigil* is the earlier film: one of several reasons for beginning with it. *Vigil* was written and directed by

Vincent Ward and produced by John Maynard in 1984. The film was his first feature after two notable shorts: *A State of Siege* (1978) and *In Spring One Plants Alone* (1980). *Vigil* was the first New Zealand feature to appear in competition at Cannes. *Crush* appeared in 1992. The team was the same as for *Kitchen Sink* (Alison Maclean as writer/director, Bridget Ikin as producer). *Crush* was Maclean's first feature film after several shorts. It was presented at Cannes and was noted as 'an interesting ... first feature'.[25]

Vigil has a particular place in New Zealand film history. (Ikin describes it as 'my only inheritance', and as a film that demonstrated to funding bodies the viability of an 'art-house style').[26] The film also has a particular place in Vincent Ward's history. *Vigil* is the first of three films directed by him that have a common central theme: the nature of encounters between people who belong to different social groups. In *Navigator*, an isolated Medieval group flees contact with plague-ridden others of the same time period, and makes unexpected contact – in a shift of time and place – with a contemporary city in New Zealand. In *Map of the Human Heart*, an Inuit boy in the 1930s meets a visiting mapmaker from Montreal, is diagnosed by him as having tuberculosis ('the white man's disease'), and flown by him from the far North to Montreal for years of treatment before an eventual return as a stranger to his own Inuit group.

In *Vigil* all four characters are New Zealanders, living and working on a small and far from prosperous farm. The four are a man, his wife, his father, and the couple's daughter: a slight, boyish-looking child of about twelve whose pleasure in her father's company is established at the start by her rushing to join him, to the mother's displeasure, in a search on fog-covered hills for some straying sheep and their newborn lambs. The woman turns out to have been a city girl, now removed to a new place by having married a man 'on the land'. The person presented as 'foreign', however, is a local, who lives outside the usual codes. Instead of being settled on a farm, he does odd jobs and poaches deer on others' property. Instead of respect for God, he insists that the hills care as much about who lives or dies as God does. Instead of fear and hatred of the hawks that threaten the young lambs, he admires them and can imitate their call.

As in many narratives, the arrival of the stranger triggers a process of change. In *Vigil*, the stage is set for change by a death. The father falls from a cliff in the search for a lamb and the stranger brings in his body. The child starts a vigil at the site of her father's death, visiting it as often as possible, planting a tree there, and wearing – both there and everywhere possible – her father's old coat and balaclava. The help of an additional person is clearly needed if the farm is not to be sold or abandoned (the main value lies in the sale of the young lambs) and the grandfather hires the stranger, ignoring the woman's coolness towards him. The stranger is an unenthusiastic worker and prefers to spend his time fixing the tractor, helping the grandfather build an elaborate construction designed to plumb a cave, talking to the child, and making it clear that he finds the child's mother sexually attractive. In the course of the lambing season, the mother and the stranger begin an affair, the grandfather's hopes come to nothing when the new machine falls apart in the first try, and the daughter ends her vigil (the stranger has convinced her that 'God does not care') and – on the eve of their leaving the farm – has her first menstrual period. The film ends with a double closure. The mother and daughter (the daughter now wearing a dress and no balaclava) walk away from the farm, their few belongings in a cart drawn by the tractor, with grandfather as the driver. The stranger drives off in the opposite direction, smashing through the gates with his truck as he leaves: gates there is no longer any point in opening and closing.

Crush is visually a brighter film than *Vigil*. *Vigil* is shot in unrelentingly cool, dark colours with an occasional splash of red. The landscape is craggy and ominous. The primary colour in *Crush* is the green of rolling hills lit by sunshine: a picture postcard landscape that fits the locals' phrase, 'God's own country'. Two women – one American, one a New Zealander – are driving towards a village, where the New Zealander (Christine) is to interview a reclusive writer who has just won an award. The two women are old friends, meeting again after some time apart. Between them there is clearly both affection and a competitive tension.

Where *Vigil* opens with a real death, *Crush* opens with a near death. Lane (the American) crashes the car shortly before they reach the village. She is unharmed but Christine is severely injured. She will need to learn again both how to speak and how to walk. She will need also to learn to cope with the bursts of rage that she now experiences and with a frustrating loss of memory.

The accident sets off a series of shifting alliances. The first of these begins when Lane cannot bring herself to visit Christine. She turns instead towards developing a friendship with the writer's daughter Angela, a girl of about sixteen who is on the verge of a sexual awakening and who finds immensely attractive Lane's sexual frankness, her air of freedom, her unimpressed response to the 'natural wonders' of the area, and her appreciation of Angela's looks: 'I thought you were a boy', says Lane, 'but you're too good looking to be a boy'.

Lane turns also to locating local entertainment, taking Angela to a disco and keeping her as a companion as she begins noting potential sexual partners, one of these being a Maori musician at the disco. The person she actively seduces at a slightly later point is Angela's father, Colin, beginning the affair in her motel room but then moving into the house shared by Angela and Colin. The daughter in turn shifts her love to the bed-ridden Christine, and works with her to recover some speech and mobility (they combine to speak of Lane as evil). Angela insists upon Christine becoming part of the family group and, on her own initiative, brings Christine to join Colin and Lane on their weekend visit to a cottage that Colin owns.

The film ends with the death of Lane during this weekend. The direct agent for that death is Christine who, in the course of a visit to a high lookout and the beginning of a possible reconciliation with Lane, is swept up with rage in her recognition of the 'evil' Lane, takes some first steps, and pushes Lane over the edge of the cliff. Shortly before that moment, the father and daughter have come to a better understanding of one another and of the need to acknowledge the relationship of the two foreigners to one another: they cannot simply be taken over. The 'double triangles' that Maclean sees as the crux of the story (Lane, Colin, Angela; Lane, Christine, Angela) have shifted once again, but the direction of the next shift, given the ambiguous source of Lane's death – at Christine's hands but in the wake of Angela's incitement of Christine to hate Lane and Colin's provocation of Angela's anger towards Lane – is left unresolved.

Who is a stranger? What marks the stranger?

This is the first of three large questions that I shall abstract from what Kristeva has written. The questions will provide a way of both summarizing Kristeva's ideas and demonstrating the relevance of the questions she raises for the analysis of film.

As a starting point, let me note again that for Kristeva a foreigner need not be of another nationality. It is not necessary to leave one's country to be regarded as foreign or to feel foreign. The shift from one province to another may be sufficient. French farmers who shift provinces, for instance, are often regarded as intruders and labelled 'Portuguese' or 'Spaniards'.[27] There may, in fact, be no need to change one's physical place. A shift in social class or in occupation may have the same effect. So also may a state of marginality in one's own country. As Kristeva notes with regard to women:

> A woman is trapped within the frontiers of her body and even of her species, and consequently feels *exiled* both by the general clichés that make up a common consensus and by the very powers of generalisation intrinsic to language.[28]

This way of defining foreigners has the particular advantage of allowing a multiplication of forms of foreignness within the one film. The one person may be a foreigner, a stranger, in more than one way. To be a woman from another country, for instance, may make one doubly alien. To be different in one's speech may compound the difficulty. Kristeva reminds us, for instance, that:

> Homer ... seems to have coined the term [*barbarian*] on the basis of such onomatopoeia as *bla-bla, bara-bara*, inarticulate or incomprehensible mumblings. As late as the fifth century, the term is applied to *both Greeks and non-Greeks* having a slow, thick, or improper speech .... For all three dramatists [Sophocles,

Aeschylus, Euripides] 'barbarian' meant 'incomprehensible', 'non-Greek', and finally 'eccentric' or 'inferior'. The meaning 'cruel'... would have to wait until the barbarian invasions of Rome showed up.[29]

To be different in one's dress and attitudes may amplify the problem still further. Kristeva recounts, for instance, the story of the Danaïdes: the fifty daughters of Danaüs who asked for asylum among the Argive. The Danaïdes, Kristeva notes, were 'foreigners for two reasons: they came from Egypt and they were refractory to marriage'.[30] Their foreignness was also visible to all, an aspect made explicit in one of the objections raised by the Argive king:

> So outlandishly arrayed in the barbaric luxury of robes and crowns, and not in Argive fashion / Nor in Greek? But at this I wonder how without a herald, without a guide, without patron you have yet dared to come.[31]

Anticipating such concerns, Danaüs's advice to his daughters was that they 'act the suppliant', carry 'white suppliant wreaths', and 'yield':

> Let no boldness come from respectful eye and modest features. Nor talkative nor a laggard be in speech / Either would offend them. Remember to yield / You are an exile, a needy stranger / And rashness never suits the weaker.[32]

In short, the foreigner is anyone who is 'other', 'different'. And any person may involve layers of foreignness. One does well then to ask of any narrative: who are the strangers? What marks them as 'different'? Is the spectator also made to feel a stranger, even in what should be his or her 'own land'?

Vigil supplies a first example. The obvious foreigner is the poacher, the one who illegally hunts deer and is persuaded to work with the sheep. *Vigil*, however, contains more than this single layer of a stranger. The film makes it abundantly clear that all the people there are strangers to the land, and that the land is not welcoming. At best, it is indifferent – 'Do the hills care?', asks the stranger. At worst, it is hostile: taking back in landslides a little each year of what has been cleared or cultivated, a natural home only to the predatory hawks. The mother especially feels an alien within this landscape. So also does the spectator, presented from the start with hills that drop away sharply, and are wreathed in fog that in seconds separates the daughter from the father and makes her becoming lost seem inevitable. A few open paddocks surround the house, but in the hills one never sees a clearing except for the small patch where the daughter plants her tree. There must be a sizeable path to this clearing since it contains also the wreck of an old car; but one never sees a path. People emerge abruptly from the hills, or move jaggedly from one rock to another. And it seems to rain constantly, making the ground seem treacherously spongy and reducing still further the visibility of any path. It is only at the end of the film, as everyone leaves the area, that we see clearly that there is a dirt road in and out of the homestead.

Crush contains still more layers of strangers, set in even more complex relationships with one another. The most obvious foreigners are the two women, Lane and Christine: journalists from 'outside'. As the story unfolds, the novelist they seek to interview also turns out to be a stranger. He has withdrawn to this small town, and he works with the locals in netting fish, but he does not come from there and Lane later makes it clear that his life was once quite different from what it is now. A life of 'impulse' is her description of his past, one he acknowledges as true but also as past.

The layer of relationships among strangers and others that especially distinguishes *Vigil* from *Crush*, however, has to do with the relationship between the indigenous Maoris and the whites – the pakehas. (*Pakeha* is a Maori term for non-Maori and is widely used by Maori and pakeha alike.) Maoris do not appear in *Vigil*, with its cast of four. They are present, however, in *Crush* and their presence instantly converts the pakehas into foreigners; latter-day settlers.

This new definition of those who 'belong' and those who have come lately presents more than an extra layer of strangers and others. It involves as well a challenging problem of representation. Here is a new narrative that has to be written. Everyone agrees that Maoris should be included in current New Zealand films, redressing their past invisibility. Including them in the New Zealand picture may make the landscape seem strange to the usual pakeha viewer, but the current social climate argues for Maoris being included in the picture.

The problem is how to do so. A way needs to be found that does not go back to 'the noble savage', that represents current times, and that is not offensive to present-day Maoris. This concern with accuracy without offensiveness – and with attention to the Maori point of view, the Maori's narrative – is new. So also is the caution with which the pakehas now proceed in their representation of the people to whom they are the foreigners. In the words of the producer of *Crush*, Bridget Ikin:

> [M]any white filmmakers shy away from any representations ...[:] it is a minefield ...[;] you just can't win ...[. Y]ou are damned if you include them in your film and damned if you don't.[33]

What are the representations that gave rise to such concern, and how are these concerns met? There are in *Crush* two male Maori characters (no women except for a glimpse of the extended family of one of the two). One Maori plays a minor role as a black-tie waiter in the restaurant to which Colin (the father of Angela, the lover of Lane) takes Lane, Angela and Christine, still grossly clumsy in her movements and slurred in her speech. For a change, it is the Maori who disapproves of the pakehas' 'poor' behaviour.

The main Maori character – 'Horse' – plays a far more complex role. His first appearance is as a musician in the nightclub/disco to which Lane takes Angela on a first night out (Angela out of her usual dungarees and wearing a red dress: one of Lane's). Horse admires, and compliments, both women. His second appearance is later the same night with Lane, observed by Angela. The two are clearly meeting as attracted equals, ready to party and to spend the night together. The third is an appearance in the hospital, where Horse is in traction after an accident. He is at first shown with family, in a scene that seems almost trite. Here is Horse surrounded, as one New Zealand stereotype suggests, by a large extended family: a family that covers several generations and is able to extend their warmth to the young pakeha girl. In contrast, here is Christine, whose closest friend (Lane) does not visit: whose only visitor, in fact, is the young girl who was previously not known to her.

Any suggestion of trite stereotypes, however, is wiped out by the next scene. After his relatives leave, Horse persuades Angela – in the hospital visiting Christine – to stay and spend time with him. At one point, he persuades her also to kiss him and then relieve an itchy spot by inserting a knitting needle under the plaster and moving it around to scratch the spot. The same sigh of ecstatic relief as this first itch is relieved is repeated when Horse then guides Angela's hand to his penis and continues to move it, with her somewhat ambivalent consent, until he reaches climax. At this point, Horse is again Lane's equal: her parallel in taking sexual pleasure wherever it may be found, happily, without overt violence, with some awareness that the other is ready to be seduced or to participate, and without much more thought beyond that.

The parallel with a white is a characterization that gives a Maori a form of equality, an acknowledgment of 'sameness', that goes far beyond any patronizing recognition of the Maori as the strangers who are now to be granted visibility in a white world. Horse is presented as a character with the same complexity and the same style as the lead female: a daring equality that replaces an earlier invisibility. For most pakeha viewers, this representation of a Maori character places before them a multidimensional character who can only be for them a stranger.

The stranger's stance as the critical feature

If a difference in nationality is not to be the defining feature of a stranger, what shall we put in its place? It is easy to say that the stranger is any 'other'. There is, also, as Noëlle McAfee and Norma Claire Moruzzi both point out, some conceptual advantage to placing the analysis of strangers under the general umbrella of defining 'self' and 'other'.[34] The difficulty, however, is that the category of 'the other' now becomes extremely broad.

If not by nationality, how shall we differentiate one type of stranger from another?

Kristeva offers an interesting possibility that takes one back to her concern with the quality of the connection between one text and another (see Chapter 1). She and Bakhtin, it will be recalled, distinguish between texts that mock established forms of literary or social order and texts that accept these forms. In similar fashion, Kristeva distinguishes between strangers who accept the demand that they allow themselves to be 'perfectible'[35] and strangers who are critical of the society in which they find themselves.

It is the latter kind of stranger, like the avant-garde, that especially attracts Kristeva's attention. These are not the suppliants, the foreigners who present themselves as 'needy'. They are instead the ones who relish their position as outsiders, who are open in their scorn, and who mock the values of the established society. For Kristeva, the foreigner as critic is a character to be found in many narratives:

> Beginning with Montesquieu's *Persian Letters* (1872) and including Voltaire's *Zadig* (1747) and *Candide* (1759), to mention only the most famous works, philosophical fiction became peopled with foreigners who invited the reader to make a twofold journey. On the one hand it is pleasant and interesting to leave one's homeland in order to enter other climes, mentalities, and governments; but on the other hand and particularly, this move is undertaken only to return to oneself and one's home, to judge or laugh at one's limitations, peculiarities, mental and political despotisms. The foreigner then becomes the figure onto which the penetrating, ironical mind of the philosopher is delegated – his double, his mask. He is the metaphor of the distance at which we should place ourselves in order to revive the dynamics of ideological and social transformation.[36]

The 'pinnacle' of these criticisms, Kristeva proposes, is to be found in the eponymous antihero of Diderot's novel *Rameau's Nephew*. Here is an insider – one of one's own nationals – who 'internalized both the discomfort and the fascinated recognition aroused by the strange and carried them to the very bosom of eighteenth century man':[37]

> Rameau's Nephew does not want to settle down – he is the soul of a game that he does not want to stop, does not want to compromise, but wants only to challenge, displace, invest, shock, contradict .... The Nephew is conscious of his strangeness ...[:] he himself prefers not to be like 'others', who actually represent only the abject consensus, the perverted mass .... The frankness he displays is a turning inside out of deceitful words, the correction of a falsehood .... The Nephew experiences the meaning of his words as a liberating process: clash of opposites, pleasure springing up, truth of laughter.[38]

The Nephew, Kristeva argues, goes beyond the 'honest' cynicism of a Greek such as Diogenes, that 'eccentric dog-man, rancorous and scornful toward Alexander as the Nephew was with respect to Rameau':[39]

The Nephew is closer to a cynic who left his imprint on literary genres by inventing a new model of satire – Menippus of Gadara, who, besides, was a corrupt usurer and ended up hanging himself.[40]

It is, however, both types of cynic who move society forward. Diogenes is seen as doing so by challenging society to discover a new 'moral imperative'.[41] The Nephew does so by challenging any status quo, setting against it always a 'stance' that is 'temporary, moveable, changing',[42] and arguing that every statement of truth or value is a moveable 'position'.[43] The critical, mocking, challenging stranger then should be the one to look for in any narrative. This is the character most likely to give excitement and tension to a story. This is the character who should shift old mores or old relationships into new patterns.

How does that view of strangers and their effects fit with films such as *Vigil* and *Crush*? How do Kristeva's ideas encourage us now to 'read' those narratives? What stands out first is the presence in both films of a mocking stranger. The stranger in *Vigil*, for instance, mocks any sentimental association with the land, or any belief that God will solve one's problems. He takes a casual attitude toward work. The grandfather's advice is that working harder would 'warm up' the widow, but the stranger would clearly prefer to spend his time – and does spend his time – fixing the tractor and joining the grandfather in building a machine whose rickety appearance makes it abundantly clear that it will never work. The machine does in fact fall apart the first time it is used, but not before the daughter has also been swept up in the excitement of the new toy, eagerly taking a first swing on it, giving it her blessing when she might have been working or formed a partnership with her disapproving mother.

The stranger also makes it clear to the daughter that life on this farm is nothing compared with the wonders of the larger world that he has known. It is with the 'magic' of this world – a demonstration of the colour that the play of light can involve – that he wins her affection and begins to weaken the intensity of her grief for the father she has lost. The tone of superiority is sustained even with the mother. She joins him in crutching the lambs and he makes light of her competence. He finds her doing ballet-stretching exercises in tights (a first sign of her eagerness to return to an outside, middle-class world that she now sees as possible to rejoin). Instead of acting as if he were out of place, he looks sardonically at the mother and says: 'Well, you're full of surprises, aren't you?' His is not the brutal cynicism that Kristeva sees in the Nephew. The stranger in *Vigil* simply refuses to take seriously, or to be bound by, the virtues and values that constrain the three others. And it is that freedom which then allows the others to set aside some of those constraints.

Crush presents an even more mocking foreigner, in the character of Lane. The film opens with her criticism of what many New Zealanders hold dear: the green, rolling hills, dappled with sunshine, that are a major part of the description Janet Frame offers in *An Angel at My Table*: 'God's own country'. Lane finds it boring and says so: 'Everything is so empty'. She is equally unimpressed by Angela on their first meeting – 'I thought you were a boy' – and proceeds to show her how she might improve her appearance and her manner. She will not be bound by conventions that limit her sexual freedom or her ability to respond with aggression to what is unwelcome (she burns with a cigarette the hand of the motel manager who breaks a window in an attempt to follow up the sexual promise that Lane seems to offer to all). She will not even be bound – although here she seems uneasy – by the conventional obligation to visit her friend Christine in the hospital, even though the accident was caused by Lane's inattentive driving (her glancing aside at the statue of an attractive young woman placed in front of a fruit-stand by the side of the road). The task of visiting Christine is one she attempts but cannot face; it becomes Angela's. Nonetheless, Lane – like the stranger in *Vigil* – is not a bitter mocker. Part of her attraction in fact lies in her general sense of pleasure in life: a particular contrast to the relative earnestness of the New Zealand life around her. In the words of the actress who played the part, Marcia Gay Harden: 'Lane is the opposite of a "people-pleaser" – she's direct, honest, brutal, acerbic, witty and wild'.[44]

Lane, moreover, is not alone in her refusal to play the grateful, silent stranger. The injured woman – Christine – also plays a mocking role, somewhat unexpectedly. At the start, Christine appears to be gently disposed towards the countryside. After the accident, she is visibly 'needy', forced to depend upon others. Nonetheless, she does not act out the role of someone who must disguise resentment or dislike in order to gain help and approval. She mocks herself and the hospital. The bond between herself and Angela is, in fact, first formed around their mutual laughter at a dignified nurse who – on her way to express her disapproval of Christine's throwing the hospital food on the floor – slips on some of that food.

In effect, the mocking of established forms of order is more explicit in *Crush* than it is in *Vigil*. Both films, however, underline the importance of strangers who dissent: strangers who do not follow the conventions with regard to how hard one should work, the way one should speak, the degree of sexual freedom one should allow oneself or should display, or the degree of gratitude one should express towards those who have allowed one to stay. Strangers may stand apart in the emotions they express: a 'tearing happiness', a marked 'ebullience and verve', or – at the opposite end of the scale – an 'emptiness', a 'love of solitude'. (Kristeva sees Mersault in Camus's *The Stranger* as the prototype of the latter kind of character.)[45]

In all cases, however, the critical feature to the stranger has to do with the stance taken towards the surrounding society. That stance significantly underlines the nature of the relationship between 'you' and 'me', tips the balance towards one of the mixed set of feelings that the foreigner evokes (indifference, angry rejection, or fascinated attraction), and provides a critical part of the tension that stranger narratives contain.

What creates the tension?

Stories involving foreigners would have no interest, at either the political or the narrative level, if their presence involved no tension. The critical question is: what gives rise to the tension? On this score, Kristeva's proposals are especially rich. I have already indicated that one source of tension may be the stranger's mocking stance, especially when this is set against the local's expectations that the stranger assimilate or be grateful. I shall now draw out two further suggestions. These have to do with the tensions between (a) hatred and the factors that constrain it, and (b) conflicting codes of behaviour.

Hatred and its constraints

Suspicion and hatred, Kristeva proposes, are natural reactions to foreigners:

> The cult of origins is a hate reaction. Hatred of those others who do not share my origins and who affront me personally, economically, and culturally: I then move back among 'my own', I stick to anarchic, primitive 'common denominator', the one of my frailest childhood, my closest relatives, hoping they will be more trustworthy than 'foreigners', in spite of the petty conflicts those family members so often, alas, had in store for me but that now I would rather forget. Hatred of oneself, for when exposed to violence, individuals despair of their own qualities, undervalue their achievements and yearnings, run down their own freedoms whose preservation leaves so much to chance; and so they withdraw into a sullen, warm, private world, unnameable and biological, the impregnable 'aloofness' of a weird primal paradise – family, ethnicity, nation, race.[46]

Hatred is also part of each person's psychic history:

> In the beginning was hatred, Freud said basically (contrary to the well-known biblical and evangelical statement), as he discovered that the human child differentiates itself from its mother through a rejection affect, through the scream of anger and hatred that accompanies it, and through the 'no' sign as prototype of language and of all symbolism. To recognize the inputs of that hatred aroused by the other, within our own psychic dramas of psychosexual individuation – that is what psychoanalysis leads us to. It thus links its own adventure with the meditations each one of us is called upon to engage in when confronted with the fascination and horror that a different being produces in

us, such meditations being prerequisite to any legal and political settlement of the immigration problem.[47]

As if this were not enough, the easy response of hatred is often justified by reference to wrongs received in past times. The God of the ancient Jews (Yahweh), for instance, exhorted the Israelites to kill Amalek: 'Now go and strike down Amalek; put him under the ban with all he possesses. Do not spare him, but kill man and woman, babe and suckling, ox and sheep, camel and donkey.'[48] The reason? Amalek 'opposed them on the road by which they came out of Israel'.[49] Small wonder, then, that enmity could last for centuries, and be reciprocated (as it was by Amalek's sons, Agaf and Haman, who issued a decree calling for the 'total annihilation of Israel').[50] Such justification of current actions by references to the past might occasionally work for the benefit of strangers ('you must not molest the stranger or oppress him, for you lived as strangers in the land of Egypt').[51] More often, the past emerges as justifying annihilation, or delayed acceptance (the 'third generation' of the Egyptians, for instance, might be 'admitted to the assembly of Yahweh').[52] Kristeva might well be describing the current enmities of Serbs and Muslim Bosnians.

> At base, the foreigner threatens one's sense of 'self'. The foreigner presents one with a potential loss of boundaries: this time 'the boundaries between *imagination* and *reality*'.[53] The foreigner also presents the self with a challenging possibility – 'the possibility or not of being an other ....It is not simply – humanistically – a matter of our being able to accept the other, but of being in his place, and this means to imagine and make oneself other for oneself.'[54]

Worst of all, it is not simply any 'other' that the foreigner represents. What one perceives in foreigners is one's own 'familiar repressed',[55] one's own 'ghosts and doubles'.[56]

Would hatred be resolved, then, if the foreigner accepted all the conditions imposed by those already in place: the conditions, for instance, of acting the suppliant, becoming converted, becoming assimilated, giving up one's difference, being 'devoured'? Not entirely, Kristeva argues. The fear remains that 'the convert can never be fully trusted'[57] that 'the assimilated foreigner works on the faithful ... from the inside'.[58] The 'clean false face' that I noted earlier as particularly abject appears once again as a particular reason for dread of the stranger.

All told, one wonders how any positive resolution – any renewal, any transformation, or any emergence of a new ethic can occur. Even short of that, what keeps the negative feelings on both sides from constantly erupting into open warfare? Kristeva's analysis points to constraints of three kinds.

The first of these is the presence of attraction as well as suspicion or hatred. The stranger elicits a 'fascinated rejection', a 'frightened joyfulness'.[59] The degree of fascination may vary with the times. There are historical periods, Kristeva points out, when we are especially inclined to be 'in love ... with national peculiarities'.[60] The German Romanticists provide Kristeva with an example:

> The Romantic leaning towards the supernatural, madness, dreams, the obscure forces of the fatum, and even animal psychology is related to the desire to group the strange, and by domesticating it, turn it into an integral component of the human. *Einfühlung* – an identifying harmony – with the strange and different then became essential as the distinctive feature of the worthy, cultivated man: 'The perfect man must be capable of living equally in various places and among diverse peoples', Novalis noted.[61]

Even without a belief in the importance of *Einfühlung*, Kristeva points out, some attraction is inevitable once the possibility is open for any recognition of the stranger as ourselves: as the parts of ourselves that we see it necessary to control, on the one hand, but on the other not to deny or reject completely. Historically, Kristeva argues, Freudian theory – especially by way of the concept of the unconscious – builds upon 'its humanistic and Romantic filiation' to produce 'an involution of the strange in the psyche'.[62]

> Hence forth the foreigner is neither a race nor a nation. Neither glorified as a secret *Volksgeist* nor banished as disruptive of rationalist urbanity. Uncanny, foreignness is within us; we are our own foreigners, divided.[63]

Does such a concept do more than point to one of the factors that keep suspicion and hatred from 'erupting' into open action? The concept helps as well, I suggest, to account for the nature of some contemporary stories. *Crush* provides an example. Why is Colin so attracted to Lane, so ready to overlook the effects upon his daughter of his open affair, an affair that Colin and Lane pursue in Colin's home? He has apparently been celibate for some time. His marriage is in the past, wrecked – he implies – by a choice he made between his writing and the care of his wife. That is one explanation. He is currently facing a writer's block, and Lane could be a way of breaking this second form of 'ice'. That is another explanation. But, the story adds, he once lived differently, was different: impulsive, even violent (Christine carries a newspaper clipping describing him as punching a critic who wrote negatively about his writing). Lane reminds him of that time: 'I thought impulse was your specialty', she says. He replies that this is no longer the way that he is. Lane, however, brings out that part of him again. He in turn brings that part of himself back into line again by treating the affair as the beginning of a long-term romance, of domesticity. To her dismay, he begins to talk of places they will explore – in this same area – 'next year'. She fights against the domestication ('I may not be here'), leaves, returns to accept love on his terms, but is then again furious when one night he turns away from her sexual initiative and reaffirms his life of 'no alcohol, no drugs', and, Lane comments with a slightly bitter irony, 'no surprises'. In effect, the narrative plays out, in a form readily understood by a contemporary audience, the attraction and the retaming of the part of oneself that 'once was me'.

Over and beyond the presence of attraction towards the stranger, what else restrains the recognition and the open expression of suspicion and hatred? Kristeva points to the power of economic need. From the time of the Greeks, she comments, the foreigner has been the workhorse of the local economy, and one needs to treat one's workhorses with some degree of care. A further factor is the power of reputation. The concern of contemporary filmmakers with the image they present of themselves as enlightened, and the concern of New Zealand funding bodies with the images presented to people within and outside the country: these are not uniquely contemporary concerns. Kristeva cites Plato's dissection of the reasons for proposing particular ways of treating foreigners:

> The intercourse of cities with one another is apt to create a confusion of manners; strangers are always suggesting novelties to strangers …. On the other hand, the refusal of states to receive others, and for their own citizens never to go to other places, is an utter impossibility and to the rest of the world is likely to appear ruthless and uncivilized; it is a practice adopted by people who use harsh words, such as *xenelesia* or banishment of strangers, and who have harsh and morose ways, as men think.[64]

It was then to retain Greece's reputation as enlightened, but also to reduce 'confusion', that Plato recommended different regulations for different kinds of foreigners: those who are 'like birds of passage, taking wing in pursuit of commerce' were to be received in public buildings outside the city by magistrates. Those who came for 'the festivals of the Muses' were to be received by priests and ministers of the temples. Those who came to learn, or – a rare case – to teach were to be given the warmest reception but even they must eventually depart, 'as a friend taking leave of friends'.[65]

Plato's proposals bring up the last of these restraining forces that I shall abstract from Kristeva's work. This restraint now comes from the presence of codes that specify the actions that foreigners and locals should display and, more subtly, the feelings they should experience or strive for. The codes that Plato refers to are in the form of written regulations. There are as well, Kristeva points out, ideologies related to 'proper' behaviours towards strangers: ideologies related to the treatment of guests or to the importance of loving one's neighbour as one loves oneself. The significant feature to these codes, Kristeva points out, lies not in their simply being present but in their being neither static (their strength changes from time to time) nor totally consistent with one another. There is, in fact, she argues, a continuous tension between the two main ideologies that mark the treatment of foreigners throughout the history of the Western world. This continuing tension deserves space of its own.

Tension between conflicting codes

The codes of particular interest to Kristeva are ideologies. Legislated rules – the regulations that specify where foreigners may live, the conditions under which they might become citizens, the circumstances under which they can be expelled or extradited, etc. – may display a fair degree of stability, with tension arising only between the law-makers and the strangers who object to the regulations. Ideologies, however, may display less stability. Moreover, they may change and conflict with one another within the person who is not the stranger.

Within the Western world, for instance, one ideology argues for acting along universalist lines. The philosophy of the Stoics, the essence of *caritas*, the doctrine of *ecclesia*, the Old Testament's advice to 'molest no stranger', Montesquieu's emphasis upon 'human sociability', the first phrasing of the French constitution in terms of the rights of man rather than the rights of citizens: all these Kristeva reviews as evidence of the recurrence throughout history of an ideological or religious code that says one should treat all people as equal, and not favour one's own.

A contrary ideology, however, argues for particularism. 'The patriot', says Rousseau, 'is hard on the foreigner', and should be so.[66] One should first look after one's own. Rights should be the prerogative only of citizens. The full sweep of history is used again by Kristeva to bring out the way in which universalist ideals eventually become trimmed to meet particularist restrictions. The story she tells of the French Revolution is a particularly telling example. In 1792, the Legislative Assembly accepted a proposal to declare as deputies a set of 'foreign writers whose works were already supposed to have abolished "the foundations of tyranny and prepared the way for liberty"'.[67] One of those accepted was the American Thomas Paine. 'Paine', in Kristeva's description, 'remained faithful to the notion of a spiritual bond that transcends all religious differences'.[68] His fate, however, was to be an ineffective deputy. He argued for not sending the king to the guillotine, and became suspect for that action, for not learning to speak French with any fluency, and for being a Quaker. How could he, Marat argued, be competent to vote on the king's fate when 'his religious principles run counter to the will to inflict the death penalty?'[69] Paine was arrested in 1793, freed after ten months in prison, and after several years of rejection for various posts, returned to the U.S.A. in 1802, 'a foreigner everywhere'.[70]

Does the tension of these two ideologies help articulate the nature of tension in *Vigil* or *Crush*? For *Vigil*, the background alerts us to an interesting presentation of reasons for treating the strangers reasonably well. The widow and the stranger are unusually frank in their acknowledgement that need and pleasure are the main factors in their relationship. There is no reference on either side to any general code of moral behaviour, or to any concern with reputation. These disguises set aside, each person's own needs are presented as the main motives, acted out, however, in a way that does no violence to the other.

The same type of question applied to *Crush*, however, makes one aware of the extent to which the narrative involves a tension between two further codes: one that says 'intervene in their disputes' and another that says 'let them sort out their own problems – don't meddle'. This is not the particular tension highlighted by Kristeva but it is in line with her general interest and certainly has its parallels in the politics of immigrants and 'locals'.

This tension starts with Angela's visit to the hospital to see and help Christine. Up to this point, Angela's involvement has been only with Lane. Angela becomes angry, however, at Lane's becoming her father's sexual partner, rather than remaining *her* friend, unknown to the father and of no particular interest except as a source of change in his daughter: 'Did she give you that?' he asks, referring to a red dress that Angela is wearing. It is in anger that Angela turns to the 'other' foreigner, the immobilized Christine, and quickly forms with her an alliance against Lane. More than that, she meddles in an especially disruptive way, encouraging Christine to regard Lane with hatred and justifying their joint anger by a moral disapproval of Lane. Lane is to be regarded by both as lost because of her sexual freedom: in Angela's words, 'she fucks everybody'; 'she's the most lying, selfish, hypocritical bitch I ever met'. Lane is also to be regarded with special anger by Christine because Lane was the driver of the car at the time of the accident. Angela goes so far as to cut out a photograph of Lane, bring it to the hospital, and point out the face to the amnesic Christine – 'She's the one who's done this to you'.

Angela continues to involve herself in the ambiguous but longstanding relationship between Christine and Lane. (In the restaurant, Lane surprises Angela by commenting that she and Christine were at school together.) The only correction to Angela's righteous stirring comes from the father, who towards the end of the film invites his daughter to walk in the woods with him for a while, leaving Lane and Christine together at the clifftop. Angela accepts the offer of a return to affection between them. She almost accepts also his advice that she not turn back from their walk to minister to Christine: 'Let's give them some time [alone]', he urges. Angela seems to accept the principle but nonetheless turns back to where she had left the pair. With increasing anxiety, she discovers that Christine is not where she had left her, and Lane is not in sight. The two had indeed begun to act like friends towards one another. At least, Lane has begun to do so. Christine falls in an effort to get out of her wheelchair. Lane picks her up, embraces her, strokes her hair and face with an expression of tenderness that is at last a break from her earlier defensive irritation towards the damaged Christine. As Angela comes closer, she sees Christine stumbling forward towards Lane who – for once admiring the scenery (another sign of her ceasing to be cynical?) – has her back turned. Angela calls out to Lane, apparently in warning, but the words come too late. The end of Angela's becoming involved, of not 'letting people solve their own problems', of widening rather than decreasing a gap, is Lane's death, and the debatable responsibility of those left alive: Christine, whose hands have been the direct agent and who cries out only 'I walked!'; Angela, who encouraged Christine to hate Lane and insisted on bringing Christine to the weekend house to embarrass Lane and break up the weekend idyll of Lane and Colin rather than to benefit Christine; and Colin, who sparked Angela's anger with himself and Lane by taking over as 'his' someone who was initially Angela's 'special friend'. Breaking the father's official code – 'let people work things out for themselves' – has carried a heavy penalty.

The representation of tension

Suppose we start from Kristeva's argument that a major source of tension in our encounters with strangers comes from the presence of mixed feelings on our part: in particular, the mixture of attraction with suspicion and hatred. To take that argument further, I shall ask two questions prompted by it: what feelings towards the stranger are represented in this narrative? Who expresses the positive, the negative, or the ambivalence?

In seeking to answer these questions, one notices that both *Vigil* and *Crush* contain the device of 'splitting', followed by a reversal of roles. 'Splitting' is most often used to refer to 'madonna/whore' contrasts in representation: all the good qualities are wrapped up in one woman, all the negatives in another, avoiding any of the ambivalence that a woman with mixed qualities would evoke. The same type of separation, however, may apply to the 'good' stranger/'bad' stranger. In *Vigil*, initially it is the daughter who finds the stranger attractive; the mother plays out the negative role. And for the mother, the stranger plays out the negative role. For her, the stranger is a lazy poacher, and his efforts to charm her daughter do not please her. It is only later that she herself turns positively towards the stranger, inviting him into the house for a meal (to his surprise: 'you aren't like the others', he comments) and making herself attractive for the occasion. It is then the daughter's turn to be repelled by the stranger and, in a tense scene, to fix him in the sights of her father's rifle.

Crush uses a similar twist. The daughter is again the one to find the stranger interesting and charming. Lane offers Angela compliments, lends her a close-fitting red dress, takes her out to a local disco, holds out the prospect of an adult life that has a fair degree of pleasure and amusement to it. The father is the one who initially wants nothing to do with Lane. 'Did *she* give you that?' he asks with reference to the red dress and, in the face of Angela's obvious pleasure in the way she looks, proceeds to say, 'it's too old for you'. He does not ask to meet Lane and, when he later finds her sharing Angela's bed, asleep and without clothes on at least the upper half of her body, his expression is one of shock: he appears ready to believe 'the worst'. The switch in roles comes when Lane seduces the father and becomes for Angela the 'bad' stranger, replaced in her affections now by the 'good' stranger, the crippled Christine who needs her and can be persuaded to join her in anger at the 'evil' Lane. Only slowly does the narrative allow both father and daughter to entertain towards both strangers a mixed set of feelings and a willingness to think in terms of a relationship that is between the strangers rather than perceiving them as within only the father's or the daughter's orbit. For most of the film, however, Angela and her father play out their feelings towards Lane in what Kristeva has described, in the history of novels, as a 'monovalent' fashion: each character represents one position towards the other, without ambivalence.[71]

What is the narrative function of the stranger?

This is the third of the questions to be abstracted from Kristeva's analysis of foreigners. In the history of nations, and of individuals, foreigners serve a number of functions. They may meet economic needs. They may – by virtue of the way they are treated – enhance or reduce the locals' reputation. They may, within fiction, provide a way of voicing criticism of one's own group. Within and outside fiction, they may bring about not only a renewal but also a move forward into a new pattern of relationships or a new ethic.

From these several possible functions, let me extract two. The first of these is the extent to which the foreigner meets the particular needs of those who are established. The proposal prompts me to ask: in any narrative how is the issue of need presented? Is it presented forthrightly, or with a cloak of kindness or generosity?

These questions make one aware of a feature I noted briefly at an earlier point: the novel treatment of need in *Vigil*. The stranger is hired because of economic need. With the father dead, an extra hand is needed for the lambing season (and without the sale of the lambs, the family will be left with nothing: the land itself has little value). The mother needs him to stay through the season, and this is one of her reasons for offering herself as an inducement to stay. Finding him packed up and ready to leave after she has angrily told him to stay away from her daughter, she removes her blouse and comments, 'you're a greedy so and so aren't you ... well take what you want'. That she enjoys the affair and that it serves to end her grief and isolation are further aspects to the part the stranger plays. At its start, however, she needs to keep him for reasons that are explicitly economic. At the end of the lambing season she can leave, but there is again no pretence. Neither party suggests that the relationship has any future. She leaves in one direction, he in another, with no scene-in-between of a personal parting. Each has met a need for the other, but that moment is over, and neither pretends – or has pretended – that anything more was involved. Economic need and a need for sex are kept separate from issues of love or pity by both parties, by both man and woman.

The second function to which I draw attention has to do with the emergence of a new pattern of relationships. This is for Kristeva the special function of foreigners. If we combine the challenges that foreigners present with a knowledge of the past, she argues, we may be able to reach towards a new 'ethic', a new way of relating to those others that we regard as foreign. The critical voice of the stranger is then the voice that provides 'the leaven of a culture', provides a moment 'when the latter is aware of and transcends itself'.[72]

Kristeva's concern with this new ethic is expressed predominantly in terms of the way locals and foreigners – differing in nationality – might combine to create an agreement, a set of expectations, or a set of regulations that allows for separateness without fragmentation, 'for equality and mutual respect rather than the domination of one group over the other, and for a willingness on all sides to contribute to the good of the whole – to the *ésprit général*'[73] rather than to serve only their own interest. The discussion might equally apply, however, to relationships within love or marriage.

What would this new ethic, this new pattern, be like or be based upon? In political terms, Kristeva sees it as one that provides a nation with 'a contractual, discursive, and transitional' future. The new future would be contractual in the sense that in order to create 'the optimal rendition of the nation in the contemporary world', we need 'a legal and political pact between free and equal individuals'.[74] It would be cultural/discursive (Kristeva uses the terms interchangeably) in the sense that a shared language and a shared literature are needed, not to produce 'elitism and meritocracy' but to create a unity based on a language act:

> To write a fiction in French, as I have done with *The Samurai* and *The Old Man and the Wolves*, is at the same time an acknowledgement of the fact that a nation (the French one) is a language act and an attempt to inscribe on it other sensitivities, other experiences.[75]

Finally, the new future would be transitional in the sense that it would be an 'open-ended' state:[76] one that can change as new relationships develop, as 'the particular' comes to be 'integrated into another particular, of greater magnitude'. The term 'transitional' comes from psychoanalysis. The 'transitional object' is that 'child's indispensable fetish' as it begins to grow away from its mother: a necessary growth – and a necessary support – if we are to gain 'access to speech, desires, and knowledge'.[77] In similar fashion, the concept of a 'nation' is a necessary step towards living effectively with others: disabling only if it stays at the level of a fetish, reducing one's willingness to become part of any larger group, and constantly evoking nostalgia for the nation that was.

The same criteria for an effective way of living together may apply also at the more personal level. I noted earlier that Kristeva's assertion of the value of foreigners as allowing a new pattern of relationships to emerge could apply both to political relationships – with foreigners defined in national terms – and to relationships of a more personal kind; between lovers or friends, or between one's past, present, and emerging self. In both *Vigil* and *Crush*, it is at the level of interpersonal relationships that the stranger brings about new patterns.

In *Vigil*, a first critical change comes from the way the stranger transforms the position of the grandfather. The latter's power is broken. The stranger proves to be the one to get the tractor moving. He is also the one who treats as a game the grandfather's interest in an underground cave, and is simply amused when the contraption he and the grandfather build collapses. The grandfather is revealed as 'an old fool', and it is this breaking of the grandfather's power that allows the mother to move the family away from the farm. The mother and daughter are transformed as well through the meeting with the foreigner. Through sexuality, the widow's grief for her husband is ended. The affair with the stranger, moreover, is marked later by laughter and playful pleasure on both sides. (The father's brief appearance at the start displays him as an earnest, conscientious man). For the daughter, the father is exorcised through the stranger's loosening of her belief that the vigil in the hills must be continued. She removes her father's balaclava and jacket and, in a change that almost overdoes the signals of 'a new life', physically moves into womanhood.

In *Crush*, the strangers again change old patterns. The father's 'ice' is broken by the pleasure he experiences with Lane. He emerges as a potentially joyful man rather than as sombre and withdrawn. A new relationship emerges also with his daughter. And again the daughter moves into sexuality and womanhood. She takes off her dungarees and gets into a red dress; her hair is cut; she lets herself, largely out of curiosity, be used by Horse. She is, moreover, faced with her own aggression and its power and with her father's vulnerability. In Kristeva's terms, she must now come to terms with the fact that each of us contains the possibility of being both 'victim' and 'executioner'.[78]

When are tensions and changes most likely to occur?

I have so far abstracted from Kristeva's analysis of strangers three questions that may be brought to bear upon the analysis of films that involve stranger narratives. The first question was: who is the stranger here? That question drew attention to the possibility that the one person could be a stranger in several ways, and to an important feature that differentiates strangers:

the presence of an accepting as against a mocking, critical stance towards the forms of order and the people already in place. The second question was: what are the sources of tension? That question drew attention to Kristeva's proposal that the 'natural' responses to strangers (hatred and suspicion) are held in check partly by the attraction also felt, and partly by ideological codes that regulate conduct between strangers and locals. The third question was: what is the function of the stranger? Both at the level of the novel and at the level of society, one major function turns out to be the setting in train of events that change the old patterns and that may contain the possibility of a new ethic: an ethic – expressed at the interpersonal or the national level – that allows both parties to be equal, that is built upon a shared language or a shared set of meanings, and that is open to change rather than being set in rigid form.

The fourth and last question that I shall abstract from Kristeva's analysis of strangers has to do with the occasions when tensions, and the changes those tensions may produce, are especially likely to occur. An increase in tension, Kristeva proposes, can stem from changes on the part of both local and foreigner. These changes may be changes in number: in the sheer probability of being outnumbered, of encountering foreigners, or being ourselves foreigners. Numbers matter, however, only if they involve a change in two other circumstances: a change in the balance of power and/or in the codes that have traditionally regulated the place and the reception of strangers, of others.

The importance of a shift in the balance of power emerges in the course of Kristeva's observation that many states have remained stable in the face of the majority of the population being slaves:

> The once solid barrier between 'master' and 'slave' has today been abolished, if not in people's unconscious at least in our ideologies and aspirations. Every native feels himself to be more or less a 'foreigner' in his 'own and proper' place, and that metaphorical value of the word 'foreigner' leads the citizen to a feeling of discomfort as to his sexual, national, political, professional identity ... [and] arouses a feeling of suspicion: Am I really at home? Am I myself? Are *they* not masters of the 'future'?[79]

That same statement expresses also the importance Kristeva places upon breaks in the codes that have traditionally regulated the place of strangers, of others. One form of break is a shift in the power of religion and its images or ideologies (an interest of Kristeva's that we shall see emerge again in her analysis of the Virgin Mary as an image of motherhood). Where foreigners are concerned, a decline in the power of religion, with its injunction to 'love thy neighbour as thyself', and a decline in the ideological attachment to egalitarianism have a common consequence: a drop in the power of traditional brakes upon suspicion, aggression and exclusion. In their place, there has arisen 'the particularistic, demanding individualism of contemporary man'.[80]

More subtly, the old codes may be questioned and rejected, not by the native, but by the foreigner. It is the foreigners, for instance, who now reject an old way of managing foreigners: by insisting upon an integration in which 'they' must become like 'us' if they are to be given asylum, protection, or tolerance.

> The violence of the problem set by the foreigner today is probably due to the crises undergone by religious and ethical constructs. This is especially so as the absorption of otherness proposed by our societies turns out to be inacceptable [sic.] by the contemporary individual, jealous of his difference.[81]

> [T]he question arises again: no longer that of welcoming the stranger within a system that obliterates him but of promoting the togetherness of those foreigners that we all recognize ourselves to be.[82]

Contemporary France is one country that Kristeva sees as caught in the grip of such changing circumstances. It is undergoing a crisis of identity – what is the place of France? – in the face of 'a double humiliation':

> The French population is subjected to a twofold humiliation: First there is the interior impact of immigration, which often makes it feel as though it had to give up traditional values, including the values of freedom and culture ... (why accept [that daughters of Maghrebin immigrants wear] the Muslim scarf [to school]?) .... [T]hen there is the exterior impact of tomorrow's broadened Europe (why should the Deutsche Mark's performance bring about the decline of French speaking communities and of French culture generally in Eastern Europe, for instance?).[83]

France is caught up also in a current emphasis – on all sides – that the solution of assimilation ('you' must become like 'us') is no longer acceptable: no longer acceptable to the people on whom it is imposed, and increasingly seen as suspect by at least a proportion of the group that once imposed assimilation without reflection and with a strong sense of doing so to the foreigner's advantage, of doing 'good'.

New Zealand does not face the degree of humiliation – the fall from grandeur – that France does. It has, however, increasingly had to face the problem of its smallness in a large world. Its refusal to allow ships carrying (or not declaring) nuclear-powered weapons brought an awareness of national courage but also of vulnerability to reprisals (a large part of its income comes from tourism and from exporting its meat and wool to the U.S.A. and Europe). In related fashion, New Zealand's insistence upon a public trial for the French security agents involved in the destruction of the Greenpeace vessel – The Rainbow Warrior – and the death of the photographer on board, brought once more a sense of how difficult it is to take a principled stance in the face of larger powers that do not do so. New Zealand had to face France's willingness to deny entry to New Zealand's meat exports (predominantly lamb) and the reality of eventually meeting

French terms. (The two French agents went to prison, but on French-Pacific soil; after a brief period, they were moved to France, officially for medical reasons, but to a government welcome that was by no means unnoticed in New Zealand or Australia.)

New Zealand's image of itself as a free agent is accordingly in public question. So also is its image of itself as a country of 'free' settlers who made a reasonable settlement with the 'natives'. In contrast to Australia, New Zealand was never a convict settlement. Australia was declared by England to be *'terra nullius'*: available for settlement or for immediate claim as England's without any recognition or compensation for the Aborigines. The possibility of a treaty and of native entitlement to land is now under discussion in Australia, but that is two hundred years after the first take-over. Settlement in New Zealand faced more organized resistance and resulted in a treaty that in theory guaranteed the Maori rights to land and representation in the New Zealand Parliament. In contrast, Australians classed as Aborigines did not gain the right to vote, or to drink alcohol, until 1967.

New Zealand, then, has some degree of pride in its 'better' treatment of the indigenous population, compared with Australia or with the U.S.A. All the more reason to be concerned now with the public emergence of Maori insistence that Maoris were in fact poorly treated (often deprived of their land by trickery and by pakeha manipulation of the law that was supposed to offer protection). All the more reason also to feel uneasy and troubled as New Zealand – along with other countries – faces the claim that its official history has been constructed by a group with an interest in a particular ideology, and in a particular version of events. All the more reason, as well, to ask – as Kristeva puts it – Who am I? What am I? What *is* my history?

Those remarks have all to do with an increase in tensions and in a concern with definitions. What does Kristeva have to say about the circumstances that increase the likelihood of change towards an improved pattern of relationship? Worth particular note is a point that is especially relevant to *Vigil* and to *Crush*. This point has to do with Kristeva's comments on the issue: Who should make the move towards bridging the gap between native and foreigner? Some possible moves forward have already been pointed to. Some are for the people in place to make. It is to them that Kristeva directs especially the advice: know yourselves and your history; recognize your tendency to devour, to erase the other, to insist on the supremacy of your own speech and your own view of speech.

Other steps are for the foreigner to make. It is the foreigners' responsibility to ask themselves why they are in France, and what their intentions are with regard to membership of the nation that France represents:

> It is time, however, also to ask immigrant people what motivated them (beyond economic opportunities and approximate knowledge of the language

propagated by colonialism) to choose the French community with its historical memory and traditions as the welcoming lands. The respect for immigrants should not erase the gratitude due to the welcoming host.[84]

Can one be sure that even foreigners, who are asking for 'integration', are aware of and appreciate that French *ésprit général* in which they seemingly wish to take their place? What are the personal, symbolic, political benefits that they expect from the French nation?[85]

Such questions and such advice stem primarily from Kristeva's concern with the contemporary crisis. I shall turn them back into the analysis of narratives, however, by asking the questions they suggest: who, in any particular story, makes the moves towards bridging a gap? And why should it be this particular person, at this particular time?

In *Vigil*, the major moves are made by the two female characters. The daughter is the one who tries to come to know the foreigner. The mother is the one who – by offering herself – stops him when he is on the point of leaving. In *Crush*, the major moves are again in the hands of women. Lane takes the initiative in coming to Colin's house, meeting Angela there for the first time. Lane takes the initiative also in seducing Colin, and in acknowledging that her feelings towards him have come to move beyond sexual pleasure. Even at the end, it is Christine's move that, however difficult to interpret, changes the relationship patterns once again. Women, in these stories, are the ones who both take steps to bridge the gap and to insist that some particular conventional bridges will not be the ones that begin or end the story.

Why should it be women who make these particular moves? The intent may lie with the filmmaker (Maclean's and Ikin's wish, for instance, to present women as agents). Kristeva takes a position that again helps one understand why feminists find her at times disappointing. Women, Kristeva argues, are particularly vulnerable to the appeal of fundamentalism, to the refusal of difference:

> Women ... are particularly vulnerable to a possible support of *Volksgeist*. The biological fate that causes us to be the site of the species chains us to space: home, native soil, motherland (*matrie*) (as I wish to say, instead of fatherland [*patrie*]). Worshipping the national language arouses a feeling of revenge and narcissistic satisfaction in a number of women, who are otherwise sexually, professionally, and politically humiliated and frustrated. A society based on the rudimentary satisfaction of survival needs, to the detriment of the desires for freedom, could encourage the regressive sado-masochist leanings of women and, without emancipating them at all, rely on them to create a stagnation, a parareligious support of the status quo crushing the elementary rights of the human person. Considerable watchfulness is thus needed in order to ward off that too facile symbiosis between nationalism and, if not 'feminism', at least a certain conformist 'maternalism' that lies dormant in every one of us and can turn women into accomplices of religious fundamentalisms and mystical nationalisms as they were of the Nazi mirage.[86]

Women, Kristeva argues, also have a particular responsibility – as 'boundary-subjects' themselves – to help move the nation towards a state where 'difference' will be accepted.

> Foreign to the unisex commonality of men, everlasting irony of the community, as the sorrowful Hegel so aptly said, women today are called upon to share in the creation of new social groupings where ... we shall try to assure our children living spaces that ... will respect the strangeness of each person within a lay community. Women have the luck and the responsibility of being boundary-subjects; body and thought, biology and language, personal identity and dissemination during childhood, origin and judgment, nation and world – more dramatically so than men are .... The maturity of the second sex will be judged in coming years according to its ability to modify the nation in the face of foreigners, to orient foreigners confronting the nation toward a still unforeseeable conception of a polyvalent community.[87]

One might as easily say that women, so much more likely to be the losers in conventional contracts, have some vested interest in building different bridges, in transforming old patterns, and in seizing the opportunity to do so. Kristeva's argument, in its current statement, has the uncomfortable sound of arguing that women once again must take up the burden of bringing culture and civilization to a world of barbarian men: a position that seems out of line with her general sensitivity to the position of women and to stereotypes about their role. The more positive implication – and the one I shall carry forward to the chapters that follow – is that one needs to ask with regard to any text: who makes the moves to bridge the gap between 'us' and 'them'? And what leads to those moves taking some particular forms rather than others?

As a first step, in the next chapter I shall take those questions forward to the analysis of a set of expansions upon Kristeva's baseline concepts, beginning with an important and novel theme in Kristeva's writings on foreignness: the stranger's experience.

Notes

1. Julia Kristeva (1991a) *Strangers to ourselves*. New York: Columbia University Press; Julia Kristeva (1993) *Nations without nationalism*. New York: Columbia University Press.
2. That concern is also marked outside these books: cf. Julia Kristeva (1986b) 'A new type of intellectual: The dissident'. In T. Moi (Ed.) *The Kristeva reader*. Oxford: Basil Blackwell.
3. Julia Kristeva (2000a) *Crisis of the European subject*. New York: Other Press, p. 117.
4. Ibid., p.117.
5. Ibid., p.118.
6. Kristeva (1991a, p.95).
7. Kristeva (1991b) in interview with Ebba Witt-Bratström: 'Främlingskap – intervju med Julia Kristeva'. In *Kvinnovetenskaplig tidskrift*, issue 3(91).
8. Roudiez in Kristeva (1993, p.xi).
9. Kristeva (1991a, p.191).

10. Ibid., p.191.
11. Kristeva (1993, p.46).
12. Kristeva (1991a, p.191).
13. Ibid., p.187.
14. Ibid., p.191.
15. Kristeva (1993, p.46).
16. Ibid., p.65.
17. Ibid., p.40. Jacqueline Rose, it may be noted, sees the change in Kristeva's concerns as reflecting less the nature of current times than the inevitable retreat, with some degree of panic, from positions of anarchy one may have welcomed at an earlier age. Jacqueline Rose (1986) *Sexuality in the field of vision*. London: Verso, p.142.
18. Kristeva (1993, p.1).
19. Ibid., p.97, emphasis added.
20. Ibid., p.16, emphasis in original.
21. Kristeva (1991a, p.104).
22. Ibid., p.50.
23. Ibid., p.104.
24. Ibid., p.91.
25. Comment made by Ikin in interview with K. Goodnow (December, 1992).
26. Ibid.
27. Kristeva (1991a, p.18, emphasis in original).
28. Kristeva (1986b, p.296).
29. Kristeva (1991a, p.51, emphasis in original).
30. Ibid., p.44.
31. Ibid., p.47: Aeschylus, *The Suppliants* cited by Kristeva.
32. Ibid., p.47.
33. Ikin in interview with K. Goodnow (August, 1993).
34. Noëlle McAfee (1993) 'Abject strangers: Toward an ethic of respect'. In K. Oliver (Ed.) *Ethics, politics and difference in Julia Kristeva's writing*. New York: Routledge; Norma Claire Moruzzi (1993) 'Julia Kristeva on the process of political self-identification'. In Oliver (Ed.). See also Noëlle McAfee (2004) *Julia Kristeva*. New York: Routledge, pp.119–126; and Norma Claire Moruzzi (2000) *Speaking through the mask: Hannah Arendt and the politics of social identity*. Ithica, N.Y.: Cornell University Press.
35. Kristeva (1991a, p.152).
36. Ibid., p.134.
37. Ibid., p.135.
38. Ibid., p.135.
39. Ibid., p.139.
40. Ibid., p.138.
41. Ibid., p.138.
42. Ibid., p.139.
43. Ibid., p.139.
44. *Crush* production notes, press release, p.7.
45. Kristeva (1991a, pp.24–29).
46. Kristeva (1993, pp.2–3).
47. Ibid., pp.29–30.
48. Kristeva (1991a, p.65): First book of Samuel, cited by Kristeva.
49. Ibid., p.65.
50. Ibid., p.199.
51. Ibid., p.67: Exodus, cited by Kristeva.
52. Ibid., p.66: Deuteronomy, cited by Kristeva.
53. Ibid., p.188, emphasis in original.
54. Ibid., p.13.
55. Ibid., p.188.

56. Ibid., p.191.
57. Ibid., pp.68–69.
58. Ibid., p.75.
59. Ibid., p.191.
60. Ibid., p.180.
61. Ibid., p.181.
62. Ibid., p.181.
63. Ibid., p.181.
64. Ibid., p.55.
65. These several passages are from Plato cited by Kristeva (ibid., pp.55–56).
66. Ibid., p.143: Rousseau, cited by Kristeva.
67. Ibid., p.156.
68. Ibid., p.167.
69. Ibid., p.166: Marat, cited by Kristeva.
70. Ibid., p.167.
71. Julia Kristeva (1990) 'The adolescent novel'. In J. Fletcher and A. Benjamin (Eds) *Abjection, melancholia, and love: The work of Julia Kristeva*. London: Routledge, p.13.
72. Kristeva (1991a, p.134).
73. Kristeva (1993, p.47).
74. Ibid., p.40.
75. Ibid., p.44.
76. Ibid., p.41.
77. All references are to Kristeva (1993, p.41).
78. Julia Kristeva (1981) 'Women's time'. In *Signs*, issue 7(1), p.34.
79. Kristeva (1991a, pp.19–20, emphasis in original).
80. Ibid., p.2.
81. Ibid., p.2.
82. Ibid., pp.2–3.
83. Ibid., p.36.
84. Kristeva (1993, p.60).
85. Ibid., p.47.
86. Ibid., p.34.
87. Ibid., p.35.

Chapter 5

STRANGERS – EXPANSIONS:
THE STRANGER'S STORY

The major part of Kristeva's analysis of strangers deals with the impact of the stranger upon the local. What needs most to be explained is the local's mixture of interest and unease, of attraction and hatred. What needs to be documented is the variety of ways in which competing codes – universalism and particularism especially – change in their relative strengths and give rise to various political solutions and various degrees of acceptance from one time to another. What needs to be understood – again by the local – is that the response to strangers has a long story to it: a history that contains a series of narratives about strangers at different times and places, narratives with a variety of endings.

It is then all the more surprising to find that the opening chapter of *Strangers to Ourselves* gives the major part of its space to a different theme. This theme is the experience of the stranger: the stranger's feelings, the stranger's position, the stranger's options. For Kristeva, the new ingredient in an old pattern is the increasing likelihood that we will all have the double experience of encountering and *being* a foreigner. This double or shifting social position must inevitably complicate any definition of 'stranger', any analysis of 'self' and 'other', of 'local' and 'foreigner'. It should also mean that narratives, as well as scholarly analyses, begin to include more of the stranger's perspective. Kristeva's analysis is in itself a marker of the need to do so.

Is there any equivalent turn in film narratives? If so, what are the questions that Kristeva's analysis would prompt us to ask about such stories? The film I shall use as a base for exploring these questions is *An Angel at My Table*. Before introducing it, however, let me note briefly two ways in which Kristeva's comments on the experience of the stranger reflect some general aspects of her perspective.

The first of these general aspects has to do with Kristeva's pervasive interest in the emergence of 'new' or 'different' texts. One of Kristeva's basic proposals is that, to a greater or lesser extent, all texts transform the texts that have preceded them. To that broad proposal, she adds the specification of some particular forms that the transformation may take.

Change may involve, for instance, the use of transposition, of combining two or more competing voices, or of deliberately violating the usual rules for the settings in which one places a story or for the way a narrative unfolds.

The second general aspect has to do with a question that again helps specify the form that a 'new' or 'different' text may take. When she examines any existing theory or any existing set of narratives, Kristeva is partial to the question: what is being left out here? What is excluded? What story is not being told? What voice is not being heard? What alternative is not being considered?

Kristeva's use of this type of question can be observed in her early studies of language. What is excluded or omitted from accounts of language that emphasize syntax and symbol systems, she argues, is everything that has to do with what is most visible in poetry: the place of rhythm, music, 'pulses', the sound of words in themselves over and above what they refer to. Omitted also is the desire for language and, especially, for the poetic aspects of language.[1] Kristeva's analysis of 'tales of love' provides a further example. Where, she asks, are the contemporary tales of love or caring, tales that go beyond stories of sexuality or sacrifice?

In Kristeva's analysis of foreignness, the missing story may be located in Kristeva's concern with the issues: what is it like to be a stranger? What is the stranger's story? When stories are told from the point of view of those at the margin rather than at the centre, what feelings and actions are likely to be represented? The emphasis upon the missing narrative, and the need for new tales, is nowhere nearly as explicit as it is within *Tales of Love*, but the recurring concern with the stranger's position, feelings, and options is in itself the provision of a different story.

With those general aspects of Kristeva's perspective in mind, I turn to a brief description of the film that will serve as a base for this chapter (*An Angel at My Table*, hereafter referred to as *Angel*) and then to an interweaving of Kristeva's comments on being a stranger with aspects of *Angel*.

Introducing *An Angel at My Table*

Angel is the story of a woman who is a stranger within her own country rather than having a different nationality. More specifically it is the story of a living writer, Janet Frame, based upon her autobiography. A novelist/poet, Frame was – until *Angel* – probably better known outside New Zealand than within it, and might well have been described as better known to critics than to the general public. Her life – watched in *Angel* or read in the volumes of her autobiography – gives rise to feelings of sorrow, anger, and admiration. It is, in the words of one journalist, a 'life-story [that] makes *One Flew Over The Cuckoo's Nest* look tame'.[2] How, we wonder, could Janet Frame have survived, as a person, as a writer? Where did her tenacious inner strength come from? At the same time, how could she have been so apparently passive and obedient, so innocent, so naive? Why is she always being rescued, as well as damaged, by 'more knowledgeable others'? What kind of world is it that treats with such cruelty those who do not fit its Procrustean beds?

Here at the start of the film is the outsider we can all recognize as a child: poor (her father was a manual labourer for the railways), tubby, and topped with a massive mop of fuzzy, red hair of the type that responds only to expert styling; hoping for friends but desperately shy; often inarticulate but fond of writing stories and poems; smart and eager for approval but caught up in a school system that seems bent only on restriction and control.

That much might be the story of many a child. So also, except in terms of degree, might be her place in her family. An older brother's epilepsy, in the days before medication, attracts the scorn of other boys in the school: a scorn that she feels is a reflection upon her. Two sisters provide moments of companionship, but neither is like her. The older sister especially is outgoing, popular, interested in clothes and boys, eager to leave school and go to work in a local factory. This sister's death – an unexpected drowning while Janet Frame is still in school – removes a bridge to the outside world that might have saved Frame a great deal of hardship.

A way forward appears to be offered by winning a scholarship at the end of secondary school, to train as a teacher. She goes off to college, boarding with a relative, and is managing despite her shyness, the drawback of teeth so discoloured by decay that she covers her mouth when she smiles, and the abandoning of her career as a teacher (she finds herself unable to speak during the visit of an inspector to her classroom while she is practice teaching and, in one move, leaves the classroom, the school, and the course; her plan later is to continue studying at the university as a general student). She makes, however, the fatal mistake of writing – in a report to the instructor in psychology, John Forrest, whom all the students admire and hope to impress – that she has attempted suicide by taking an overdose of aspirin (this is after the inspection).

Frame's motives for the overdose are unclear. In the film, she appears to feel that a suicidal type of gesture is part of being a writer: all great artists seem to suffer despair and to inflict wounds upon themselves. The psychologist's understanding is also not made explicit in the film, but the next action that emerges is a visit to her house by members of the college staff. They recommend that she take 'a rest' in hospital: in reality, a psychiatric ward. Offered the chance to leave and go home to 'rest', she insists on staying where she is, not realizing that this refusal will lead to transfer to a mental asylum, with a police matron at her side.

Diagnosed as schizophrenic (her psychology textbook describes this as involving 'a deterioration of the mind, with no cure') she spends almost all of the next eight years as a hospitalized 'mental patient'. During that time, she is given electric shock treatment (two hundred times) and is at risk of a leucotomy (the 1950s was a time when leucotomies and lobotomies were frequently used as a treatment for depression or schizophrenia and one of the gruesomely Dickensian scenes is of a line of women – all women – walking from one ward to another with their heads swathed in bandages). The family's poverty and naivety, on top of Frame's own, offer no counter to the rolling-on of a heedless system. Frame's rescue comes when her first book wins a highly regarded prize. Her talent recognized, she is released, wins a scholarship, goes overseas, survives the challenge of coping with a new set of experiences (including a misjudged affair with an American writer when both are in Ibiza), and begins coming to terms with the judgement of an eminent London psychiatrist that she was never schizophrenic.

The film ends with Frame's return to New Zealand upon the death of her father (her mother had died before Frame went to England). It is not clear why his death leads to her prompt and permanent return. His death does, however, release her from a new set of expectations that again threatens her individuality. Her English publisher wants her to write a 'bestseller' (the books written in England have been well received by critics) and to become 'smart' (little black dress, high-heeled shoes, etc.). She returns to clean out the old cottage, to find an eager young journalist asking for a story ('local writer comes back', etc.), and to settle into a modest fame and a writing life, working in a caravan in the garden of the home of her younger sister. She now has a sense of family (the cheerful noise of her sister's children can be heard in the garden), respect for her need for solitude, and a sense of 'my place':

> now that writing was my only occupation, regardless of the critical and financial outcome, I felt I had found 'my place' at a deeper level than any landscape, of any country, could provide.[3]

What light can Kristeva possibly throw on such a narrative? True, both she and Frame may be regarded as foreigners. Kristeva is a Bulgarian who came to Paris in her twenties: she is not a native Frenchwoman. But Kristeva, by the world's standards, is an immensely successful foreigner. She is described as making an instant mark on the French intellectual scene, rapidly recognized as a trenchant critic of established thought and as having something original to say. She 'married well' (she married Philippe Sollers, the editor of *Tel Quel*, for which Kristeva often wrote). She has had a child and describes motherhood as a happy and sensational experience. Her books are readily published. She is widely known internationally. She is regarded by the outside world as one of '*the* French feminists'. She has demonstrated her control of French by writing in that language not only academic works but also a novel (*The Samurai*) and a book for children (*The Old Man and the Wolves*). She is a public figure. Her photographs on the covers of her books show a transformation from an earnest, Left-bank type (*Desire in Language*) to a well-groomed, smiling figure standing by a museum sculpture (*Strangers to Ourselves*), to a smoothly poised, elegant woman in a studio-portrait pose (*The Samurai* and *The New Maladies of the Soul*). One cannot imagine that she is a person who was ever easily put down, easily depressed, or willing to stay in the shadows if people would simply allow her to write and would recognize that on paper she had something to say.

In short, someone more remote from Janet Frame seems hard to imagine. All the more interesting, then, to find that Kristeva's analysis of the experience of being a foreigner, both historically and in current times, does provide a way of helping us read Frame's narrative. It does so by the way it prompts – and answers – a set of three questions that one may bring to any narrative of being a stranger, even Janet Frame's: what is the foreigner's position? What are the foreigner's feelings, both towards the old 'home' group and towards the new? And what are the foreigner's options? I shall take these up in turn, interweaving Kristeva's proposals with aspects of the narrative in *Angel*.

The stranger's position

Early in her account of foreigners throughout history, Kristeva reminds us that the position of foreigners is far from being a protected one, even when they meet some particular economic needs of the local group. As needs change, so also can the degree to which strangers are tolerated.

Kristeva's account starts with the foreigners to whom the Greeks gave the term 'metic':

> Marie-Françoise Baslez rightly calls him the homo economicus of the Greek city-state .... Often artisans but farmers, too, metics were also bankers, owners of personal property, and shippers.[4]

Nonetheless, metics – for all that they were granted residence – paid special taxes. They 'could only exceptionally take part in competitions, choruses, or national defence (when a war drags on)'.[5] Acting as the equal of a citizen was dangerous:

> In case they illegally assumed the privileges of a citizen, metics were degraded to the condition of slaves. Plato ... advocated that metics be expelled from the polis when their capital became equal to that of the farmers who owned their land.[6]

The metics' type of position, Kristeva points out, still occurs: 'Economic necessity remains a gangplank ... between xenophobia and cosmopolitanism'.[7] It is, however, a gangplank that may be withdrawn depending upon one party's definition of need: one party's definition of times when 'the foreigner is in excess' or 'we need the foreigner'.[8] Even the laws and regulations that may at first appear to be above need may turn out not to be so:

> Moreover, such permissions and other regulations pertaining to subjective rights stem from the opinion such and such a government has arrived at concerning the country's economic and political interest, and this endows the objective rights granted to foreigners with a very peculiar legal status.[9]

The general lack of protection, and the 'peculiar legal status', Kristeva points out, may give rise to some particular formal arrangements. The ancient Greeks, she notes, designated particular people to function as official 'middlemen' between those who were foreign and the local establishment. A king could become such a protector – such a proxenus – but so also could a variety of lesser functionaries.[10]

More broadly, the foreigner's position creates a particular reliance upon others. When one does not know the procedures of a new world (or even understand well the procedures of the world one is born into), the place of go-betweens, of more knowledgeable others, becomes crucial. The result is a life in which decisions are often made by others, sometimes to one's benefit, and sometimes not.

It is this dependence upon the decisions of others that Janet Frame exemplifies. Frame was certainly not knowledgeable about many of the 'ways of the world'. Neither were her parents. Inevitably, decision-making others play a large part in her life. The list begins with the psychology instructor, John Forrest. As I noted earlier, his precise role in her being recommended to take a rest is not made clear. He is, however, certainly the person who shows Frame's poems and stories to a publisher he knows. He offers her as well an alternate way of viewing her diagnosis as schizophrenia, assuring her that 'Hugo Wolf ..., Van Gogh ...: lots of artists have suffered from schizophrenia'.[11] And he recommends someone else as a contact for her: a woman with whom she could talk and who could help her. (He is himself about to leave to study for a Ph.D. in the United States.)

This woman, Mrs Chandler, is the next significant other. Frame turns to her on Forrest's departure. It is Mrs Chandler who arranges for Frame's decayed teeth to be taken out (this is the request that Frame formally makes) and recommends Sunnyside Hospital where 'they have a new treatment which seems to be successful'[12] with Frame's 'no cure' disease. Thereafter, Frame's existence hinges mainly upon the decisions of knowledgeable males. There is the psychiatrist at Sunnyside who recommends a leucotomy and then rescinds the recommendation when Frame's first book, *The Lagoon*, is published, wins a prize, and is the subject of a newspaper article. There is the writer Frank Sargeson who, after Frame's release from hospital, offers Frame the space to write (a hut in his garden); arranges for her to meet other writers; gives her new authors to read (Proust, Yeats); and arranges for her to receive sickness benefits so that she has some financial support. There is the psychiatrist at Maudsley who also arranges for welfare support while she is receiving psychotherapy, who urges her to write about her life as therapy (official encouragement to write!), and who takes away the label of 'schizophrenia' (to Frame's mixed feelings – how is she now to account for her difference from others?). It is never clear how Frame's visit to Maudsley was arranged; it seems odd that anyone as shy or as naive as Frame could have organized this step. One suspects that Forrest may have again played a part: he stayed in the United States, joining the faculty of the John Hopkins University Medical School and acquiring an international reputation for his studies of sexuality. In this list of significant and often 'medical' males (one begins to feel that the story is *Now Voyager* again), it is a relief to note that it is Janet's sister June and her husband who introduce Frame to Sargeson.

One might well be forgiven for thinking that this is a classical 'victim's story'. Frame's life may easily be read as a response to the initiatives of others, as if she were a pawn, insistent only upon the fact that she must write, hopeful that others will listen, unalert to the dangers of letting others 'improve' her. A brake upon this easy interpretation, however, comes from reading Kristeva.

To start with, Kristeva prompts one to think a little carefully about what seems to be a terrifying obedience to the expectations and decisions of others. How is Frame's acceptance of others' decisions to be accounted for? A Freudian-style explanation rises quickly to mind: the nature of Frame's early life. The family did include a father who insisted upon obedience and who physically beat the children who disobeyed or disappointed him; but so did many other fathers of his time, and not all the children were so obedient (the older sister did not go underground so readily). Hers was also a school system that insisted – again brutally – on obedience and, later in Frame's life, a hospital system where Frame might well feel that, in her words, 'you did what you were told or else'.[13] The hospital scenes in *Angel* certainly convey that same sense of lost control and imminent punishment that is evoked by a film such as *One Flew Over the Cuckoo's Nest*, with its narrative of shock treatment and lobotomy as part of a possible future for those who did not respond to other hospital routines – who were 'difficult'.

To these possible explanations, Kristeva adds another that is quite different in style. The stranger, the outsider, she proposes, can also be thought of as going along with events in the hope of finding the magic key, of learning the magic procedures, of acquiring some understanding that will make sense of what is happening; will enable one to feel, 'so that's how it's done, that's how others manage'; or will open up a new world in which one does feel at home:

> Being fooled is not what happens to you either. At the most, you are willing to go along, ready for all apprenticeships, at all ages, in order to reach – within

that speech of others, imagined as perfectly assimilated, some day – who knows what ideal.[14]

That comment provides a first check, a first brake, to the easy categorization of Frame's story as a 'victim's story'. This is indeed the story of a woman who has been a victim, who exemplifies the terrible things that can happen when one is naive. It is also, however, the story of someone whose mishaps are part of an active searching for how to proceed.

A second counter-balance to the interpretation of 'victim's story' comes from Kristeva's insistence that the stranger often acts by choice – is indeed often an exile by choice, is often deliberately silent, and resistant to 'correction'. Frame's story needs then to be seen as the story of a woman who has managed to write, to be published, and to remain in some essential ways herself, to keep her own style. There is strength here (in Campion's words, 'She's been out there alone for years').[15]

Frame's story also needs to be seen as a story of survival and resistance. She leaves the Teachers' College before she is asked to leave. She does not accept the pressure of Patrick (the friendly Irishman who helps her find lodging in England) to 'give away the writing game' and find paid factory work instead. She also resists the disapproval of her Spanish landladies, who at first show their pleasure in her being a celibate 'good woman', different from 'the other foreigners'. She may move into the elegant apartment that her English publisher provides for her while she is to write a 'best-seller'. And she may listen to – even experiment with – the new clothes, the new hairstyles, the new looks that others are constantly recommending to her, but she does not stay with them. Timid, shy, thin-skinned, and unprotected in any formal sense, she nonetheless does not end up transformed into the conventional 'good woman' or 'Barbie doll' of others, and she writes in her own voice. The text of strength and resistance needs to be recognized as well as that of suffering and disadvantage.

The stranger's feelings

In her exploration of what the stranger feels, Kristeva comments on two sets of emotions: one related to the group that has been left, the other the group into whose territory one has moved or been moved. Both are worth keeping in mind when one turns to the analysis of a stranger's narrative.

The foreigner's relationship to his or her past is first of all a mixture of joy and apprehension, a sense of both having gained all and having gained nothing:

> Happiness seems to prevail, in spite of everything, because something has definitely been exceeded; it is the happiness of tearing away, of racing, the space of a promised infinite. Such happiness is, however, constrained, apprehensively

> discrete ... the foreigner keeps feeling threatened by his former territory, caught up in the memory of a happiness or a disaster, always excessive.[16]

> Free of ties with his own people, the foreigner feels 'completely free'. Nevertheless, the consummate name of such a freedom is solitude .... Deprived of others, free solitude, like the astronaut's weightless state, dilapidates muscles, bones, and blood. Available, freed of everything, the foreigner has nothing, is nothing.[17]

The price of freedom, of turning away from the past, is also some sense of guilt ('How could I have abandoned them? – I have abandoned myself'[18]) and a sense of constant search:

> He disclaims, fiercely, 'It is I who chose to leave' ...[;] a stranger to his mother ...[;] the son of a father whose presence does not detain him ...[;] if one has the strength not to give in, there remains a path to be discovered ...[;] the foreigner is ready to flee ...[;] he seeks that invisible and promised territory, that country that does not exist but that he bears in his dreams.[19]

Are there then rewards for this flight, counteracting the loss? There is at least a stronger sense of self:

> There remains, however, the self-confidence of being, of being able to settle within the self with a smooth, opaque certainty – an oyster shut under the flooding tide or the expressionless joy of two stones.[20]

And there are the moments of liberation before 'orphanhood' catches up:

> Those who have not experienced the near-hallucinatory daring of imagining themselves without parents – free of debt and duties – cannot understand the foreigner's folly, what it provides in the way of pleasure ('I am my sole master') .... Eventually, though, the time of orphanhood comes about.[21]

At this point, the stranger comes to resent the extent to which the locals act as if one's parents did not exist, or were unimportant. In recoil, he or she turns again to a sense of a shared identity with the past ('the indifference of others with respect to my kin makes them at once mine again'[22]), only to find: 'I have nothing to say to them, my parents. Nothing. Nothing and everything, as always .... I am ... foreign to them.'[23]

Any narrative on the experience of the stranger, we are now encouraged to expect, should tell us something about the way the stranger feels towards those left behind. What, then do we observe in *Angel* about the way Frame feels towards those she leaves? (She repeatedly leaves one place for others: to go to Teachers' College, to go to England, to go to Ibiza, and to return to New Zealand.)

There is, indeed, no lack of complexity in Frame's relationship to those she leaves. Her relationship to her 'Dad' stands out in this respect. His attitude towards her as a child is clearly one of affection and a wish to be supportive. He brings her, for instance, a large and precious notebook in which to write her stories – no small expense given his income and the size of the family. Later, he builds her shelves for her books. At the same time, he cannot help her, or protect her. He says, 'you're not going back to that nut-house', but he is powerless to prevent it. He is proud of her achievements but finds her new life incomprehensible. In the film (the scene is actually not in the screenplay), one of the most poignant visual scenes is when Frame's father comes to say goodbye to her on the verge of her leaving for England. On the one side is her father, on the other is Sargeson. Her father is uncomfortably dressed in his best clothes: a solid, decent, working man, with little that he can say. Sargeson is dressed in downmarket Bohemian fashion: a spry little man of the father's age, at ease socially and definitely not at a loss for words. He appears casually holding a glass of wine (an unusual gesture in New Zealand at the time) and Frame's father's response is instant suspicion. His beloved daughter is about to move into a world of affectation, snobbery, and – highly probably – immorality. The gap between the two men and the worlds they represent is immense. Frame cannot stay within her father's world. Nor can she bridge the gap.

Are, then, the relationships to people in the new world straightforward or a total joy? Kristeva makes it abundantly clear that we should also not expect this to be the case. She lays out, in fact, an alternative theme, documenting how the stranger may come to feel suspicious of the native under what may appear to be even the best of circumstances. To the local's claim of similarity, the foreigner may well respond: 'I am not like you .... Recognize me'.[24] Faced with the conditions of acceptance (assimilate), the foreigner may well feel that the demand is to disappear, to be devoured: 'The faithful devour the foreigner, assimilate him and integrate him under the protection of their religion's moral code'.[25]

To the host's claim of having generously extended legal protection, the foreigner may well respond with a sense of having no real right to decide, of being treated as an object:

> In the course of time a number of rights ... have been granted foreigners. The fact remains that the denial of the right to vote actually excludes foreigners from any decision ... that might be made with regard to them .... As Danièle Lochall notes, the foreigner is thus reduced to being a possible object.[26]

Above all, the foreigner has the sense of speaking in a voice that is never truly heard. This part of the foreigner's experience is clearly of particular importance to Kristeva, in line with the general importance of language to her. Language is, for instance, the springboard she first uses in order to ask: what is being excluded from our theories and our lives? Our conventional theories of language ignore the nature of poetry, and the extent of our desire for language.[27] Our emphasis on syntax, logic, and rationality ignores the importance of sensation and sensory pleasure.

Language is also, for Kristeva, a source of pleasure in itself (a position that makes it difficult for her to take a positive view of silence), a potential bridge between people, and – under some circumstances – a barrier and a source of difficulty. Difficulties are inevitable, Kristeva argues, when the native attaches value only to speech that is exactly like his or her own. The difficulties increase when the attitude is one of 'worshipping the national language'[28] and insisting that acceptance is contingent upon its polished use or upon the equivalent degree and kind of worship, a demand that in France gives rise to:

> a national stability (devotion to the literary tradition) as well as a plasticity (taste for stylistic inventiveness) that brings about admiration and irritation on the part of onlookers.[29]

France might represent an extreme. However, even without the insistence of those in place that their language must be learned (and often that the foreigner's language must disappear), the foreigner is likely to experience anger and disappointment at finding that his or her own speech makes unlikely any full membership in the new society. Power and standing are equated with local speech:

> No one listens to you. You never have the floor, or else, when you have the courage to seize it, your speech is quickly erased by the more garrulous and fully relaxed talk of the community. Your speech has no past and will have no power over the future of the group: why should one listen to it ...[?] Your speech, fascinating as it may be because of its very strangeness, will be of no consequence, will have no effect, will cause no improvement in the image or reputation of those you are conversing with.[30]

How do such comments apply to, or illuminate, the story of *Angel*? Here, after all, is a woman whose native language is the language of the group. She has no 'foreign accent'. Moreover, she is a person whose facility with the English language is extraordinary. She is a writer. Words are her tools of trade; tools she uses in imaginative and inventive fashion.

This fluency and inventiveness, however, are only to be found in Frame's written language. Socially, and especially when it comes to 'small talk', her use of language is clumsy. It does mark her as an outsider. It also makes her feel a stranger, watching from the margin the ease with which others speak to one another. Scenes bringing out this clumsiness and unease occur throughout the film. The Janet represented at primary school is largely silent, attempting to buy friends with sweets rather than with talk. The Janet represented at secondary school sits on one set of stairs with the 'bright' students who are talking about academic topics. The group she watches with longing, however, is the group on a neighbouring set of stairs who are engaged in social chatter and friendly bantering. At the party given to mark the end of secondary school, she cannot manage small talk with the teacher who tries valiantly to 'bring her out'. Nor can she join the group of students singing around the piano.

This type of scene is repeated in London, where she is invited to a literary party but cannot rise with any social fluency to the praise and admiration offered for being a published author. Most painful of all is a scene in Ibiza where she makes the most awkward attempts to become part of an expatriate group of writers sitting at an outdoor café. Here, surely, she seems to feel, she should feel at home. These are all artists: officially people of her kind. They, however, personify the 'garrulous and relaxed talk of the community'[31] that Frame so visibly lacks. She is, in fact, more at ease with her Spanish landladies who know she cannot speak Spanish and who accept with approval her nods and smiles, and her halting attempts at speech.

How can such a lack of social language come about? Again Kristeva suggests a possibility that offers an alternative to the easy assumption of a deficit in Frame's skills, occasioned perhaps by her temperament or her background. The possibility arises in Kristeva's comments upon what 'novelistic writing' entails. One requirement, Kristeva proposes, is an 'open psychic structure'. And one part of the process lies in the use of writing as a way of keeping open and elaborating that internal space. Writing covers this function, serving as a way of 'screening from another's appraisal':

> Through its solitary economy, writing protects the subject from phobic affects, and if it enables him to re-elaborate his psychic space, it also withdraws that space from reality testing. The psychic benefit of such a withdrawal is obvious, but does not bypass the question of managing the rapport with reality for the subject himself.[32]

The stranger's options

The analysis of any narrative of the stranger, I have proposed, will benefit from asking about the stranger's position and the stranger's feelings towards the old and the new group. Helpful also will be attention to the question: what options do the stranger's position and feelings allow? How could this narrative proceed? What would each option involve? I shall consider briefly five options mentioned in Kristeva's discussion: assimilate, leave physically, leave psychologically, reject the local codes, or challenge what one finds objectionable.

Assimilate. One possibility is that the stranger becomes like the locals. He or she accepts the advice or the pressure to acquire the 'small talk', wear the clothes that provide protective colouring, fix their hair and teeth, etc. The problem with this option is that the price can get to be too high. For Janet Frame, is acceptance worthwhile if it means that she has to 'give up writing'; give up her own voice?

Moreover, this option assumes that the assimilation route is always open to the stranger. That is certainly not always the case, as Frame finds when she attempts, in England, to train as a nurse. 'With your medical history?' is the response. Even if the route is open, however, the assimilated stranger will still be second-class. Worse, he or she may be judged as yielding beyond the point of honour. I have in mind Kristeva's account of the fate of the two Danaïdes who, in one version of the legend, did not strangle their assigned husbands on their wedding night. (The fifty daughters of Danaüs had been assigned in marriage, against their will, to their cousins: the fifty sons of Aegyptus.) Did these two, the Greeks asked – and it was a legal question – have the right to renounce vengeance? One was saved by the god Poseidon; the other was helped by Aphrodite and Hermes. Both escaped the court's judgment, but only by entering the service of the gods, remaining outside human marriage.[33]

Leave physically. Most of the foreigners that Kristeva describes are foreigners by choice: expatriates, economic immigrants, rather than expelled or displaced 'others'. Often, in fact, it is as if the stranger always had the option to leave one place for another in a constant search for the ideal, driven only by the sense that 'this is not it'.[34] Leaving physically is an option Frame does exercise take on several occasions, only to face the inevitable question: are these other places so different? Sooner or later, a sense of orphanhood will emerge. There will still be the oppression of others' expectations, often not so different from before. As I noted earlier, Patrick is even less understanding than her father of the identity Frame seeks. Patrick argues openly for an end to writing as a career, holding out as a dreadful alternative a 'steady job' working in a biscuit factory.

Leave psychologically. Without a violent break from the law, one may redefine oneself; accept being different; if possible, make a virtue of it – I am a 'writer' and writers are often different. One may take advantage of the fact that the several definitions of foreigner allow one to claim membership in groups not defined by legality or convention. This is the route suggested by Kristeva in her note on de Kooning's claim that because he is an artist, he has 'a greater feeling of belonging to a tradition': '[a]fter all, I am a foreigner, I am different because I am interested in art in its totality. I have a greater feeling of tradition'.[35]

In similar fashion, Janet Frame enjoys the sense of a similarity to other great artists: she enjoys Forrest's suggestion that she is like 'Hugo Wolf or Van Gogh, artists who combined talent with schizophrenia'.[36] The possibility is appealing. It carries within it, however, a danger. The danger is that this claim of a new membership has to be validated by others. They have to agree that you are an artist and/or 'ill' through no fault of your own. That danger helps one understand the poignancy of Frame's mixed response to the verdict 'you were never schizophrenic': '[a]t first, the truth seemed even more terrifying than the lie. How could I now ask for help when there was nothing wrong with me?'[37]

Reject the local codes. The stranger may stay but refuse to follow the local laws, sometimes violently. If laws are open to being changed when it suits the host country to do so, why should one observe them?

> To the welcomer's symbolic and legal holding back of the foreigner, the latter respond with a tendency not to accept the legislation in force. This is expressed not only through various infringements of the law ... (breaches of the labor laws, and so forth) ... but also by a refusal ... to accept the symbolics of the law, as well as the culture and civilization of the welcoming country .... [A] new form of individualism develops: 'I belong to nothing, to no law, I circumvent the law, I myself make the law'.[38]

This is not an option Frame takes, but it is clearly one to consider in any narrative of strangers.

Challenge what one finds objectionable. Surely there must be the option of objecting when the way one is treated becomes extremely negative. And surely that option should apply to Frame. Frame was not by nationality a foreigner, or by birth an orphan. Why did she not 'speak up'? Kristeva reminds us that the foreigner speaks well neither the psychological language of the old country or of that of the new: 'Thus, between two languages, your realm is silence'.[39]

More challenging is the notion that the foreigner may seek silence, may refuse speech, may feel that silence is the best defence:

> Come now! Silence has not only been forced upon you; it is within you; a refusal to speak, a fitful sleep riven to an anguish that wants to remain mute, the private property of your proud and notified discretion .... Nothing to say, nothingness, no one on the horizon. An impervious fullness: cold diamond, secret treasury, carefully protected, out of reach.[40]

The theme of refusal – of silence as a strategy – emerges again when Kristeva explicitly asks: why do we not 'argue ...[,] challenging the natives' assurance?'[41] The answer Kristeva offers has to do with the mixed feelings of the stranger. All foreigners, Kristeva suggests, feel both a sense of humility in the face of their not knowing exactly how things are said or done, and a sense of superiority to those who have not travelled or stepped outside convention – how could they understand?

> No. Those who have never lost the slightest root seem to you unable to understand any word liable to temper their point of view .... What is the point of talking to those who think they have their own feet on their own soil? The ear is receptive to conflicts only if the body loses its footing .... Yet when the foreigner – the speech-denying strategist – does not utter his conflict, he in turn takes root in his own world of a rejected person whom no one is supposed to hear.[42]

In short, the surface text may be one of victimization, of disadvantage imposed, of forced departures, and of repeated nonacceptance by those in power. The subtext Kristeva invites us to consider is one of refusal, of resistance, of deliberate silence, of pride in one's difference and insistence upon maintaining a difference even in the face of anguish over the cost and the sorrow that it brings.

Angel's impact upon the spectator

Up to this point, I have concentrated upon the form that narratives written from the stranger's point of view might take, using Kristeva's comments to establish a pool of possibilities and then observing how some of these are realized and played out in the story of *Angel*. Kristeva's perspective, the argument has been, helps one read the narrative: helps one observe what might otherwise pass unnoticed, helps one pull back from the easy interpretations that would reduce the central character to the one-dimensional status of victim and the story to one more repetition of conventional victim narratives, sparked only by the potentially melodramatic near-miss of a leucotomized brain and the announcement of 'never schizophrenic'.

Suppose, however, that we turn from the narrative per se and take as our focus the question: how are we to account for the impact of the narrative upon the spectator? What does Kristeva have to say that would help illuminate the extent to which we find *Angel* powerfully moving, the very opposite of some glib account of a woman misjudged, ill-treated, and finally recognized as a national treasure?

Part of the answer, Kristeva's comments suggest, lies in the increasingly widespread likelihood that we will be aware of being strangers. By choice as tourists or by assignment in our occupations, we move into being – even if temporarily – in marginal positions, being regarded as 'other'. Even if we never leave home, our sense of place – and our position within it – may be rendered 'different' by an influx of others, opening again the question, 'who am I?': a question that might have been thought to have been answered once and for all. To repeat a comment quoted in Chapter 4:

> Every native feels himself to be more or less a 'foreigner' in his 'own or proper' place, and that metaphorical value of the word 'foreigner' ... arouses a feeling of suspicion: Am I really at home? Am I myself? Are *they* not masters of the 'future'?[43]

Part of the answer, extrapolated from Kristeva's comments, must also lie in the way that *Angel* reminds us of feelings of vulnerability. To take but one area of insecurity, we are all reliant upon medical decisions. That reliance is comfortable as long as we have the sense that those decisions are likely to be sound and well-informed. Medicine, we like to think, is a science. To the extent that it has a history of 'bad old days', they are well into the past. Here, however, is a woman who passed away only recently. Her story would be less threatening if it came from Dickens's time or from, say, the 1930s. It is, however, a 'modern' story, and it taps into a fear that we also could be at risk of misjudgement. If Frame is rescued from leucotomy only by the extreme, and public, evidence of a book being published and praised, what would be the fate of someone without such evidence?

Those possibilities, I suggest, take us part of the way towards understanding the impact of *Angel*. There is as well, however, a further way in which *Angel* taps into our uncertainties and offers no glib way of avoiding the feelings it evokes. *Angel* is a reminder that we can be strangers within our own country. There is no need to be a foreigner to be an 'outsider'. More subtly, *Angel* suggests that the state of being a stranger is an inevitable and recurring part of human existence. None of us, it can be argued, feels completely 'at home', completely at ease with others. If the feeling is ever achieved, it will be fleeting. At the same time, each of us feels the force of the myth that there are others who feel completely at home. Like Frame, we observe people who appear completely relaxed with others, who seem to have no doubts about their status or their value. They know 'who they are' and they act from this central assurance even if there are moments when others fail to recognize or to reflect back their identity and their virtues.

In *Angel*, there is as well an absence of the storylines that soften the impact of our doubts, or that leave untouched the myth of settled identities. We are accustomed to having stories of painful shyness placed firmly in periods of adolescence, periods we can expect to leave behind us as we move into being adults. To be faced with an adult who continues to be painfully shy and to feel that she is socially the equivalent of 'two left feet' cuts away at the security offered by the implication that we 'grow out of' our uncertain identities.

We are accustomed also to stories of dramatic transformation: Cinderella stories of heroines who overnight or by the waving of some magic wand turn into successes. *Now Voyager* is a classic version. Frumpy Charlotte Vale (Bette Davis) is transformed by her psychiatrist and a borrowed wardrobe into a beauty who charms a handsome man and is quickly loved by him. The story does not allow her the final success of being able to stay with him, or of being able to love and marry the very acceptable Bostonian who finds her new self attractive. She does, however, remain transformed into a poised and beautiful woman who now has the strength to face down her once intimidating mother.

Frame, in contrast, remains thin-skinned and awkward. Even when she achieves fame in New Zealand, and is sought out by a young journalist eager to have the first story, *he* is the one who tells her where to sit, how to sit, and how to smile for the photograph he takes. She is not totally transformed. Nor is she, like the heroine in *Frances*, completely destroyed (Frances *is* leucotomized and loses her individuality: changed in a way into a person who is found by most others to be acceptably pleasant, but who is also flat emotionally and has lost the individuality that prompted the hero of her story to rescue her from confinement in an insane asylum represented as even more destructive than that occupied by Frame).

Kristeva, I suggest, would link the lack of black and white transformations and their impact to her general way of regarding identity. We are, she argues, always subjects-in-process. Transformation is constant. The 'I' is never settled. Moreover, the 'logic of identity' is always suspect. We may act as if there were settled identities, assigning them even to infants. The film *Look Who's Talking Now*, for instance, assigns a steady identity and an adult voice to a baby. We may have the sense that hidden within us is some firm, unchanging 'I', an 'I' that watches the variety of disguises we wear in the course of social and personal life, and that is well aware of the dramaturgical quality of interactions that analysts such as Erving Goffman highlight.[44] Kristeva's perspective is part of a rejection of the logic of identity by several philosophers.[45] One rarely sees that rejection played out, however, at the level of a commercially successful film. Frame, as a 'cured' adult, remains unsettled, unsure of herself, always reassessing herself in the light of other's views, sensitive to critics, vulnerable, and a mixture of moments of assurance and moments of doubt. There is, her story says to us, no time when those uncertainties disappear, when that fluidity and vulnerability go away forever.

Perhaps, it might be said, that type of portrayal of identity is likely to be especially appealing to women; especially likely to remind them of their position. We do know that women have responded to *Angel* in at least two ways, both reported by Bridget Ikin. One takes the form of women approaching Ikin to thank her for producing *Angel*, for telling *their* story. The other takes the form of insisting that this is *not* a woman's story and should perhaps even be avoided. This is, for instance, the response of the feminist who was negative towards funding *Angel* on the grounds that Frame was 'an inappropriate heroine for the nineties'.[46]

My own sense is that women are especially likely to be *represented* as vulnerable and as unsure of who they are. The people at risk in *Angel*, *Now Voyager*, and *Frances* are all female. There is, as a possible counter-case, *One Flew Over the Cuckoo's Nest*. Here the people at risk of savage medical procedures are male. They are not represented, however, as internally vulnerable or as searching for an identity. The character that Jack Nicholson portrays, for instance, is not 'troubled' within himself. Others are troubled by him and his position is precarious. Others judge him and can damage him. The story, however, is almost a variation upon prison stories. The men are confined more because of their rebel status than because they themselves feel unsure of who they are.

In contrast, Frame's story is one that bypasses rebel status or magical transformation. The film stands in opposition to conventional transformations, to plot-points that turn the story's kaleidoscope at expected intervals and leave an ending that we can feel is a true ending.

Angel unsettles us by consistently taking the point-of-view of the stranger, by making that person a 'stranger in her own country' rather than the obvious foreigner, by its reminders of our own vulnerabilities, and by the insistence that the issue of who one is and where one really belongs is never settled once and for all, even though our fictions of transformation may imply that this sense of sureness and stability is a desirable and achievable state.

Notes

1. Julia Kristeva (1980) *Desire in language: A semiotic approach to literature and art*. New York: Columbia University Press.
2. Candida Baker (1990) 'The sweet smell of direct success'. Review of *An Angel at My Table*. In *The Age*, 22 September, p.6.
3. Laura Jones (1990) *Screenplay for* An Angel at My Table. London: Pandora, p.93.
4. Julia Kristeva (1991a) *Strangers to ourselves*. New York: Columbia University Press, p.53.
5. Ibid., p.53.
6. Ibid., p.53.
7. Ibid., p.54.
8. Ibid., p.88.
9. Ibid., p.102.
10. Ibid., pp.48–49.
11. Jones (1990, p.45).
12. Ibid., p.48.
13. Ibid., p.50, in film as voice-over.
14. Kristeva,(1991a, p.15).
15. Jane Campion (1990b) in interview with Peter Castaldi: 'Castaldi on Campion'. In *Culture*, issue 9, October, p.10.
16. Kristeva (1991a, p.4).
17. Ibid., p.12.
18. Ibid., p.10.
19. Ibid., p.5.
20. Ibid., p.8.
21. Ibid., p.21.
22. Ibid., p.21.
23. Ibid., pp.22–23.
24. Ibid., p.22.
25. Ibid., p.75.
26. Ibid., p.101.
27. See, for example, Kristeva (1980).
28. Julia Kristeva (1993) *Nations without nationalism*. New York: Columbia University Press, p.34.
29. Kristeva (1991a, p.44).
30. Ibid., p.20.
31. Ibid., p.29.
32. Julia Kristeva (1990) 'The adolescent novel'. In J. Fletcher and A. Benjamin (Eds) *Abjection, melancholia, and love: The work of Julia Kristeva*. London: Routledge, p.10.
33. Ibid., p.45.
34. Ibid., p.17.
35. Ibid., p.32.
36. Jones (1990, p.45).

37. Ibid., p.87.
38. Kristeva (1990, p.103).
39. Kristeva (1991a, p.4).
40. Ibid., p.16.
41. Ibid., p.19.
42. Ibid., p.17.
43. Ibid., pp.19–20, emphasis in original.
44. Erving Goffman (1971) *The presentation of self in everyday life*. Harmondsworth: Penguin.
45. Jacques Derrida (1973) *Speech and phenomena and other essays on Husserl's theory of signs*. Evanston: Northwestern University; Jacques Lacan (1977) *Écrits*. London: Travistock.
46. Commented on by Ikin in interview with K. Goodnow (August, 1993).

Chapter 6

LOVE – BASIC CONCEPTS

In the next two chapters, I shall take up Kristeva's proposals with regard to love. I shall be particularly concerned with proposals that refer to sexual love and maternal love, although Kristeva's discussion – and some of the material I shall abstract from it – extends also to religious love and friendship.

Love is a topic that appears in many parts of Kristeva's writing, including her novel *The Samurai*. Its lack is part of *The New Maladies of the Soul*. Its presence is part of her analysis of Colette (*Colette*) and of Barthes. (*Intimate Revolt*). Two books, however, stand out. One is *In The Beginning Was Love*, a book mainly concerned with the relationship between psychoanalytic therapy and love. The other is *Tales of Love*, a review of both historical forms of love and contemporary case histories.

The topic brings a change in the kind of effect that is at the centre of Kristeva's concern. Just as the analysis of strangers showed points of continuity and change in relation to the analysis of horror, however, so too the discussion of love overlaps with, expands upon, and diverges from the analysis of the earlier topics. I shall accordingly begin, as I did in Chapter 4, by noting some of those points of continuity and change.

Aspects of continuity and change

To start with, the method used is much the same as for horror and foreignness. Kristeva again combines the analysis of literary and religious texts with insights from psychoanalysis. The psychoanalytic references, however, are now not only to written texts, but also – in case-study form – to 'tales' from her own psychoanalytic practice. More prominent in this material also are references to Kristeva's own experience, particularly as a mother.

Several of the conceptual concerns are also similar. There is again a concern with order, disturbances of order, and the instability of boundaries:

> In love 'I' has been an other ... a state of instability in which the individual is no longer indivisible and allows himself to become lost in the other, for the other.[1]

> (There is) dread of transgressing not only proprieties or taboos, but also, and above all, fear of crossing and desire to cross the boundaries of the self.[2]

There is again also a concern with the ways in which contact with what is disturbing is kept under control while still allowing it to take place. In the discussions of horror, the emphasis was upon control enforced by the construction of boundaries and the creation of ritualized contact. In the discussions of foreigners, the boundaries took primarily the form of definitions and regulatory codes. In the discussions of love, control is exercised primarily through ethical codes and social contracts such as marriage, but also through a marginalization of love:

> The trend leading to the subordination of passions to thought, already in evidence with Thomas Aquinas, was masterfully completed in the Cartesian corpus, which extols the supremacy of thought ... and knowledge ... over passions.[3]

Third, there is a continued emphasis on the mixed feelings that arise in the meeting between self and other, and between the sexes:

> I begin by speaking of love and end by speaking of hate. I can't finish the paragraph without speaking about hate because they are so mingled.[4]

Fourth, there is a continued concern with an issue that appeared especially in the analysis of foreigners – the difficulties of bridging the gap between individuals, this time between lovers. For Kristeva, the lovers who face one another in Matisse's painting are 'split by a whole world .... They are truly foreigners for each other'.[5] The gap between them, however, need not be a problem as long as there is an attempt to bridge it:

> [T]here is both infinite distance and the attempt to be together. I often say that the most stable couple are day and night, as they don't have anything to do with one another ... but they belong together anyway ...[;] both have their autonomy, which for me is something positive.[6]

Finally, there is a continued concern with the relationships between past texts and present discourses. In the analysis of horror, these past texts primarily shape the ways in which we define 'the abject', identify 'abominations', and come to expect that the abject will be represented only in particular forms and particular places. In the analysis of strangers, the past texts serve these purposes plus others: in particular, the political and potentially healing functions of showing us that the problem of 'foreigners' is not new and has been responded to in a variety of ways over the centuries. In the analysis of love, Kristeva uses the analysis of past codes to bring out a constant and a particular. The constant is the presence, over the centuries, of the difficulties that love presents to oneself and to others. The particular is the current gap between the circumstances we face and the tales at our disposal. 'We want stories of love', says Kristeva.[7] Moreover, we have a particular need of them in current times. Just as the 'values crisis' and the decline of religion (as described in the discussion of foreigners) leave us with a sense of disorientation and a return to the security of the small ethnic or family group, so also the loss of codes that once both allowed and regulated love creates a gap. Sex and technology, Kristeva argues, have driven out love, caring, trust, and passion.

What, then, is different? One new feature is the argument that bridging the gap between self and lover is necessary for the individual. The experience of horror is not a necessity, although the lack of encounter with the semiotic through the sensation of horror could lead to a sterile life. Encounters with foreigners, or the experience of being a foreigner, are also not necessary, although they enrich both the individual and the general society. Life without a meeting with love, however, is dangerous for the individual. Love is the starting point for all growth: one reason for Kristeva's substituting 'In the Beginning Was Love' for the more Biblical phrase 'In the Beginning Was the Word'. Life without love is for Kristeva a form of psychic death, a route to melancholia and psychosis: 'Love ... prevents me from being smothered to death beneath ... subterfuges and compromises'.[8]

The nature of the link between past representations and present discourses is also different from what we have seen in the analyses of horror and of strangers. We need, Kristeva argues, not only to return to past texts but also to develop new stories. Moreover, the way to do this may not be by the avant-garde transformation of old texts but by turning, at least as a first step, to a wider audience, to all who are dissatisfied with the current bank of images and tales, and asking them what it is that they want.

Finally, there are some new points for which elaboration is needed if a Kristevan perspective is to be fully useful to film analysts. In the analysis of horror, the main elaboration had to do with the circumstances surrounding the reception of the horrific: the site of encounter, the nature of the audience, the implicit contract between 'speaker' and 'addressee'. In the analysis of strangers, the elaboration concentrated upon the emergence of new narratives: narratives that present the point of view of the stranger, particularly the stranger who is not foreign by nationality but by gender and by definition as 'odd', or as possibly 'mad'. Love, it will emerge, continues this concern with the emergence of new texts or new discourses. If Kristeva is right in urging that we need 'new tales of love', we shall need to ask: who will write them? What form will they take? And how will they come about?

For this chapter, the first of the pair on love, the sequence roughly parallels the sequence of Chapter 4 (on strangers). The chapter presents first an outline of the films that serve as a focus (Jane Campion's *Sweetie* and *The Piano*). It then proceeds to an account of Kristeva's proposals with regard to love, concentrating on those related to the forms of love, the sources of difficulty in achieving and sustaining love, and the ways in which change comes about. Each section abstracts proposals from Kristeva and asks how they fit with, or how they help us understand, the shape and the impact of the two films chosen as a focus.

Sweetie and *The Piano*: An introduction

Sweetie was Jane Campion's first feature after producing four shorts, including the acclaimed *Passionless Moments* and *Peel*. (The latter won the Palme d'Or at Cannes in 1986.) It is the first of a trio of features, with the later two being *An Angel at My Table* (discussed in chapter 5), and *The Piano*. The script for *Sweetie* was written by Campion and Gerard Lee. The film was produced in Australia by Maynard's Arena Films. It received no prize at Cannes, but was admired by many serious critics, invited to several other festivals, and given rave reviews by *The New York Times* and by *Vanity Fair* ('the most original film of the year').[9]

A summary of the story will be in order, even though *Sweetie* received a fairly wide distribution. The setting is suburbia, pictured in all its ordinariness and somewhat claustrophobic air (one seldom sees a camera shot that provides any expansive view). The story centres on two sisters – Kay and Sweetie – and their relationships to their parents and their lovers. The film opens with Kay, a bank clerk, receiving advice from a psychic that she will soon meet a man with whom she is fated to be together. Kay will recognize him by a question mark on his forehead. At work Kay sees a man who has just become engaged to one of her co-workers. The fiancé, Louis, has a lock of hair and a freckle which combine to give the appearance of a question mark. Kay advances with a sense of fate. Louis is overwhelmed by her intensity and sexual openness. The two begin a relationship in which Kay's sexual love cools fairly quickly. (The images of houses collapsing, earth surfaces being broken up, and tree roots undermining the foundation of buildings, imply that she is afraid of love becoming too unsettling, too undermining of her usual control.) The lovers are then faced with the dilemma: how are they to deal with her loss of interest? A great deal of intellectualization is engaged in by both, satisfactory to neither.

At this point, the film seems to have stalled. It is jolted into life again – along with its characters – with the appearance of Sweetie. Sweetie is Kay's flamboyant sister, who normally lives at home (Kay does not) and takes medication to keep her 'on course'. Sweetie has joined up with a junkie, Bob, whom she calls her 'producer'. The two of them have grand plans to get Sweetie to the top of the music industry if they just could get a break (and get out of bed early enough). Sweetie and Bob move into Kay's house, initially by breaking down the door, later through attracting Louis's sympathy. Kay's father, Glen, also moves into Kay's house after being abandoned by his wife, Flo (the mother of Kay and Sweetie). Flo has had enough of living at the beck and call of Sweetie and of her husband. She announces that she wants a 'trial separation' and leaves for the outback, for a job cooking for a group of cattle- and sheep hands ('jackaroos').

Kay, Louis and Glen decide to drive to where Flo is working, hoping to persuade her to return. That, at least, is Glen's intention. Sweetie is tricked into staying behind. Flo is obviously enjoying her outback sojourn (here the camera does offer open vistas). She is, however, persuaded to return on the promise that new arrangements will be made, with Sweetie moving out. This arrangement is never put into place. Instead, it is quickly upset by Glen's distress on the trip back to the city: distress over what he sees as the breaking up of the family. Sweetie has moved back home but is again a major challenge to suburban decorum. During the others' absence, she has turned the tidy house into what looks like a disaster area, and she herself has reverted to a refusal to speak except in barks and growls. She makes her presence known to the whole neighbourhood by painting her well-fleshed, naked body and trumpeting from her childhood treehouse. Her father refuses to let anyone phone the fire brigade (they would bring a ladder that could reach Sweetie). Instead, they phone Kay for help, and Glen places a ladder against the treehouse. Sweetie pushes it away and jumps up and down in violent triumph upon the old boards. They give way. Sweetie falls, badly injured. Kay's 'kiss of life' is to no avail and Sweetie dies within a few moments. The film ends with no indication of where the parents' marriage now stands. Kay and Louis, however, are pictured as together again, and as moving towards a reopening of their sexual relationship.

In all, the style of *Sweetie* is modern. The camera angles are often askew, the actors placed in corners or edges of the frame, and outdoor shots in particular have a 1950s Kodachrome look. Jane Campion herself felt, upon seeing the first cut of the film, that 'it looked like it had been made by Martians'.[10] Shots are often held long after the dialogue is completed (an upsetting technique that Jim Jarmusch has also used, for example in *Stranger Than Paradise*). The acting style is dry, the lines presented in a Bressonian-style rather than experienced intensely, as in the American, method-acting style.

In contrast to *Sweetie*, the style of *The Piano* is lush. This big-budget period movie has a totally professional finish, together with a mixture of actors from New Zealand and the United States: the female lead is played by Holly Hunter, the two male leads by Sam Neil and Harvey Keitel. The film was financed in Australia with script support coming from the

Australian Film Commission, The New South Wales Film Board, and the French construction company CIBY 2000. Jan Chapman was the producer, following up her other success, *Chez Nous*. *The Piano* won the Palme d'Or at the 1993 Cannes Festival, making Jane Campion the first woman to win this award.

The story of *The Piano* is probably better known than the story of *Sweetie*. It has been a box-office success and it has been followed by a large number of analyses.[11] A summary will still be in order. Primarily the film is about love, passion, and the options open to women and men in colonial New Zealand in the mid nineteenth century. The film begins with a voice-over. Ada, a young woman in her late twenties, tells us that she is speaking to us directly from her mind as she chose to stop speaking at the age of six. No reason is offered. Ada tells us also that her father has given her in marriage (by proxy) to a man she has never met: a man in New Zealand. The images under this voice-over are clearly from an English park, where a little girl is learning to ride a pony and a young woman is sitting beneath a tree (a gentleness of landscape unlike that which will be faced in New Zealand).

Ada has one passion in addition to her daughter, Flora – a piano. Through this piano her feelings are expressed. (She communicates also by writing notes.) The piano is shipped to New Zealand with a few other belongings but is left on the beach upon arrival. Ada's husband, Stewart, does not bring enough bearers with him to take everything on the tortuous trip through the muddy bush to his homestead and he clearly regards the piano as an unnecessary 'extra'. He is unmoved that Ada clearly feels at a loss without her piano, and her relationship with Stewart founders from the start.

Ada's piano is restored to her through the actions of an illiterate neighbour, George Baines. Baines has a better relationship with the Maoris than Stewart does and has the piano transported to his hut. He also has it tuned, to Ada's immense surprise and pleasure. Stirred in a way he finds strange by Ada and by the depth of Ada's and Flora's response to the piano (Ada plays as soon as they arrive at the beach), Baines offers Ada a bargain. Ada may earn back her piano, black key by black key, if she allows Baines to 'do things' while Ada plays the piano. (Officially, he is taking piano lessons from Ada.) These acts begin fairly innocently with the stroking of an arm, the revealing of some leg, but develop as Baines becomes more impassioned by Ada. Ada does not initially return his desire and Baines, 'sick with love' and ashamed at an arrangement that he sees as one turning Ada into 'a whore', finally returns the piano to her and asks her not to visit him any more. Ada then reveals that she has come to be drawn to him as well. She visits him on her own initiative, unaware that her husband has become suspicious of their arrangement and has followed her. He watches them make love, confronts her with this afterwards and tries to possess her first through rape, then by boarding up the house with her inside.

Baines, hurt that Ada does not return, decides to leave the area. Ada attempts to send him a message but is foiled by her own daughter who takes the message to Stewart instead. Stewart, in fury, drags Ada out to the farm's chopping block and removes one of her fingers. This he sends to Baines by Flora with the message that, if the lovers continue to meet, he will remove Ada's fingers one by one.

Ada survives the attack and Stewart breaks down over what he has done. He lets Ada and Flora – whose alliance with the mother has now been re-established – leave with Baines. Baines carefully packs Ada's piano onto the Maori canoe they depart in, but Ada requests that it be buried in the sea. At first, she seems ready to die with the piano. She allows herself to be dragged overboard by the end of the rope around it. Under water, she decides to live and surfaces. The film ends with her playing a new piano (a metal finger has replaced the one she lost). The voice over speaks of her teaching the piano to others in the town (she comments that she is still regarded as 'a freak') but also of her beginning to practise speech.

All told, the story weaves together a number of Ada's changing relationships: with her daughter, with Stewart, with Baines, and with the conventional Victorian society around her. Set in contrast to these pakeha relationships are the Maoris: people who offer a contrast in their attitudes to the land, to sex, and to the body in general. Stewart and his fellow colonists have no point of contact with the Maoris except by way of attempts at an exploitative relationship. Baines has come to know them, to feel sympathy with them, and – as a sign of his acceptance – to wear some of their body tattoos.

There are, then, several refusals of the conventional order: from Ada, from Baines, and from the Maori. The refusals from all three contain an acceptance of sensuality and physicality rather than the denials of puritanism. Potentially, all three could form an alliance, although in the narrative only Baines forms an alliance with the Maori. Ada and the Maori join forces only in the moment when the Maori are the ones who understand Ada's feeling that the piano is 'contaminated' and must be dumped at sea. In effect, the story of people who are foreigners to each other by way of nationality is subordinated to the story of people who are strangers to one another by virtue of their acceptance or rejection of a puritan ethos in which love and physicality are cast out by restraint and respectability.

What are the forms of love?

With a sense of the film narratives in hand, let me turn to Kristeva's proposals about love, interweaving them with the films by way of questions that are contained in Kristeva's discussion, and starting with the question: what are the forms of love?

In Kristeva's account, the forms of love are clearly several. In *Tales of Love*, for instance, Kristeva's historical account begins with the legend of Narcissus and ranges through the troubadour era of the Middle Ages, the story of Don Juan, and the writings of Baudelaire and Stendhal. The tales cover love directed towards other adults, towards children, towards oneself and towards God. To these accounts, Kristeva adds as well – interspersed through the volume – case studies drawn from her own psychoanalytic practice, that illustrate contemporary enactments of similar definitions and difficulties of love. Still further case studies, and again a particular concern with the transference love that usually occurs in the course of psychoanalysis, are offered in her shorter book, *In the Beginning Was Love*. The variety prompts two questions: how then shall we define 'love' in general? And how are we to distinguish among these many instances?

For the first question – the general nature of love – one would not expect from Kristeva an explicit definition that carefully marks the boundaries between 'love' and 'not love'. That would be out of keeping with her overall style. If a definition is needed at the start, one might note that for the individual, love is a state of feeling marked by several qualities: by the idealization of the object of love, by a wish for 'oneness' with what one loves, and by the sense of being swept up in something larger than oneself. Love is also, however, a social phenomenon: that is, it cannot be defined only in terms of what the individual feels. This is a state of feeling for which there are several social conventions and ideological codes that specify what is expected of lovers and of the ways in which sexual pleasure may be taken: expectations that may range from marriage to a limit on the proper objects of love or the proper length of time for the 'excesses' that are part of being 'in love'.

The more effective understanding of love comes through considering its varieties. Kristeva offers several distinctions, basing these upon the perspectives of both psychoanalysis and history. I shall abstract two that have particular relevance to the analysis of difficulties and achievements and to the analysis of film: one related to the object of love, the other to the expected course of love.

The object of love

Love may be directed towards physical objects, towards self, towards other people, or towards God. Where the attachment is to people, it may be to child or adult, to male or female, to those younger or older than oneself, and to the whole person or to some part singled out as the 'essence' of the loved one.

In themselves, however, these distinctions have no particular dynamic to them. The advantage of working from Kristeva's perspective is that one moves on to asking: is the object of love in keeping with the prevailing codes of love? Is it, in the light of the prevailing codes, legitimate, appropriate, tolerable, or unacceptable? Among the Pharaohs of Egypt, for instance, marriage between brother and sister was legitimate, even expected. In Medieval Europe, the Lady who was the object of 'courtly love' could be the wife of another. In *The Piano*, sexual pleasure is taken by children, rubbing their bodies against the trunks of trees. To Maori adults, the practice is acceptable. To Ada's husband – a conventional, Scots-born male – it is not. When Ada's child follows the Maori example, he responds with disgust and makes her whitewash every contaminated tree. In short, what counts is the extent to which the chosen object is in keeping with or out of line with the established order.

What counts also – if one thinks further along Kristeva's lines – is the way in which the prevailing codes specify particular consequences or punishments for a choice that falls outside the established order. It is these allowable or excessive consequences, and the extent to which a character or a narrative conforms to them, that can give a particular dramatic value to adultery. In earlier Inuit times, for example, the man who offered his wife as an overnight gift to a guest could hardly be said to involve her in adultery or to set up a moment of tension in Inuit society. For the moment to have dramatic value, the action needs to be a violation of what are regarded at the time as one party's (often a man's) rights to exclusive ownership or the other party's (often a woman's) rights to act as a person, an agent, a subject, rather than an object to be passed from hand to hand.

What matters also must be the extent to which the consequence of going outside the code falls within a range of acceptable punishments. In some settings, a 'wronged' husband may kill his wife and/or her lover, and be acquitted because the action involves a question of 'honour'. In other settings he may legitimately divorce her, beat her, or restrict her to the house. To any narrative of love, then, one may bring not only the question: is this object of love in keeping with what is expected?, but also the question: does the response to a violation of what is expected fall within the conventional range?

It is the latter question, for instance, that makes one aware of the narrative significance of the punishment Stewart administers to Ada. No Anglo or Scots code in the mid nineteenth century, when *The Piano* is set, said a man might mutilate his wife in the way that Stewart mutilates Ada: chopping off a finger, and threatening to take one away for each time that she sees her lover. This 'punishment' not only deprives Ada of the sexual pleasure she experiences with her lover, but also deprives her of the pleasure of music: a pleasure that predates both men and is, as her husband well knows, the core of her being. In some societies of honour, the punishment that Stewart administers might be thought to be restrained: Ada still has her life. Within contemporary Western codes, however, Stewart's action strikes the viewer as both cruel and against the law. Moreover, within Stewart's own code his action is so barbaric, depraved, excessive, and 'primitive' that he – like Ada's lover, Baines, at an earlier point – comes to feel that it is better to yield Ada than to continue trying to gain a prize that carries so high a price, that threatens to destroy his image of himself and the image others may hold of him, that invites him to commit both acts of cruelty and murder. In effect, the grossness of the code violation makes sense of his yielding Ada to another: an action that up to this point he has regarded as unthinkable.

How is it, then, that the story of *The Piano* allows Ada to violate the conventional code and yet, at the end, succeed in love? She does not die. She is allowed to leave her husband and to live with her lover. They are happy with one another, and Ada's daughter is content (the final scene is a kiss between Ada and Baines that combines both affection and sensuality; while they kiss, the camera shows Flora playing happily in the garden). Ada is even restored to music: not the original piano, but a piano she can play with the new, metal finger. Living 'outside marriage', she will continue not to be part of the local church circle; but she is not condemned to a loveless life with a husband who can accept her only if she denies herself and conforms to his image of what she should be. Here, then, is a text in which, for a change, the heroine can have 'a little romantic cake and ... eat it too'.[12]

The expected course of love

The love varies not only in its object, and the legitimacy of that object, but also in the course that it is expected to follow. Part of the expected course is laid out by the prevailing codes. The tales and rituals of love spell out for us, in a given time and place, the expected periods of courtship, the trials that should be undergone, the proofs that should be offered, the anticipatable periods of difficulty (the seven-year itch; the decline of interest in sex after motherhood; the special problems of mid-life crises for both partners, etc.).

The course to which Kristeva draws particular attention, however, comes more from her psychoanalytic interests than from her interest in the codes contained within the text of culture and history. It is her psychoanalytic perspective that leads her to distinguish especially between two courses of love: the course of love between mother and child, and the course of love between adults.[13] It is her psychoanalytic perspective that leads her also to relate the nature of the course of love to some particular sources of difficulty that may arise.

In essence, the love between mother and child begins with oneness: a oneness felt by both mother and child. Both must experience separation, although typically it is the child's experience that is given the greater attention. The course for the child is one of moving from auto-eroticism and 'the paradise' of the original mother–child 'dyad' to a state where love is directed towards others, perhaps by way of 'transitional objects' (the breast is replaced by the bottle, the dummy, or the thumb; the mother's body by an object that may be carried around, clung to, sucked at will, etc.). The problems for this kind of love, then, are problems of achieving a successful separation: one that leaves the child able to love others, not 'tied to its mother's apron strings', forever looking towards the past in a state of constant nostalgia.

In contrast, love between adults begins with separateness, with the gap that Kristeva notes so explicitly in the analysis of Matisse's painting cited earlier. The course of closing the gap, or reducing it, calls for finding a place 'between the two borders of *narcissism* and *idealization*'.[14] Both narcissism and idealization are a necessary part of the course. Some degree of narcissism – of self-love – must be present before one can love an other. Some degree of idealization – some overvaluation of the other and of one's own image in the eyes of the other – must also be present. So, also, must be the capacity to accept, without hatred, bitter disappointment, or flight, the inevitable intrusion of the real into this state of fantasy: the inevitable discovery of the other, or of the reflected image, in some degree short of the idealized perfection.

For Kristeva, understanding the necessary course of love helps clarify why love is often difficult to achieve. A position of unadulterated narcissism or unadulterated idealization, for instance, dooms adult love. The course of love, in her analysis, is also part of our cultural/historical expectations about the way love – in life or in a narrative – should unfold, and part of our unease, shock, anger, despair, or concern when this does not occur. *Sweetie* provides an example. This time (a contrast to the mother–son pair in *Psycho*, for instance), the spectator's unease is sparked by a father who holds back a separation from a daughter. Sweetie remains for her father a little girl, turning in cute little performances that he applauds (performances appropriate for a six-year old, now presented by a young woman). He treats her as a wayward child, encouraging her in her retreat from words to growls and barks. There is a clear overtone of the erotic in their relationship (the older sister Kay sees or recalls a scene in which an adolescent/adult Sweetie soaps her father's body in the bath – in a sense, he now acts the baby). The more constant note, however, is one of sustained infantilization for both father and daughter. He wants to remain an infant. His wife, when she leaves, labels a set of meals for him to heat up while she is gone, but even this is beyond him and he turns up – to stay – at his daughter Kay's house. In his scenario, Sweetie also will remain infantile, uncritical of her own inadequate performance, acting out her baby place in the family that the father sees as 'happy' and hopes to maintain, ignoring the cost to his wife, to the older sister, and to Sweetie herself.

The difficulties of love

All good narratives are stories of difficulties, bravely borne, tragically experienced, sometimes crushing, sometimes magically or heroically overcome. And all such stories invite analysis in terms of the kinds of difficulty, their sources, their impact, and their possible resolution.

Kristeva is a rich source of proposals for the difficulties that love meets: difficulties in establishing it or maintaining it. I shall abstract four of particular interest, and link each to a feature of *Sweetie* or *The Piano*. The four have to do with the disorderliness of love, the incompatibility between marriage and love, the invitation to games of power, property and sacrifice, and the lack of stories of love. When one adds these to the two sources of difficulty already mentioned – the restrictions placed by society on the objects of love, and the difficulties of achieving or overcoming a separation between self and other – the list becomes formidable. The wonder is that love ever occurs or is ever sustained.

Love as 'disorderly'

As always, 'disorder' has a special place in Kristeva's analysis. She brings out both the forms of order that are threatened and the solutions often sought. In broad terms, love alters the balance between what Kristeva summarizes as symbolic and semiotic forms of experience. Love is:

> a ... destabilization between the *symbolic* (pertaining to referential signs and their syntactic articulation) and the *semiotic* (the elemental tendency ... that privileges orality, vocalization, alliteration, rhymicity etc.[)][15]

What specifically does the disorder of love upset? Love may first of all destabilize the order that usually prevails between one's 'head' and one's 'heart'. 'Reason' loses its dominance:

> [T]his state of crisis, collapse, madness ... [is] capable of sweeping away all the doors of reason ...[,] capable ... of transforming an error into a renewal – remodelling, remaking, reviving a body, a mentality, a life. Or even two.[16]

The usual power of words is also destabilized. Love involves both a 'vertigo of identity' and a 'vertigo of words'.[17] At one and the same time one experiences 'the impression of speaking at last, for the first time, for real'[18] and an awareness of how inadequate and misleading words can be:

> [I]n the rapture of love, the limits of one's own identity vanish, at the same time ... the precision of reference and meaning become blurred in lovers' discourse. Do we speak of the same thing when we speak of love? And of which thing? The ordeal of love puts the univocity of language and its referential and communicative power to the test.[19]

Love alters as well our usual commitment to conventional 'projects' and the careful use of time. These effects are made especially explicit in the feelings attributed to the character Olga in Kristeva's novel *The Samurai*:

> My child ...[,] what word is there for the link that binds me to you ...? A body ...? ... A love ...? ... [T]ime? That might be nearer to it .... You have opened the present to me .... I just let things and words and people pass me by .... I loiter, I don't rush around any more, I don't pursue any goal .... You've reminded me of the past .... My own childhood ... comes back .... And you've turned the future into a riddle: it's not a plan anymore.[20]

> Suppose you've spent twenty, thirty, or forty years of your life among words and ideas, libraries and debates, books and travelling. You've become quick-thinking, lucid, decisive, disillusioned, broken and repaired, sharp, blunt, flexible but thick-skinned, sensitive but adaptable, immune from anguish and depression, yet secretly cultivating their latent, suave, and well-controlled sources. And then a little boy who was a baby but is now growing up sometimes too slowly, sometimes too fast, starts to open your eyes, your ears, your skin .... He does something silly and you are part of that. He gives an innocent laugh and you are part of that too ...[;] touching, ridiculous and trivial little things become full of meaning.[21]

Such a sweeping away of time applies also to sexual love:

> [T]he nontime of love that, both instant and eternity, past and future, abreacted present, fulfils me, abolishes me, and yet leaves me unsated ... [t]ill tomorrow, forever, as ever, faithfully, eternally as before, as when it will have been.[22]

These several forms of destabilization, however, might be regarded as a problem only for the individual. No form of order in Kristeva's analysis, however, exists without a connection to other forms of order. A private madness cannot exist. There is inevitably a threat of destabilization to the established social order. The love of Romeo and Juliet, for instance, threatens more than their own sanity. It threatens also the factional structure of the city, the established separation of Montagues and Capulets. The mystical withdrawal of Jeanne Guyon into silence, into quietism, threatens a religious order. Even the *Song of Songs* attracts a sermon detailing love's impact upon the proprieties:

> What a violent all-consuming, impetuous love! It thinks only of itself, lacks interest in anything else, despises all, is satisfied with itself! It confuses stations, disregards manners, knows no bounds. Proprieties, reason, decency, prudence, judgment are defeated and reduced to slavery.[23]

No form of disorder, in Kristeva's analysis, exists without concurrent attempts to control it, to avoid its being overwhelming. To any narrative then, one must bring the questions: how do people deal with their own disorder? And how do they deal with the destabilization of order that the loves of others can cause?

One solution highlighted is flight or exclusion. The sickened lover may flee. This is, for instance, Baines's solution (*The Piano*) for the wretched state to which his love of Ada reduces him. 'Go away', he tells her – and then prepares to go away himself. (Ada turns out to be the character with the strength to hold on to her own obsession. She will *not* abandon her piano: in fact, she comes close to preferring to die with it rather than lose it.)

Flight is also Kay's solution in *Sweetie* when she faces the possibility of love taking root and getting into the 'foundations'. Louis plants a small tree in the back yard; she dreams of its root system spreading widely, cracking up the concrete surface of the yard, and unsettling the house; she hides the torn-out tree under the bed where she and Louis usually sleep, and then cannot make love. Instead, she retreats to another room and to feeling like a 'sister'.

Flight is a solution that others may also adopt when confronted with a form of love they find disturbing. Sweetie, for instance, is a threat to everyone else's order. Her first appearance in the tidy suburban home rings alarm bells. She is fat without any sign of concern with her size, colourful and untidy in dress, impulsive and clumsy in movement, cheerful, affectionate, and demanding in a mindless 'here I am' kind of way. Her absurd idealization of her lover (the spaced-out man she presents as 'the producer' who will build for her a career in the entertainment industry), her infantilized relationship with her father, her demands that she be allowed to do what she wants, the threat 'I'm going to do something': all these make her sister's and mother's lives intolerable. Sweetie has appeal. She is in many ways the perpetual puppy; the six-year-old next door finds her a rewarding playmate; and her serious sister – Kay – would like to love her, even though one glance at Sweetie is enough to prompt the question: 'are you off your pills?' Sweetie is the child-within-us grown large and not under control. Her return to the family is the last straw, which leads to her mother's flight and then to the flight of her father, Kay and Louis. They leave behind Sweetie, who was determined to join them in their journey to where the mother is working. Sweetie, however, is tricked into staying behind: a trick she repays by rapidly reducing the house to a state matching her own disorder.

Flight from the scene of disorderly love, however, is not likely to be a society's preferred way of dealing with the problem. In what ways, then, does a social order act in order to control or contain this form of madness?

One way, I suggest, consists of building up a bank of stories saying that sad endings await all those who act excessively or inappropriately. The 'tales of love' are then not only codes of love. They are also cautionary tales for those who may be tempted into a wrong love or an excess of love. They will become 'sick with love'. They will invite their death and the death of others (Romeo and Juliet). They will invite castration and banishment to a life of celibacy (Heloise and Abelard). They will invite disapproval and ridicule, and will inevitably be caught up in a 'crucible of contradictions and misunderstandings'.[24] If it were not for the eventual unification of Ada and Baines, *The Piano* might indeed be such a cautionary tale: one warning after another against excess. As it stands, however, only 'excess' of love wins in the end; an 'excess' of hatred and jealousy loses; and an alternative is offered to the more usual cautionary tale.

Kristeva says little explicitly about texts of love as cautionary tales. She does, however, point to three other ways in which a society copes with the disorderly aspects of love. One way is to sanctify the madness. For this to happen, however, the 'disorder' must occur within a given place and be directed towards the right object: God. The ecstasies of a mystical union with God may be allowed but only within limits:

> Theology alone, and only within its mystical deviations, allows itself to be lured into the trap of a blessed loving madness.[25]

A second way is to banish, exclude, isolate, or remove those who create the disorder. A third, one to which Kristeva gives more attention, consists of legitimizing love. Love can be allowed to exist, but only within the bounds of marriage. The danger then, Kristeva argues, is that love may die.

Marriage as the enemy of love

How does Kristeva come to regard marriage – the union of people within 'the law' – as the enemy of love? She makes the point more than once:

> the loving couple is outside the law, the law is deadly for it.[26]

> [M]erged with the ... practice of law, marriage – a historically and socially determined institution – is antimonic to love.[27]

Part of the effect, Kristeva proposes, stems from the way that marriage may present both parties with a possible loss of power. For men, marriage may mean some loss of phallic status, some loss of image as conqueror and prime mover that may affect both partners. The man may be tempted into flight:

> [T]he man flees from being swallowed up by the matrimonial couple in an attempt to secure his phallic power; he does so through the successive mirrors of more or less transgressive conquests that are reassuring.[28]

The woman may also be less than happy with her domesticated partner. ('And no surprises', says Lane in *Crush*, in response to Colin's reiteration of his new regime – 'no drugs; no stimulants'). More often, the woman seems likely to become the victim of the law's 'tyrannical facet, woven with daily constraints and ... repressive stereotypes'.[29] For women especially, the 'joys of marriage' ... run a great risk of being reduced to the masochistic submission ... of a household servant. An entire chapter of libido soaked up by the housewife's worries.[30]

A further part of the difficulty, Kristeva suggests, is that love is not sustainable in its initial state. Society has no investment in sustaining it:

Out of this amatory 'we' in a delightful state of destabilization, the law then produces a coherent set, a mainstay of reproduction, of production, or simply of the social contract.[31]

Moreover, any state of ecstasy cannot be prolonged forever. Its short life is inevitably incompatible with the view that marriage should span some reasonable period of time.

The interesting question, Kristeva argues, then takes the form: what sustains the myth of 'forever'?

If desire is fickle, thirsting for novelty, unstable by definition, what is it that leads love to dream of an eternal couple?[32]

The answer, she proposes, lies in this dream being largely the province of adolescence and of those whose goal is one of 'recreating the paradise of the lost dyad'.[33] The mature adult should not expect that the first, fine flush of love will last: an expectation perhaps underlined by stories such as the tale of Romeo and Juliet. For the romance to be all-powerful, the story needs to end in the lovers' early deaths, before the moment fades.

Another interesting question, I would add, is: if marriage has part of its negative effect because it opens the way to petty tyrannies and oppressive constraints, why do these tyrannies and constraints occur, and what alternatives are there? Is it possible for marriage not to be tyrannical? Yes, Kristeva suggests, if both partners are equal, if both are agents, if both are 'speaking subjects', and if both manage to avoid the games that marriage conventionally invites: games of power, property, and sacrifice. I shall take up these positive possibilities in the later section on links to change. For the moment, however, let me document some further interesting aspects of Kristeva's account of the difficulties of love.

Games of power, property, and sacrifice

Are there, Kristeva asks – as all of us must ask – forms of marriage that are not 'antimonic to love'? They can occur, Kristeva suggests, only if we resist the temptations to enter games of power, property, and sacrifice. Of the three, games or relationships of power are given the least attention by Kristeva in her analysis of love. (Power is certainly not an issue she ignores and one might argue that power subsumes issues of property and sacrifice. Power, however, is not the pivot for her analysis of relationships to the extent that it is for Foucault).[34] Nonetheless, love, in Kristeva's view, 'probably always includes a love for power',[35] with easy shifts into 'the havoc of the master–slave game'.[36]

Rather than document power plays, Kristeva asks: what is there in the marriage contract or in the codes of love that invites the man's exercise of power and the woman's sacrificial submission? The answer, she suggests, lies in the way past tales and images of love and marriage are written in terms of dominance and submission. 'To love, honour, and obey' has a long history in marriage ceremonies.

Like power, the perception of people as property is not a strongly articulated theme in Kristeva's account of the difficulties of love. These perceptions, however, are clearly out of line with there being two 'speaking subjects' rather than one person as subject and the other as object. Kristeva would have no difficulty in seeing *The Piano* as a prime story for asserting that the definition of women as the property of husbands is antithetical to love. Ada is handed from a father to a husband to be part of what he owns. She is then expected to be open to physical penetration by her owner. That sense of property goes beyond ownership of Ada's body. It applies also, for example, to ownership of the piano. Baines, to take one small but telling instance, gives the piano back to Ada. Her husband, Stewart, then sees no strangeness in objecting, 'I don't want a piano', leaving it for Baines to point out that the piano was given to Ada, not to Stewart: a distinction within the marital 'we' that clearly sounds odd, certainly novel, to Stewart's ears.

Stewart is, in fact, throughout, the symbol of how difficult it is – regardless of a nature that is potentially loving – to rise above the conventional definitions of his time. He cannot see Ada except as his. Prepared to wait for her to become sexually 'affectionate', as an older woman puts it, he is stung to an attempted rape only when he finds that Ada has been 'friendly' with Baines. Rather than yield what is 'his', he will cut off a finger, use Ada's daughter (a child of about nine years) as a messenger to take the bloody package to Baines, and shut both Ada and her daughter into a boarded-up house so that they cannot leave. Only the sense of his own descent into 'madness' brings him to any willingness to 'give up' Ada, as if she were still his to give. Stewart, in fact, is hemmed in not only by his conventional definition of Ada as his property. In his relationships with the Maori, he cannot rise above a view of them as lesser beings. They treat with scorn his attempts to buy their labour with buttons and their land with blankets, as if they were children or ignorant savages, but Stewart cannot find another way forward. Nor can he find a way to treat the land by any means other than clearing it and fencing it in. For Stewart, in Campion's words, 'things ... had to be transformed for him to accept them'.[37]

Where Kristeva does elaborate on dominance and submission is in her analysis of the sacrificial contract that is a core part of many Western images of motherhood. This analysis is a major part of her dissection of an image of motherhood that has long been dominant but is now regarded by many women as irrelevant or suspect: the Mater Dolorosa.

On the face of things, Kristeva points out, the Blessed Virgin occupies a position that many women might envy. Here is a mother who 'experiences a fate more radiant than her son's: she undergoes no Calvary, she has no tomb, she doesn't die ...[,] she is transported' into heaven.[38] She is a 'guardian of power':[39] 'a substitute for effective power in the family'.[40] She possesses a beauty that is 'enough to make any woman suffer, any man dream'.[41] She is 'alone of her sex'.[42]

At the same time, the Mater Dolorosa – this woman whose status was often marked with 'milk and tears' – is outside language: 'milk and tears ... are the metaphors of nonspeech'.[43] The Mater Dolorosa is also essentially an image of sacrifice. Hers may be 'a suffering lined with jubilation'[44] but the message remains that the route to approval – to a status as the most blessed and most admirable of women – is one of mute sacrifice.

The Mater Dolorosa may seem remote from contemporary life. Consider, however, the expectation that the father/husband makes of his wife in *Sweetie*, and the way in which he uses a moment of romance to undo her decision to leave a marriage based upon sacrifice. Tired of caring for Sweetie and for a man who cannot even make a meal for himself, she leaves. He follows and, in a scene of great tenderness, he asks if he may join in her dance. She is cooking for a group of station hands: men not renowned for their gentleness or their openness to the 'softer' side of experience. When she puts on a dance record, however (a waltz), they ask to be shown how to dance and are prepared to look like beginners (even, in conventional masculine terms, a little foolish) in order to learn. It is into this scene that the husband returns, asks if he may cut in, and reveals himself as a smooth dance partner. The partnership continues into the kitchen where he joins in the washing-up, and into the good resolutions that lead to his wife's agreeing to return. What breaks the move to the new relationship? It is his use of tears, and his wish that Sweetie should live with them, that everything should be 'the way it was'. The momentary breach in the sacrificial contract is precisely that: momentary. They will look after Sweetie. They will keep it all 'in the family': this refusal to turn outside for help eventually costs Sweetie her life.

The lack of stories of love

The last major difficulty to be abstracted from Kristeva's account of love has a particular relevance to the emergence of new texts. It has to do with the lack of a satisfactory discourse, of satisfactory ways to talk about love. That lack, Kristeva proposes, is especially the case in contemporary Western society. We have, she argues, marginalized love in our pursuit of knowledge and our valorization of reason:

The trend leading to the subordination of passion to thought, already evident in Thomas Aquinas, was masterfully completed in the Cartesian corpus, which extols the supremacy of thought ... and knowledge over passions. The subordination ... of love to true knowledge ... contrasts with the medieval thesis postulating a truth that only stemmed from the love of God. The dethronement of faith by reason is accompanied by a mutation of love, which slips away into knowledge.[45]

Moreover, we have lost the old codes and not replaced them:

We have lost the relative strength and security that the old moral codes guaranteed our lives either by forbidding them or determining their limits. Under the crossfire of gynaecological surgery rooms and televisions screens, we have buried love within shame for the benefit of pleasure, desire, if not revolution, evolution, planning, management – hence for the benefit of politics[, u]ntil we discover under the rubble of those ideological structures – which are ... nonetheless ambitious, often exorbitant, sometimes altruistic – that they were extravagant or shy attempts intended to quench a thirst for love.[46]

All told, we lack current 'tales of love':

There are no love stories anymore. And yet women want them, and so do men when they're not ashamed of being tender and sad like women. But men are all in a hurry to make money, and to die .... They're always taking planes, high-speed metros, high-speed trains, space shuttles. They don't have time to look at that pink acacia stretching out its branches toward the clouds and the strips of sunlit blue silk in between.[47]

In short, the possibility of achieving love and of sustaining it in any enriching form seems slight. There is, fortunately, a more positive side to Kristeva's analysis: a side that emerges when she begins to comment on the steps that may be taken towards love, or towards changes in the status quo.

Links to change: Steps towards love

As moves towards reducing racism and establishing better relationships with foreigners, Kristeva offered several positive suggestions: recognize the presence of differences; accept and respect those differences (as long as they are not incompatible with an *état général*); know the past and benefit from the examples that it offers (at the least, come to recognize that the problem is not new); know yourselves (what is rejected in the foreigner is often an unloved aspect of ourselves); and take, when you can, the point of view of the stranger, if only because all of us will at some time be strangers. Some of the same types of recommendation emerge when Kristeva mentions moves that may increase the likelihood of achieving and sustaining love. There are as well, however, some steps that are more specific to the relationship of love and it is on these that I shall concentrate.

It will come as no surprise that Kristeva argues for the development of a new discourse. That is so large a part of her argument, and so provocative a part of it, that I shall simply mention it here, reserving for the next chapter a sustained look at the questions: what would a new discourse be like? How might it be developed? How can the new voice be heard? Films such as *The Piano*, I shall argue, may be regarded as part of the search for a new discourse.

Beyond developing a new set of texts, or resurrecting some of those buried 'under the crossfire of gynaecological surgery rooms and television screens', what are the steps Kristeva proposes? One step consists of moving towards a new legality, towards forms of authority that would reduce the extent to which legal unions are 'enemies of love':

> There is no reason not to think of other settings of legality in the matrimonial relationship ... and at the same time trim its superegoistic powers ... without ... setting itself up as an authority checking our desires .... It is not that the family might become a place unencumbered by authority. But is not an authority that one might idealize rather than fear ... an authority to be loved?[48]

A further step consists of a step away from self, a step that allows one to develop a relationship of 'caring'. This step comes through most clearly by way of the comments placed in the mouth of the psychoanalyst, Joelle:

> Caring gives back the ability to enter into it all. The simple happiness of shared facts, like the happiness of breathing. Or like the humble but vital springiness of trodden grass: ordinary, pleasant, reliable .... Happiness ... doesn't need to last: a perfect moment achieves eternity. But the full experience of the moment includes both love and the insignificance of love, the intensity of my pleasure ... and the foolishness of it.[49]

A third step consists of letting oneself become more open: open to one's own body and to others. We have, Kristeva argues (as do several other contemporary scholars) become caught up in a mind/body distinction with the body taking second place.[50] We now need to learn to know our own bodies; to recognize that it is on the basis of touch and skin as well as sight that we develop a sense of self and a sense of others; to rescue the body from our perception of it as often abject.

That form of opening-up may carry little risk, or be relatively controllable. Opening up to others involves far more hazard. There is, to start with, the danger of doing so in ways that are regarded by others as inappropriate. Only on the analysts' couch, Kristeva argues, are we currently allowed to reveal our injuries, to rage against past wrongs, and to weep for what we have lost.[51] There is also the danger of one's openness being exploited, or – more subtly – not reciprocated. It is the nonreciprocal nature of her relationship to her analysands, Kristeva comments, that gave rise to her writing the novel, *The Samurai*. Now she would take the step of revealing herself, and her fantasies, as the analysands are expected to do.[52]

Finally, one step towards love consists of recognizing the need for some degree of separateness, and the value of small gifts, small moments. Within *The Samurai*, that message is delivered towards the end of the book through the voice of Olga, commenting on maternal love. The same message is delivered also, at the very start of the book, through the voice of the analyst, Joelle:

> They're together because they're separate. What they call love is this shared fidelity to their individual independence. It keeps them young, they look like teenagers, children almost. What do they want? To be alone together. To play at being alone together, tossing the ball back and forth between them now and again to show there isn't any resentment in their solitudes.[53]

What do such ideas bring out for us when we turn to films such as *Sweetie* or *The Piano*? They bring out first of all the sad initial position of Kay: able to move towards Louis only because a tea-leaf reader has said a man with a certain kind of appearance is her 'destiny' (the question mark on his forehead), and eager to keep the disorderly Sweetie out of her life. It is only at the end that she is able to move towards Louis with sexual affection, and that comes after becoming finally able to express her love for Sweetie. When the treehouse collapses under Sweetie's violent jumping on its boards, and she falls injured, it is Kay who moves to give Sweetie the kiss of life while her parents stand frozen.

The more difficult extension would appear to be to *The Piano*. How do any of the possibilities for change that Kristeva suggests – the development of a different legality, refusals of the old contract, the cultivation of caring and greater openness to others and to one's own body – fit with an image that Ada presents? Part of the story of Ada fits with Kristeva's picture of a new pattern. Touch and sound are central to her. Moreover, she personifies a refusal of the old contract. Ada claims a status of her own and the right to take the initiative in love with her husband rather than to be only his object, responding only to his desire. Ada claims also the right to grant her body to another in order to gain back the piano that is, until late in the film, what she desires above all else. And it is Ada who claims the right of refusal that is part of being a subject rather than an object: the right to refuse sex, the right not to be taken in by the romantic surface of a wedding dress that is only part of a photographer's equipment, the right not to abandon her piano at her husband's command, the right not to play the 'jig' music that is the level of her husband's taste. These are modern assertions – assertions of a new view of marriage – that the Victorian frame makes all the more striking.

What are we to make, then, of the most striking option that Ada exercises in *The Piano*: the refusal of speech? Here, in a deliberate move, silence has become 'a refusal to speak …[:] a secret treasury, carefully protected, out of reach'.[54] From a Kristevan point of view, this might seem the least effective option of all. Without a voice, Kristeva has argued – more specifically, without the entry into the symbolic order that language provides – the positions one adopts have little or no persuasive value. At the level of the world at large, this may be true. At the level of love between two people, however, Kristeva suggests, words can create difficulties, reducing one's awareness of the world of touch, rhythm, and sound. (One might add one's awareness of the visual world, but this is not part of Ada's characterization.) Words lead one quickly into a world of rationality, of thought overriding passion. Adult love, in *The Piano*, develops only between the two characters whose reliance on words has been undercut: between Ada, with her refusal to speak, and Baines, whose inability to read means that even Ada's brief written notes are ruled out as a form of contact. Their love must be without spoken words on her side and without written words on his, until Ada makes two gestures.

The first gesture towards a reconciliation with words comes after Ada has been locked up by Stewart. She sends Baines a key from the piano, engraving it – with a hot stylus – with the message: 'You have my heart forever'. (Rather, she attempts sending it, but the daughter, the messenger, takes it instead to Stewart.) The second gesture is her beginning to practise speech again, at the end of the film. By that time, she can be sure that this man understands and respects her view of the world. Stewart has found her sensuality unacceptable (he leaps out of the bed after *she* has begun to caress *him*). Baines is clearly as sensual as she is, and accepting of sensuality in others (both in Ada and among the Maoris with whom he spends more time than he appears to do with the other settlers). Baines also understands Ada's attachment to the piano. Its fate is again in question when Baines, Ada, and Flora leave. It is difficult to load the piano into the Maori canoe. Now Baines, however, is the one to insist. 'It must go', he says. 'She *needs* the piano.' By cutting herself off from speech, Ada may make no impact upon most of the others around her: others portrayed as straight-laced Scots devoted to their church. With two people, however – her lover and her daughter – she gains a close communion that would appear to be unachievable if she were to follow the mores of her time and her society.

Times of difficulty and change

At the end of Chapter 4, I asked: in Kristeva's analysis, when are tensions and changes most likely to occur in relationships between 'strangers' and 'locals'? An analysis of difficulties may help us understand the course and the tension points of a narrative. We need, however, to go beyond that, to ask when difficulties and particular resolutions are likely to occur.

In her comments on strangers, Kristeva's argument discounted the significance of numbers and pointed instead to shifts in the balance of power, in the need of each party for the other, and – an aspect of particular significance – in the acceptance by each side of the codes that once regulated the positions and feelings of each towards the other: codes of law, codes of religion, and codes of custom.

Does the same type of argument apply to the analysis of love? Some of the same themes occur but there are some variations. The dissatisfaction felt with the old codes now appears especially in the form of a dissatisfaction with the 'tales of love' that are available; with the discourse that frames the talk of love. This dissatisfaction is described as felt most strongly by one particular group: women. And the dissatisfaction is seen as particularly focused on the issue of motherhood.

Why should it be women who feel particular dissatisfaction? They are, Kristeva notes, caught in a particular bind. All lovers may 'crave legitimation'. 'It is a fact that the lover (especially the woman lover) desires his or her passion to be legal'.[55] But mothers especially need the protection that the legitimacy of marriage provides. 'Motherhood – another love that is dissolving and death-bearing, ecstatic and lucid, delightful and painful – needs support,[56] a need that places mothers then at particular risk when marriage turns out to be oppressive or to bury love in the midst of domesticity's demands.

In Kristeva's analysis, women are also 'the discontents of our civilization'[57] because the past tales of motherhood are no longer satisfactory. Men and women may both lack stories of love, but women have the further lack of satisfactory representations of motherhood:

> When women speak out today it is in matters of conception and motherhood that their annoyance is basically centred.[58]

Central to this 'annoyance', Kristeva proposes, is a particular dissatisfaction with the kind of representation contained in images such as the Mater Dolorosa – the sad, mute, sacrificing Virgin Mother. Kristeva asks:

> What are the aspects of the feminine psyche for which that representation of motherhood does not provide a solution or else provides one that is felt as too coercive by twentieth century women?[59]

The dissatisfactions, Kristeva notes, are several. The mother without words may be easily excluded from power. In addition, the image contains several gaps. Left out of this image of motherhood, Kristeva proposes, is 'the war between mother and daughter': 'a war masterfully but too quickly settled by promoting Mary as universal and particular ...[,] as "alone of her sex"'.[60] In fact, no relationship to any other woman is part of the story. Left out, also, is any attention to the way motherhood is related to sexual love for another adult. The image of the Virgin Mary does not invite analysis 'from the standpoint of the rejection of the other sex that it comprises'.[61] Small wonder, then – Kristeva argues – that 'motherhood ... today remains, after the Virgin, without a discourse'.[62] The task, one may note – like the task of building up more effective relationships with foreigners – is again perceived as calling for the particular involvement of one group. It 'demands the contribution of women':

> These ... questions ... concerning motherhood ... suggest, all in all, the need of an ethics for this 'second sex', which, as one asserts it, is reawakening .... Spinoza excluded women from his [ethics] (along with children and the insane). Now ... a contemporary ethics ... demands the contribution of women[: o]f women who harbour the desire to reproduce (to have stability)[; o]f women who are available so that our speaking species, which knows it is mortal, might withstand death[; o]f mothers ...[–] an *herethics* .... [H]erethics is ... love.[63]

What form might the new ethics, the new discourses, take? And what conditions influence their emergence? Those are the questions I take up in the next chapter.

Notes

1. Julia Kristeva (1987b) *Tales of love*. New York: Columbia University Press, p.4.
2. Ibid., p.6.
3. Ibid., p.297.
4. Kristeva quoted in Rosalind Coward (1984) 'Julia Kristeva in conversation with Rosalind Coward'. In L. Appagnanesi (Ed.) *Desire*. London: ICA documents, p.27.
5. Julia Kristeva (1991b) in interview with Ebba Witt-Bratström: 'Främlingskap – intervju med Julia Kristeva'. In *Kvinnovetenskaplig tidskrift*, issue 3(91), p.46.
6. Ibid., p.46.
7. Julia Kristeva (1992) *The samurai*. New York: Columbia University Press, p.1.
8. Ibid., p.2.
9. See David Stratton (1990) *The avocado plantation: Boom and bust in the Australian film industry*. Sydney: Pan Macmillan; and Jane Campion (1990c) in interview with Susan Chenery: 'A real sweetie'. In *GH (Good Housekeeping)*, June.
10. Campion (1991) in interview with Stratton: 'Preface'. In G. Lee and J. Campion *Sweetie: The screenplay*. St. Lucia: Queensland University Press (p.x).
11. Harriet Margolis's edited book *Jane Campion's* The Piano (2000, Cambridge: Cambridge University Press) consists entirely of analyses of the film. The film is also the basis of Felicity Coombs and Suzanne Gemmell's edited book *Piano Lessons: Approaches To* The Piano (1999, Sydney: John Libbey) and is the specific topic of Maria Margaroni's 2003 extension of Kristeva's emphasis on the speaking subject (Maria Margaroni (2003) 'Jane Campion's selling of the mother/land: Restaging the crisis of the postcolonial subject'. In *Camera Obscura*, issue 18(2)).
12. Jane Campion (1993b) in interview with Milo Bilbrough: 'Jane Campion – *The Piano*'. In *Cinema Papers*, issue 93, May, p.8.
13. I have omitted a third course to which Kristeva gives a great deal of attention: the course of love during a period of psychoanalysis. The participants are now adults but the course often repeats the path of childhood – love first attached to the analyst and then transferred to others – as well as containing the hazards of adult love: an inability to love oneself or to go beyond self-love, and a lack of resilience in the face of an impossible

idealization that cannot be sustained. See Kristeva (1987b, Chapters 1 and 2), and also the long essay *In the beginning was love* (Julia Kristeva (1987a) *In the beginning was love: Psychoanalysis and faith*. New York: Columbia University Press).
14. Kristeva (1987b, p.6).
15. Ibid., p.16, emphasis in original.
16. Ibid., pp.3–4.
17. Ibid., p.3.
18. Ibid., p.3.
19. Ibid., p.2.
20. The voice is that of Olga, in *The samurai* (Kristeva, 1992, pp.318–319).
21. Ibid., pp.331–332.
22. Kristeva (1987b, p.6).
23. Ibid., p.151: Sermon on the *Song of Songs* 79:1, cited by Kristeva.
24. Ibid., p.2.
25. Ibid., p.8.
26. Ibid., p.210. This quotation and the seven that follow are from the chapter on 'Romeo and Juliet: Love-hatred in the couple'.
27. Ibid., p.209.
28. Ibid., p.225.
29. Ibid., p.209.
30. Ibid., p.226.
31. Ibid., p.209.
32. Ibid., p.225.
33. Ibid., p.225.
34. E.g., Michel Foucault (1980) *Power/knowledge: Selected interviews and other writings 1972–1977*. Brighton: Harvester Press.
35. Kristeva (1987b, p.9).
36. Ibid., p.81.
37. Jane Campion (1993a) in interview with Lynden Barber: 'Playing it low-key'. In *The Sydney Morning Herald*, 3 August, p.24.
38. Kristeva (1987b, p.243).
39. Ibid., p.244.
40. Ibid., p.245.
41. Ibid., p.245.
42. Ibid., p.253.
43. Ibid., p.249.
44. Ibid., p.260.
45. Ibid., p.296.
46. Ibid., p.5.
47. The voice is that of Joelle in *The samurai* (Kristeva, 1992, p.1).
48. Kristeva (1987b, pp.209–210).
49. Kristeva (1992, pp.283–284).
50. See Elizabeth Grosz's essay in J. Fletcher and A. Benjamin (Eds) (1990) *Abjection, melancholia, and love: The work of Julia Kristeva*. London: Routledge, for other scholars and for some possible additions to Kristeva's argument, although most of Grosz's account of Kristeva's attention to 'corporeality' comes by way of reviewing the essay 'Stabat mater'. It is critical to note that Kristeva's attention to the body is elaborated only in relation to pregnancy and motherhood. It is, however, a novel extension of a rising interest in the place of the body and the way images of the body (e.g. 'the ideal body') are socially constructed.
51. See, for example, *Tales of love* (Kristeva, 1987b, p.6, p.12), or the essay 'In the beginning was love' (Kristeva, 1987a).
52. See interview in Julia Kristeva (1993) *Nations without nationalism*. New York: Columbia University Press, pp.92–93.

53. Kristeva, 1992, p.2.
54. Kristeva, 1991a, p.16.
55. Kristeva (1987b, p.209).
56. Ibid., p.227.
57. Ibid., p.236. This quotation and the six that follow are from the chapter 'Stabat mater'.
58. Ibid., p.236.
59. Ibid., p.259.
60. Ibid., p.261.
61. Ibid., p.261.
62. Ibid., p.262.
63. Ibid., p.263.

Chapter 7

LOVE – EXPANSIONS: OLD AND NEW DISCOURSES

The expansions in this chapter stem from three questions. What form would a new tale of love take? To what extent do *Sweetie* and *The Piano* exemplify new discourses? What other forms might a new tale of love take? Turning to these expansions parallels the turn taken in the second of each of the earlier pairs of chapters – one on horror and one on strangers: a turn towards expansions that film analysts would especially wish to add to Kristeva's basic concepts. Since the expansions in this chapter build upon those noted in the earlier expansion chapters, let me first briefly review the main points that those chapters contained.

Aspects of continuity and change

In Chapter 3, the expansions were mainly based upon two questions about horror in the face of the abject: (a) Is this response timeless? If not, what particular historical circumstances are related to change? (b) Is this response universal? If not, what particular dimensions of difference among people are related to variations in what they feel?

Both questions, I noted, provide ways of filling in some gaps in Kristeva's analyses. Both, for instance, take steps towards linking together the two forms of order that Kristeva consistently proposes as linked: the social order and the established order of representation.

In Chapter 5, the expansions were mostly based upon questions about the emergence of new texts. I asked especially about the form of any new text and, taking a lead from Kristeva, argued for one important form being stories dealing with the experience of the stranger: with the stranger's position, feelings, and options rather than with the more usual focus on the impact of the stranger upon those who are already 'in place'.

The analysis of love continues with the same emphasis upon the emergence of new texts. What shape are they likely to take? What circumstances influence their emergence and their being heard? We shall see again, for instance, the argument that the emergence of a new text or a new discourse is related to a breakdown or a weakness in the codes that previously held sway. The relevant codes, however, are now the tales of love (sexual love and maternal love especially) that dominate a culture's storehouse of texts, rather than, say, the religious codes that keep 'abominations' at bay (horror) or the legislated negotiations that specify how foreigners and locals shall behave (strangers). A shift in what Kristeva considers as the old forms of order is then a first change from the expansions offered upon the basic concepts of horror and strangers.

Changed also is the degree of attention given to why the old forms of order – the old rules embedded in narratives – are unsatisfactory, who finds them especially unsatisfactory (women), and what the new tales of love might be like.

Current discourses and their weaknesses

In Kristeva's analysis, the problems for those seeking satisfactory tales of love stem predominantly from two sources: from the subordination of sensuality to an emphasis upon thought, rationality, and 'projects', and from the burial of love and caring under tales of lust and clinical approaches to sexuality.

The difficulty, Kristeva argues in her essay *Women's Time*, is felt especially by contemporary Western women. It is women especially who feel the need to examine the social contracts that surround them and that are embedded in the tales 'bequeathed' to them 'by tradition':

> [F]or women in Europe today, whether they are conscious or not of the various mutations (socialist or Freudian) which have produced or accompanied their coming into their own, the urgent question on our agenda might be formulated as follows: *What can be our place in the symbolic contract?* If the social contract, far from being that of equal men [sic] is based on an essentially sacrificial relationship of separation and articulation of differences, what is our place in this order of sacrifice and/or of language? No longer wishing to be excluded or no longer content with the function which has always been demanded of us (to maintain, arrange and perpetuate this socio-symbolic contract as mothers, wives, nurses, doctors, teachers ...), how can we reveal our place, first as it is bequeathed to us by tradition, and then as we want to transform it?[1]

That discontent is with women's social position generally. The dissatisfaction with old tales of sacrifice, however, is one that Kristeva regards as being especially sharp when it comes to tales of maternal love. The dissatisfaction felt with images such as the Mater Dolorosa, she comments, stems not only from a general decline in the religious codes that once held this image high, but also from the sense that this image has a number of specific weaknesses. The Mater Dolorosa, to summarize her argument, is an image of 'milk and tears'. The image implies no eroticism to the Virgin's body (it is a mother's body, its breast a source of milk), no voice of her own, no power except through her son, and no place for mother–daughter relationships. Any new discourse, one might expect, would break these several silences.

At the same time, Kristeva argues, there must be dissatisfaction also with stories or discourses that perceive motherhood only as a vehicle for the oppression of women and the maintenance of patriarchy. This dissatisfaction underlies Kristeva's negative comments upon feminist positions that argue for the complete rejection of motherhood as an experience, just as it underlies the softer dissatisfaction expressed by feminists such as Hirsch with an exclusive emphasis upon 'sisterhood' as a rewarding relationship. In Kristeva's terms:

> Now, when feminism demands a new representation of femininity, it seems to identify motherhood with (an) idealized misconception, and because it rejects the image and its misuse, feminism circumvents the real experience that fantasy overshadows. The result? – A negation or rejection of motherhood by some avant-garde feminist groups. Or else an acceptance – conscious or not – of its traditional representation by the great mass of people, women and men.[2]

For Kristeva, the advocacy of motherhood without fathers is equally unsatisfactory:

> [I]n the refusal of the paternal function by lesbian and single mothers can be seen one of the most violent forms taken by the rejection of the symbolic ... as well as one of the most fervent divinizations of maternal power – all of which cannot help but trouble an entire moral and legal order without, however, proposing an alternative to it.[3]

Small wonder that Kristeva is not looked upon with favour by all feminists. Entry into 'the symbolic order', into any position of status, power, or centrality in the social system appears to be made equivalent to the establishment of a 'standardized household'.[4]

The list of objections to the available tales of love – the dissatisfactions felt with tales of sacrifice on the one hand, and oppression or subordination on the other – needs no further amplification. The critical question takes the form: what might take the place of the old tales?

For that question, I shall interweave points from Kristeva with features of *Sweetie* and *The Piano*, treating these as new stories of love. It is true, as Moi points out, that 'so far Kristeva herself has not really followed up her own programme for research into maternity'.[5] For that research, Kristeva has advocated turning to today's mothers rather than, or in addition to, a society's storehouse of stories:

> There might doubtless be a way to approach the dark area that motherhood constitutes for a woman; one needs to listen, more carefully than ever, to what mothers are saying today, through their economic difficulties ...[and] through their discomforts, insomnias, joys, angers, desires, pains and pleasures.[6]

I shall treat Kristeva as one such voice, paying particular attention to the statements on the left-hand side of the page in 'Stabat Mater' (a side given over to existential statements about motherhood made shortly after the birth of her son), and to later statements (1993) made by the character Olga in *The Samurai* with reference to her sense of motherhood. These are, however, limited voices. For further voices, I shall turn to the women involved in *Sweetie* and *The Piano* (the women in the stories and the women who made the films), noting what they imply or say about new stories of sexual and maternal love. For these films to strike a chord with today's audiences – for *The Piano* especially to be one of 1993's great commercial successes as well as a source of critical acclaim – the stories they tell must be meeting some current needs for particular tales of love.

The shape of new tales of love

In all, I propose, the new tales are likely to be marked by five features: features that one can abstract from Kristeva's discussions. One is a refusal of sacrifice and subordination. A second is a place for passion combined with caring, for romance combined with reality. A third is an insistence upon one's own voice, on being a speaking subject. A fourth is a place for mother–daughter relationships. A fifth is a place for both men and women to be represented as in some ways equivalent as victims or as supplying nurture and love to others.

A refusal of sacrifice or subordination

I begin with *Sweetie*, a narrative that documents both invitations to sacrifice and attempts to avoid them or leave them. The wife, Flo, presents at the start a standard picture of 'a good wife'. Her world seems to have revolved around family and home, a home that is painstakingly decorated. She looks after her husband, Glen, to the point of providing for him, when she departs for a trial separation, a freezer full of meals, one marked per day. She has also looked after their adult daughter, Sweetie, allowing her to live at home in a room filled with the small objects and the pink, frilly decorations of a young child. The novel feature to Flo is her stepping away from this contract, despite her husband's upset and his failure to understand why she wants a 'trial separation'. Flo leaves for a job in the country and is persuaded to return only on condition that Sweetie moves out to an apartment of her own. Sweetie is to live near her parents but not with them. Flo's husband fails to respect that agreement, but Flo has made the break once and may well make it again.

The film presents her decision as completely reasonable, and sympathetically shows a cheerful, 'new' woman emerging after the break.

The film also makes it clear, however, that the refusal of sacrifice means coming to terms with some conventional framing of the old ways. The husband sees the old ways only as 'the good times', the times when they were 'a happy family', 'together'. The wife is the one who has to counter that framing with her picture of them as 'just another couple muddling along'.

Finally, *Sweetie* makes it clear that it is not only mothers who are faced with the expectation of sacrifice. The same expectation is made of the 'good child', Kay – and again refused. When Flo leaves, both Sweetie and Glen turn up on Kay's doorstep. Kay's father pleads incompetence and asks for pity. He even brings with him the frozen meals that his wife has left for him. Kay's sister simply assumes that a place will be made for her and for her lover: an assumption they act out by breaking the glass in the front door in order to let themselves in. The demand that Kay be kind to Sweetie comes from their father, from Kay's lover (Louis), who believes Sweetie's story of a sickly childhood, and from Sweetie herself. Sweetie enforces her demands for special treatment by her threats that she is 'going to do something'. After an argument with Kay, for instance, Sweetie breaks and attempts to swallow one of Kay's prized porcelain horses: an episode that ends with Louis's urging Kay not to be 'hard' towards Sweetie.

To break from this framing of what is expected of her, Kay takes the only route that seems open: turning the expectation back to the person who once met it. They will all go in search of the mother, but without Sweetie. (Being faced with Sweetie, it seems generally agreed, would simply strengthen Flo's resolve to stay away.) Flo does return, but this solution does not completely settle Kay's difficulties. To be able to love Louis, the film shows her as needing both to refuse the demand that her life be given over to Sweetie and to accept Sweetie as being someone whose needs she can recognize and – at a point where the 'kiss of life' seems called for – at times meet with affection. In effect, the narrative implies, refusal without some degree of recognition of the other's needs (even while one refuses) will be insufficient.

What does *The Piano* add to this earlier tale by Campion of the ways in which women might meet invitations or demands for a sacrificial role? The Victorian society in which Ada moves is one that expects women to be subordinate to men, to respect their wishes, to live within the narrow confines of what is expected of 'good women'. In this society, Ada is expected to be pleased that her father has found for her a husband who does not object to her being mute (who sees, in fact, some advantages to this state) and who is willing to accept a woman with a child (and a possibly dubious past). In this society, Stewart – the man she has married by proxy – has the right to expect that she will abide by his decision to leave the piano on the beach, that she will in time become sexually 'affectionate' in response to his initiative, that she will be pleased by his arrangements for a wedding photograph, and that she will accept the reasonableness of his wish to – as he puts it – 'clip her wings' when she turns towards Baines, as if she were a bird that needed only to be grounded in order to become docile.

The striking feature to *The Piano* is Ada's refusal of all these expectations. She does not accept Stewart's decision about the piano. She turns aside his sexual initiatives and terrifies him at a later point by taking the initiative herself. Visually, an especially striking refusal comes in the episode of the wedding photograph. The photographer arrives with a dress that Ada is expected to pin in front of her – the same dress, the same prop, that the photographer uses for all such photographs. The dress, and its lace, are greatly admired by the other women who come to visit for this substitute for a wedding. They exclaim over the delicacy of the lace, the unmarried daughter of a neighbour clearly envious of Ada's 'success'. Ada briefly allows it to be pinned to the front of her own clothes, but then tears the dress roughly from her, refusing the sham of the dress as she refuses the sham of the marriage.

Is there then no support for Ada's refusal? Initially, that support comes from her daughter Flora, who refuses to call Stewart 'Papa'. Support comes also from her lover, Baines, although clearly he – an illiterate settler who is 'friendly with the natives' – does not rank highly in the local pakeha group. And implicit support comes from the general Maori enjoyment of living and tolerance for sexual freedom. In the main, however, the message from *The Piano* is much the same as it was with *Sweetie* and *Angel*: to refuse, to resist the roles that society lays out for you, you will need to draw heavily upon your own strength. In the end, says the narrative for *The Piano*, you may be rewarded by a love that accepts your needs, and your demands to be what you really are. Ada does not go to the bottom of the sea with her piano, and – in a scene added to the screenplay by Campion in the course of production – she and Baines kiss in a contentedly sensual manner, with Flora happily playing nearby. Resistance and refusal have met with a happy ending. In the words of the producer, Jan Chapman:

> What I think is modern about [*The Piano*] is that, unlike the ending of Wuthering Heights or other romantic novels where there is a deep and dark move into an abyss, Ada comes back up and takes on life and tries to find another way of expressing her will.[7]

A place for passion combined with love, romance with reality

Does Kristeva ever suggest alternatives to the death of love within marriage or within domesticity? Three alternatives are briefly suggested for sexual love between adults. The first of these has already been mentioned in Chapter 6: the maintenance of some degree of separateness. Day and night, to take Kristeva's provocative comment in an interview, may be the 'perfect couple', forever linked in their separate orbits.[8]

The second alternative involves allowing time for recovery from the inevitable sense of injury:

> Love is said to last when the adventurers involved manage to bind up their wounds, when the skin heals, and they start to look at each other again like Narcissus contemplating himself in the water. It calls for a lot of patience and a great respect for time. Where love's concerned, you have to take good care of time. Not time in the sense of duration – that's just a spin-off from the art of loving – but time in the sense of the magic that transforms a moment of perception, disquiet, or happiness into a gift. The gift of a word, a gesture, a look.[9]

The third alternative emerges in the course of Kristeva's account of a case study. The analysand (Genny) finds herself compulsively turning to affairs after marriage, while her husband settles into monogamy and, instead of his original indecisiveness, into 'the bearing of a master'. Part of Genny's being 'addicted to *jouissance*' is perceived by the analyst as resting in Genny's ambivalent feelings about becoming a 'mother' to John (her husband). A further part is perceived as resting in John's lack of an 'imaginary': his lack of interest in maintaining any of the spontaneous, 'disorderly' aspects of love. Genny maintained some of her fantasies; John did not:

> Conversely, the maternal, phobic-obsessive, security-giving, law-full John, has no imaginary. The law without imaginary is the enemy of the couple. It rests on husbands who merely perform their duty, and nothing more; joined with their own frigid mothers, impeccable spouses and housewives, such husbands establish an abode, not a couple. Their sexual performance, often respectable, does not prevent their wives from being depressed, nymphomaniac, or suicidal.[10]

A change in John, then, might preserve this couple as a romantic couple. John, however, is not in analysis. It is then Genny who comes to the realization that,

> in reality, John suits me better, if one truly has to, if one must, live with someone. Because we are, each of us, incomplete, and the couple completes, otherwise it makes no sense. While with Henry (Genny's current lover), there are never two of us, there are two copies of the same, the print and the negative.[11]

To maintain touch across some degree of separateness, to accept that difference and complementarity may have their benefits, and to keep alive some of the spontaneity and unconventionality of romance: these are the possibilities suggested for a couple's continuing romance.

In comparison, the possibilities that Kristeva suggests for maternal love are far more vivid. Here the positives are continually refreshed by the child's constant change. The list of pleasures begins with the assertion that motherhood may bring a spurt of creativity:

> Maternity ... can favour a certain kind of female creation, provided the economic constraints are not too heavy, at least in so far as it lifts fixations, and circulates passion between life and death, self and other, culture and nature, singularity and ethics, narcissism and self denial ...[. R]eal female innovation (in whatever social field) will only come about when maternity, female creation, and the link between them are understood.[12]

This statement hovers on the unnecessary implication that the only route to creativity on the part of women lies in the experience as well as the understanding of motherhood. Less easily misunderstood is the list of pleasures that Kristeva describes on the lyrical left side of the pages of 'Stabat Mater': a paean to motherhood that in itself represents Kristeva's expression of a new discourse.

Part of the joy of motherhood, she begins, comes from the sheer aesthetic pleasure that gazing at a child provides:

> A child? An angel, a glow on the Italian painting, impassive, peaceful dream .... And then the mother-of-pearl bead awakens: quicksilver.[13]

That source of pleasure, however, is not unique to mothers. More special to them are the way the interaction between mother and child brings a relaxed sense of self:

> Head reclining, nape finally relaxed, skin, blood, nerves warmed up, luminous flow: stream of hair made of ebony, of nectar, smooth darkness through her fingers .... Narcissus – like touching without eyes, sight dissolving in muscles, hair, deep, smooth, peaceful colours. Mamma: anamnesis.[14]

Part of the mother's joy stems also from the affirmation of life and of the desire to live. To give birth may be intensely painful,

> [b]ut calm finally hovers over pain, over the terror of this dried branch – that comes back to life .... The calm of another life, the life of that other who wends his way while I remain henceforth like a framework. Still life. There is him, however, his own flesh, which was mine yesterday. Death, then, how could I yield to it?[15]

Part comes from the sense of one's own strength:

> Scent of milk, dewed greenery ... inflates me like an ozone balloon, and I hover with feet firmly planted in order to carry him, sure, stable, ineradicable, while he dances in my neck, flutters with my hair, seeks a smooth shoulder on the right, on the left, slips on the breast, swingles, silver vivid blossom of my belly.[16]

A final part of pleasure comes from the reminders of a 'recovered childhood, dreamed peace restored', a reunion with the mother in a trio: 'Alone: she, I and he'.[17]

What do *Sweetie* and *The Piano* add to these indications of what the new discourses of love might contain? To start with, *Sweetie* is itself a recognition of the difficulty of maintaining sexual love. The comments by the writers on the way the script evolved (it was co-written by Campion and Gerard Lee) begin with this difficulty: 'What do you do when you lose passion and love in a relationship?'[18]

> I really started with Kay and Louis trying to look at the problems I saw and had experienced in my life – how it's really great to fall in love but it's really hard to maintain it. There seemed to be a gap. We all knew how to meet people, we all knew how to get into bed but we didn't know how to keep being sexually excited with someone after you have been living with them for a while. That was the starting point. All that stuff about the sisters, that came later.[19]

The love story for Kay and Louis begins with a quick move into sexual intimacy and living together, followed by Kay's withdrawal into being a 'sister' after Louis takes a step – planting a small tree – that to her symbolizes the potential disruption (by way of its roots spreading underground) of the house and the earth. Secretly tearing out this tiny plant does not remove the problem. Indeed, throwing the dead remains under the bed on which she and Louis have been sleeping makes the problem even worse. Only an acceptance of her own 'disorderly' self – personified by Sweetie – holds out a future promise. Kay offers 'the kiss of life' to the injured Sweetie, and it is this move, rather than Sweetie's death in itself, that seems to allow Kay to return to sensuality.

In short, there is little in *Sweetie* that points to the pleasures of maternity: if anything, the reverse. For every 'good child', one may give birth to a Sweetie. There is little also in *The Piano* about the joys of giving birth or of caring for the very young. Flora is already about nine years old when she first appears: a poised, articulate nine-year-old at that.

Within *The Piano*, however, there is a great deal about the maintenance of romance in combination with reality. Campion's comments speak to the issue:

> The instinctive game that I felt we needed to play was that while the epic style of the film and landscape suggests the romantic genre, at the same time people seem very real – so that you're never quite let out by any sense that the action is taking place in a fairy-tale romantic world. One of the clichés of romance is that the heroines are classic beauties but I wanted there to be a reality to our actors that counters pure romanticism.[20]

It is to keep the romance anchored in reality then that Campion insisted upon Ada not looking glamorous and having the 'greasy hair' that Campion noted as typical of the period.[21]

For similar reasons, Campion does not allow the Victorian time-setting and the colonial place to lull the reader into the sense of an 'easy' romance in a faraway 'new world'. The 'new world' is mysterious and lush, but also muddy and squalid. (The women lift their crinolines to walk along narrow boards laid across the mud.) The Victorian time is used both to convey 'the romantic impulse' and to heighten the contemporary nature of her message:

> My not writing in [Victorian times] means that I can look at a side of relationships that it wasn't possible to do [then]. My exploration can be a lot more sexual, a lot more investigative of the power of eroticism which can add another dimension. Because then you get involved in the actual bodyscape of it as well, because the body has certain effects, like a drug almost, certain desires for erotic satisfaction which are very strong forces too.[22]

This, then, is to be no Mills and Boon paperback romance:

> I feel a kinship between the kind of romance that Emily Brontë portrayed in 'Wuthering Heights' and this film. Hers is not the notion of romance that we've come to use, it's harsh and extreme, a gothic exploration of the romantic impulse. I wanted to respond to those ideas in my own century.[23]

Women speaking with their own voice

In her deliberations on the biblical 'Song of Songs', Kristeva discusses the passive/active roles of wives in relation to their husbands. She proposes that the Shulamite, who loves, and more importantly, speaks to her God, 'is the prototype of the modern individual':

> She, the wife, for the first time ever, begins to speak before her king, husband, or God; to submit to him, granted. But as an amorous loved one. It is she who speaks and sets herself up as equal, in her legal, named, unguilty love, to the other's sovereignty. Through such a hymn to the love of the married couple, Judaism asserts itself as a first liberation of women. By virtue of being subjects: loving and speaking.[24]

The Piano is the film that takes this possibility further. Ada finally takes the sexual initiative, caressing Stewart while he stays passive, playing upon his body as if he were another musical instrument. Campion describes the scene as meant to shock:

> Ada actually uses her husband Stewart as a sexual object – this is the outrageous morality of the movie – which seems very innocent but in fact has the power to be very surprising. I think many women have had the experience of feeling like a sexual object and that's exactly what happens to Stewart. The cliché of the situation is generally the other way around where men say things like 'Oh sex for sex['s] sake'. But to see a woman actually doing it, especially a Victorian woman, is somehow shocking – and to see a man so vulnerable. It becomes a relationship of power, the power of those that care and those that don't care. I'm very interested in the brutal innocence of that.[25]

Ada's choice of alternative expression – through music – is also both her own and one charged with feeling. Music, from Kristeva's perspective, has a particular place in our experience, representing the semiotic rather than the symbolic order. With speech removed, it needs to carry – along with sign language – the full burden of what Ada wishes to communicate.[26] To use a statement from Michael Nyman, composer of the music for *The Piano*:

> Music is absolutely crucial to the film. Since Ada doesn't speak, the piano music doesn't simply have the usual expressive role but becomes a substitute for her voice. The sound of the piano becomes her character, her mood, her expressions, her unspoken dialogue. It has to convey the messages she is putting across about her feelings towards Baines during the piano lessons. I've had to create a kind of aural scenography which is as important as the locations, as important as the costumes.[27]

A place for mother–daughter relationships

This is the third possible feature of new discourses suggested by Kristeva's analysis of past stories. It appears in Kristeva's account of weaknesses in the kind of image contained in versions of the Madonna – the Mater Dolorosa, the serene, nursing Virgin Mary. Mother–daughter relationships are not, however, part of the tale that Kristeva herself contributes. Instead, she concentrates upon the challenges to the woman's identity and the gaps between self and other that mothering any child – male or female – involves. Some statements from the left-hand side of 'Stabat Mater' make the point:

> What connection is there between ... my body and this internal graft and fold which, once the umbilical cord has been severed, is an inaccessible other? My body ... and him. No connection. Nothing to do with it. And this, as easily as the first gestures, cries, steps, long before *its* personality has become my opponent.[28]

> I confront the abyss between what was mine and is henceforth but irreparably alien. Trying to think through that abyss: staggering vertigo. No identity holds up.[29]

> The child, whether he or she, is irremediably an other.[30]

For some more concrete realization of what new tales of mother–daughter relationships might look like, *Sweetie* and especially *The Piano* are richer sources.

Sweetie's main theme may be quickly noted. In essence, it is a repetition of the question: how can mothers and daughters avoid a sacrificial contract? Especially when a husband and father are insisting that sacrifice represents a normal 'happy family'? The mother–daughter relationship, it is clear, is one that cannot be written about alone. Its connection to other relationships (mother/ father, father/daughter) is an essential part of the story.

The Piano casts the net still further. Not only does the mother/daughter story need to include these other, within-family relationships; it needs to cover as well the nature of the link with general society and its conventions. Part of the coherence of *The Piano* stems, in fact, from the way in which Ada's relationship to her daughter, and the mother–daughter tale in general, is a further aspect of the general contrast between the need for freedom, spontaneity, trust, and a genuine respect for the other and, opposed to that need, the demands of a closed-minded, conventional society. The tale of Ada and Flora begins with their oneness. 'The relationship of Flora to her mother was scripted by Campion to be one of mirror-like closeness, a kind of symbiosis.'[31]

The two use the same mannerisms. They share a bed; they play together. Like her mother, Flora is tiny and in love with music. When her mother first plays on the beach, Flora's improvised dance is as much a revelation to Baines as is Ada's intense feeling for the music she plays. Flora is also her mother's voice, her interpreter: the two can sign to one another, can talk together in a way that excludes others. In a delightful scene, Flora is also a fanciful interpreter to the local ladies of why her mother does not speak, creating a grand, romantic, and improbable tale.

Flora's defection to Stewart (she begins to call him 'Papa' and approves of Ada being prevented from leaving the house) is prompted in part by jealousy of Baines. It is prompted also by the attraction of portraying an angel, with wings, in the coming Christmas play. The conventional world might, after all, have its delights – might have something to offer to 'good girls' who obey their fathers and live 'normal' lives. One of the most effective visual scenes is a brief shot as Ada and Flora prepare to leave Stewart. Ada emerges pale and distressed, her hand bandaged and held close to her. Flora is not seen, but the camera zooms in upon the angel wings, discarded and floating in a puddle at the back of the house. Flora's being 'good', taking Ada's love message to Stewart rather than to Baines, has led to Stewart's mutilation of Ada and to his brutal use of Flora as the bearer of *his* message to Baines (Ada's severed finger). Flora's re-alignment with Ada and, the last scene implies, her acceptance of Baines, mark the end of Stewart as her 'Papa' and of her attraction to the wings of angels as a reward for abandoning her alliance with her mother.

Similar roles for males and females

This will be the last feature for new tales that I shall abstract from a combination of Kristeva's suggestions and the narratives of *Sweetie* and *The*

Piano. There is, in fact, little from Kristeva on this score. As I noted earlier, in her analyses of both strangers and love, it is women who are singled out as having a particular responsibility for taking steps to reduce the gaps that separate people from one another, and to resist the temptations to fundamentalism and excessive conventionality. The exception is a statement to the effect that one of the current needs for conceptualization consists of analysing 'the potentialities for *victim/executioner* which characterize each identity, each subject, each sex'.[32]

The Piano picks up part of that last statement, in the sense that it is oriented towards presenting a picture of both men and women as potential victims of their time. The husband, Stewart, is not cast as a villain, but as caught up in a social contract that smothers him just as it threatens to smother Ada. Campion's intention is that he should appear as victim as well as executioner:

> I don't condone what he does, but I see it as entirely understandable because of the time he lives in, and he is a man of his time.[33]

Campion allows him also to be puzzled by Ada, rather than condemning her out of hand, as she does him. In the absence of the piano, he finds her playing on a kitchen table as if it were a piano. He asks the local ladies for advice: 'a table is a table'; is it possible that Ada is 'deranged'? He does not yield to that conclusion, but his genuine difficulty in making sense of such 'outlandish' behaviour is evident.

Sweetie is the film that takes the stronger step of presenting both men and women as potentially nurturing, potentially open to each other. When Flo goes to the outback, she finds a different contract from the one she had at home. Her job specifies that she cook for the jackaroos. It does not specify, however, that she play music for them and that they ask her to teach them to dance. To quote Campion again:

> I wanted to make a film with likeable men ...[:] this was a bit like Snow White and the Seven Dwarfs. Mother goes out there and these men heal her: it's a celebration of the gentle side of men ...[. T]he girls on the crew loved that scene: they all wanted to help select the men to play the jackaroos.[34]

It is that same scene which tempts Flo's husband to step briefly back into openness, only to return to a love-deadening demand for 'a happy family' that will include his old relationship with Sweetie. Like Stewart in *The Piano*, Glen is presented as irredeemable. The jackaroo scene in *Sweetie* makes it clear, however – as the character Baines also does in *The Piano* – that not all men are so lost to a love that takes the other's needs into account and is open to new possibilities.

The special case of motherhood and maternal love

Maternal love is a form of love that Kristeva, and others, have noted as especially in need of conceptualization and of new tales. For Kristeva, that need has several sources. It arises partly from her own negative reaction to the rejection of motherhood that some feminist positions implied. It stems also from her sense that what is oppressed by patriarchy is motherhood rather than 'femaleness' in general (it is the reproductive power of women that men are threatened by and seek to control). More conceptually, Kristeva's interest stems from the conceptual challenge presented by pregnancy and motherhood to the distinctions we draw between 'self' and 'other' in everyday experience or in scholarly discourse. When a woman is pregnant, what is 'self' and what is 'other'? Here 'is an identity that splits, turns in on itself, and changes without becoming other'.[35] Here is an other that cannot be separated from self, a change within oneself for which there is no easily named distinction ('and no one present ... to signify what is going on'[36]).

Despite this multifaceted significance of motherhood and maternal love for Kristeva, there is little elaboration of the form that new tales of motherhood and maternal love might take. Kristeva certainly suggests several features that might mark new tales of maternal love. These tales would break away from images such as that of the Mater Dolorosa and from the sacrificial contracts. They would also begin to bring out the possibilities of pleasure as well as pain within mothering, of combining motherhood with sexuality, of investment in mother–daughter as well as mother–son relationships, combined possibly with representations of the way motherhood both restores one's childhood and its pleasure and revives the relationship to one's own mother (the trio, 'she, I, and he').[37]

For an expanded discussion of what might represent a further achievement in new tales, I shall turn to Ann Kaplan's analysis of representations of motherhood and to films other than *Sweetie* and *The Piano*. Kaplan's examples are drawn from books, films and videos from the nineteenth and twentieth centuries, concentrated for the most part on the melodrama genre but by no means restricted to it. Her perspective, like Kristeva's, combines concepts from psychoanalysis with attention to sociohistorical conditions (the current changes, for instance, in reproductive technologies). Like Kristeva also, she is strongly concerned with questions about identity. Kaplan's vision of the possible form of new texts that would meet the needs and interests of contemporary women, however, is somewhat different from Kristeva's. It also draws our attention to some further possibilities for new texts.

To use Kristeva's interests as a starting point, Kaplan notes the rise of films that present mothering as pleasure and fulfilment rather than duty. In the course of the 1980s,

[f]ilms began to image satisfaction in mothering, and the choice of mothering over career, as in *The Good Mother* and *Baby Boom* .... *Heartburn* also shows pleasure in mothering, and the choice of children over an unsatisfactory marriage .... *Raising Arizona* shows the extreme lengths (in this case, kidnapping) that parents will go to in order to have a baby.[38]

Nonetheless, Kaplan comments, these films still show a 'polarization of sex, work and motherhood in the social imaginary'.[39] *The Good Mother*, to take one example, brings out the fact that, although mothers in general may now be allowed to be sexual beings, sexuality on the part of the single mother, outside marriage, is far from being a 'liberating' discourse. A mother, Anna, loses custody of her child, Molly, because Anna's involvement with a lover is taken by the courts as evidence that she is not 'a good mother'. Moreover, the loss of the child is presented as the loss of everything. Anna now rejects her lover, takes up no new professional interests and, in Kaplan's phrase, 'acts almost as if the child has died'.[40]

Kaplan notes as well the emergence of interest in mother–daughter relationships that are not antagonistic in form. That these representations still leave much to be achieved is strikingly brought out by Kaplan's description of a 'mother–daughter ... pageant' presented on U.S. television in 1989 and repeated in 1990. Here 'we find mothers and daughters proudly united, and publicly declaring their enduring love for one another'.[41] The manner of their doing so, however, is 'bizarre':

> [T]he show verged on the grotesque: mothers and daughters paraded in a series of elaborate, look-alike gowns, and indeed were themselves made up to look the same ...[. T]he show exemplified ... the denial of aging (mothers became daughters, in a reversal of time), the denial of difference (all couples were thoroughly white, Anglo-Saxon and middle class), and the two beings ... looked like one .... In eliding the specificity of mothers different from, and differently positioned, than, daughters, the show denied the need for separation, individuation or entry into the Symbolic .... The show grotesquely pastiched some feminists' ... dream of close mother–daughter (or even adult woman–woman) bonding.[42]

If this bonding is an example of widely appealing texts, the representation of mother–daughter relationships clearly has some distance to go.

From Kaplan also I shall take a further achievement that has yet to fully appear within new tales of motherhood. This is the analysis of what 'mother' means as an identity: an analysis that Kaplan sees as in fact undercut by some current trends. One of these trends takes the form of 'writing out the mother'[43] by making the foetus the subject. That shift Kaplan sees as strongly represented in the photographs presented by Lennart Nilsson of life within the womb. Those widely acclaimed photographs, Kaplan points out, 'displace' the mother and her body: 'through incredible magnification, pictures look like those of the moon or outer space'.[44] Moreover, the foetus is presented as already a full-blown subject, a baby, rather than as an entity *in process* .... Further, the fact that this is all taking place in the mother's body is, in *Life* magazine's reproduction, ignored. The photos have no boundary to them .... The mother is not simply a part of anything. Significantly, Nilsson's *A Child Is Born* ran on two tracks, one of which was that of the mother-in-the-world. But even there, the tracks were hardly united, as in reality they ought to be.[45]

The films *Look Who's Talking* and *Look Who's Talking, Too* (both appearing in 1990) give the foetus an even more independent status. In both, the foetus is 'made a full subject, with thoughts and language, long before birth .... The world of the film is seen from their point of view'.[46] Such films, Kaplan notes, are quite different from a film such as *The Good Mother*. *The Good Mother*, 'however oppressively, situates the mother as a subject'.[47] *Look Who's Talking*, however, marginalizes the mother, renders her as 'irrelevant' to the foetus except as a temporary site, and 'redefines subjectivity'.[48] If one adds, to this way of writing out the mother, the possibility of reproduction outside the womb (no mother present at all), the representation of motherhood as a source of satisfaction and a form of fulfilment seems unlikely to have a stable future.

Even less likely, one suspects, is the second feature that Kaplan would hope to see in new tales of motherhood. Most representations of motherhood, she comments, 'essentialize' the identity of 'mother'. A person either is or is not a mother. Kaplan takes a different view:

> [I]sn't the maternal indeed a relationship, as Kristeva says, and as such not inhering on either party alone? I am only a mother in relating to my child, not outside of that relation. It is precisely patriarchal culture that has essentialized and fixed the concept 'Mother' to my being-in-the-world, instead of permitting it to be a mobile part of my being that comes and goes depending on whether I am in relation or not to the child.[49]

In an ideal future, then, one may see represented in film the 'de-essentializing of subjectivity ... and of identity', a move that should open up new tales of motherhood:

> For women, one of the most subordinated *and* fetishized positions has been that of 'mother'. Once this position is opened up as only part of any specific woman's subjectivity, not the all-consuming entirety of it; once any specific woman is seen to be constituted 'mother' only when interacting with her child; once 'mother' is no longer a fixed, essentialized quality, then women may be freed from ... (current) discursive constraints and burdens.[50]

Until that point is reached, the available tales of maternal love seem indeed likely to display a strong undercurrent of the 'maternal paradigm'[51] and a 'plethora of contradictory mother-discourses'.[52] The need for new tales will remain. How far that need will be met, however, seems to be distinctly uncertain.

Notes

1. Julia Kristeva, 'Women's time' [1981], in T. Moi (Ed.) (1986) *The Kristeva reader*. Oxford: Basil Blackwell, p.199.
2. Kristeva, cited in E. Grosz (1989) *Sexual subversions: Three French feminists*. Sydney: Allen and Unwin, p.95.
3. Kristeva in Moi (1986, p.199).
4. Julia Kristeva (1986e) 'Stabat mater'. In Moi (1986, p.133).
5. Moi (1986, p.161).
6. Kristeva (1986e, p.179).
7. Chapman in taped interview with K. Goodnow (August, 1993).
8. Julia Kristeva (1991b) in interview with Ebba Witt-Bratström: 'Främlingskap – intervju med Julia Kristeva'. In *Kvinnovetenskaplig tidskrift*, issue 3(91).
9. Julia Kristeva (1992) *The samurai*. New York: Columbia University Press, p.2.
10. Julia Kristeva (1987b) *Tales of love*. New York: Columbia University Press, p.232.
11. Ibid., p.232.
12. Julia Kristeva (1986b) 'A new type of intellectual: the dissident'. In Moi (1986, p.298).
13. Kristeva (1986e, p.173).
14. Ibid., p.166.
15. Ibid., pp.168–169.
16. Ibid., p.171.
17. Ibid., p.172.
18. Gerard Lee and Jane Campion (1991) *Sweetie: The screenplay*. St. Lucia: Queensland University Press, p.vii.
19. Jane Campion (1990d) in interview with Alexander McGregor: 'Women in prime'. In *Blitz*, May.
20. Campion (1993) in press release for *The Piano*, p.3.
21. Ibid., p.3.
22. Ibid., p.7.
23. Ibid., p.7.
24. 'A holy madness: She and he', in Kristeva (1987b, p.100).
25. Campion (1993) in press release for *The Piano*, p.6.
26. Julia Kristeva (1984) *Revolution in poetic language*. New York: Columbia University Press, p.24.
27. Michael Nyman in press release for *The Piano* (1993, p.16).
28. Kristeva (1986e, p.178, emphasis in original).
29. Ibid., p.179.
30. Ibid., p.179.
31. Press release for *The Piano* (1993), p.5.
32. Kristeva 'Women's time'. In *Signs*, issue 7(1), p.35, emphasis in original.
33. Campion (1993), in press release for *The Piano*, p.11.
34. Campion (1991) in 'An interview with Jane Campion' by David Stratton in *Sweetie: The Screenplay for*, p.ix.
35. Kristeva (1986b, p.297).
36. Julia Kristeva (1982) *Powers of horror: An essay on abjection*. Translated by Leon S. Roudiez. New York: Columbia University Press, p.237.
37. Kristeva (1986e, p.172).
38. E. Ann Kaplan (1992) *Motherhood and representation: The mother in popular culture and melodrama*. London: Routledge, p.194.
39. Ibid., p.200.
40. Ibid., p.195.
41. Ibid., p.200.
42. Ibid., pp.200–201, emphasis in original.

43. Ibid., p.204.
44. Ibid., p.203.
45. Ibid., p.204.
46. Ibid., p.209.
47. Ibid., p.209.
48. Ibid., all quotes from p.209.
49. Ibid., p.41.
50. Ibid., p.219, emphasis in original.
51. Kaplan (ibid., pp.76–106) provides a detailed account of the way this paradigm has been played out, with particular reference to melodrama in the nineteenth century, its 'representational heyday' (p.76).
52. Ibid., p.219.

Chapter 8

THE TEXT OF SOCIETY AND HISTORY

Each of the chapters so far has been devoted to Kristeva's baseline concepts and their application to three particular topics: horror, strangers, and love. The next two chapters cut across the three topics. The present chapter does so by concentrating on the text of society and history. That text may be written large, or written small. Written large, it has a broad sweep and can cover large historical periods. This is Kristeva's forte. She documents frequently the storehouse of representations that history contains, drawn upon to read any new text or to create something new.

This way of regarding the text of society and history is easily extended to film and television. Christine Gledhill, for example, describes some of the easy ways in which appropriation and change can occur. A series such as *Cagney and Lacey*, for instance, takes a known genre – cops as buddies – and recharges it by making the cops women and their 'buddy' relationship one of solidarity between women as well as between police officers. A film such as *Coma* also updates an old genre by a change in gender (women as doctors in addition to men) and a modification of the plot. The plot is basically familiar: *Coma* exemplifies

> the suspense thriller, a melodramatic sub-genre which involves a race against time between 'villain' and 'hero' – the one to conceal and get away with, the other to solve and expose, a criminal plot.[1]

The updating then comes from a change in gender (women as doctors) and from the inclusion of some content that is even more 'modern': the ethics of organ transplants.

Neither of those departures from the familiar genres meets Kristeva's expectation that the new representation should shatter the old. In contrast, for Kristeva, is a film such as *The Dictator*. This she regards as a 'specular shattering'.[2] Here laughter brings about a situation where 'identity collapses and all dictators are toppled'.[3] Here is 'a spectacular that would not ... be deposited in the bank account of order'.[4]

The text of society and history written small receives far less attention. Kristeva does draw attention to more immediate moments of background in her insistence that every word, every text, engages both 'speaker' and 'addressee', and in her remarks indicating that the addressee may at times be in the position to judge or control what the speaker is able to produce. She gives some attention also to the importance of the 'economic and ideological' backgrounds to any new text. As mentioned in Chapter 1, Kristeva notes with approval Autal's detailed analysis of that kind of background but sets it aside:

> I would simply emphasize that one cannot understand such practice without taking its socioeconomic foundations into account, nor can one understand it if one chooses to reduce it only to these foundations, thereby bypassing the signifying economy of the subject involved.[5]

A similar kind of comment appears in her analysis of Giotto's work. She was not indifferent to the role of economic/materialist aspects. Giotto's work, she notes, did need funding in order to make it possible. At the same time, that aspect of background was not her primary focus: 'this sociological aspect, however important it may be to the history of painting, shall not concern me here'.[6]

Setting that part of the text aside, however, means that there is a gap when it comes to the analysis of any form of representation. It is a gap that a focus on film can help to fill. Filling it is made all the more feasible if we take films at a time when there are still people available to comment and to make concrete the combination of circumstances – economic and ideological – that provide the immediate background to representations, especially those that are regarded as 'different'.

To bring out the text of society and history written in this smaller fashion, I shall raise questions that stem partly from Kristeva. Who are the interested parties for this production? What are their interests? How far did their interests and ideologies reflect competing codes? Did they, for example, agree on who has the rights to tell the story? To those I shall add some further questions. How did the initial movers – the 'filmmakers' – proceed in their translation of hopes into funded realities? What alternatives were open to them? Where were the difficulties? How were those difficulties resolved?

With this much introduction, let me turn to a set of 'proximal histories'. I start with *Kitchen Sink* and *Vigil*. These formed a pair where decisions about what the film would be like were made by a limited number of people who saw eye-to-eye, funding was readily available, and those providing the funding offered no interference. These were times that have been described, by an Australian, as times when, among the New Zealand group, 'loyalties and connections were strong, networks labyrinthine', with 'few attempts at co-productions with Australians'.[7]

Later films drew on a larger mix of people and places. *Crush* (set in New Zealand) was directed by Alison Maclean and produced by Bridget Ikin – both New Zealanders based at that time in Australia. *Sweetie* was directed and produced by New Zealanders: Jane Campion and John

Maynard, but made and set in Australia. *An Angel at My Table*, set in New Zealand, was written by Campion and Laura Jones, and produced by Ikin and Maynard. *The Piano* was written and directed by Campion, made and set in New Zealand, but produced by Jan Chapman (an Australian), and funded by a French construction company.

The paths for *Kitchen Sink* and *Vigil*

Kitchen Sink

The first feature in this path was the presence of a limited number of people who saw eye-to-eye. One person was both scriptwriter and director (Alison Maclean); the second person was an independent producer (Bridget Ikin), unrestrained by studio policies. Both were New Zealanders. They had also worked together on an earlier short, *Talkback*, produced in 1987. Both also wanted to produce something new. Maclean wanted to make a film that had something of the style of a writer she admired – Jane Bowles:

> Her stories are this disconcerting blend of the banal and the grotesque. They're full of eccentric women and have a surreal, drop-dead kind of humour. On the surface they're light and funny but there's a sense of enormous tragedy underneath.[8]

Ikin wanted to work with someone who was at the early stages of her career and needed help in making sure that the work got done. She also describes herself as 'interested in making films that challenge'.[9] In effect, neither wanted to make the easy kind of appropriation described by Gledhill (see above). Instead, they wanted to make more of a radical change from the usual genres.

For funding, they turned to one source only. This was the New Zealand Film Commission. Again there was a nice matching of interests. The New Zealand Film Commission expected new filmmakers to start with shorts. Maclean was 'new talent', with a couple of well regarded shorts to her credit (*Talkback* and *Rud's Wife*). The new work could then be a base for demonstrating what they could do, with help given by the New Zealand Film Commission to enter competitions to test their worth.

Maclean and Ikin submitted a proposal that met these criteria and was also what they wanted to do. Their proposal was for a short film, with a low budget, a simple setting, and a small cast. Critical for them was their wish for minimal interference. In the words of Ikin,

> the less money that you have at your disposal the less responsibilities you have ...[:] it gives you more freedom ...[. Y]ou are able to take risks with the work that you do ...[;] there is less interference and fewer people whose vehicle this is for making money and wanting to make compromises with the cast or the script or whatever.[10]

The difficulties for *Kitchen Sink* lay in finding the right audience: more specifically, finding a means of distribution that would fit the film to the audience. *Kitchen Sink* requires an audience that is prepared for, and primed to enjoy, something 'different'. To see it without advance warning that it is a 'horror' short is distinctly unsettling. The viewer starts with what appears to be nondescript suburbia and a nondescript female, and then everything, in a quite flat, 'everyday routine' style, turns out to violate those expectations and to revive within us a set of fears and unacknowledged 'facts of life' that we normally keep at bay. The short requires as well an audience that recognizes the grainy, black-and-white, unadorned style as deliberate: as, in fact, an asset rather than an indication that the producer and director could not afford anything 'better'.

Those requirements led Maclean and Ikin to turn down an offer from TVNZ (Television New Zealand), who wished to buy the short and to show it as one of a set:

> They were desperate for it at one stage when they had one of these slots of shorts coming up. It was even before we had screened it theatrically and I absolutely refused to sell it to them at that time .... They say that they have nowhere to screen it now.[11]

The right of refusal was exercised again after the short was purchased by Disney Productions for conversion to a full-length feature. Both Maclean and Ikin refused to be part of that adaptation.

How, then, did *Kitchen Sink* come to be seen? It was distributed theatrically with *Sweetie* in Australia and with *Crush* in the U.S. The audience on these occasions would be more self-selected than the usual television or film audience: self-selected in the sense that they knew they were about to see an 'arthouse', 'different' film that was not the product of a big, commercial studio. Their reception of the short would then be quite different from that of the unsuspecting viewer who hopes, perhaps, to see shorts specializing in tales and pictures of the New Zealand countryside.

Vigil

Vigil was chronologically the first of the 'New Zealand New Wave' films. The circumstances related to it were similar to those for *Kitchen Sink*. Here again was a small group of people whose interests were nicely matched. Vincent Ward wrote the script and directed the film, and John Maynard produced it. Ward wanted to produce a film that was more in line with European than with U.S. tradition: a film with a strong visual style, 'arthouse' in its quality, and oriented towards the inner experience of his characters rather than towards action in a landscape.[12] Ward's interest in producing something new was shared with the producer John Maynard. Maynard, with a background in visual arts administration, brought to the film also a strong sense of requirements in both production and distribution. For *Vigil* he had a clear idea about the audience:

> [*Vigil*] went to a pretty focused audience. When you went through the door you knew what you were seeing. It never broke into a wide audience and [the distributor] never tried to ...[reach one. I]t went to an audience who were, for want of a better word, cinema literate, who were interested in a new cinema.[13]

The funding required was not massive. The narrative called for four characters and one location within New Zealand. Some of that funding came from private investors. *Vigil*, produced in 1984, was made shortly before the end of a period of tax breaks in New Zealand. (During this period, which lasted from approximately 1978 to 1984, investors could receive up to 150 per cent in tax credits for their film investment.)[14]

Those investors, Maynard has commented, offered little creative interference. A lack of interference was also the case for support from the New Zealand Film Commission. The support of the Film Commission could not be expected to be major. It had a low budget (N.Z. $10.7 million in the year 1991/92, with the goal of stretching that to cover four features and eight short films). Its interest was in films that had some particular features. They would be full length. They would bring some financial benefit to the country as a whole: 'the film industry ... continues to contribute to the economy throughout the country', both directly and by way of drawing attention to New Zealand and increasing tourism.[15] They would also yield a social benefit. New Zealand should promote its own film industry, encouraging its own people. Funding increased the likelihood that local filmmakers would stay in New Zealand rather than departing for Australia or the United States, and that the stories told would be New Zealand stories. These stories were especially valued. They were regarded as a form of 'cultural expression', a 'record of our times, since what is on film becomes part of our permanent cultural legacy'.[16]

That emphasis on indirect financial benefit to the country, and on creating 'cultural legacy', again meant minimal interference. The result, in Maynard's description, was one that allowed Ward to have his own way, time to do so, and to produce in the end a 'gem' of a film:

> It's a very small diamond but it's been beautifully cut and polished. There's been a lot of time and care spent on this one .... He never ... compromised with a long shoot and quite often he spent long periods of time getting quite small things right .... It was certainly a long post-production so it does have that element of care and craft and knowledge of itself as a small and beautiful little gem. It always bears examining in one way or another.[17]

A rockier path: *Crush*

Crush continued the collaboration of Maclean as writer/director with Ikin as producer (the team responsible for *Kitchen Sink*). The history for *Crush*, however, brings out the significance of (a) the extent to which the several stakeholders have a common goal, (b) the particular points of development for which funding is sought and control is exercised, and (c) the presence of alternative routes when one path is blocked.

The proposal for *Crush* was for a feature rather than a short. The first place to turn to, then, was the New Zealand Film Commission for funding to allow script development. That funding was initially not forthcoming. The reasons given were twofold. One was that the script was seen as 'underdeveloped'.[18] The other reason given had to do with the representation of Maori characters. We shall see this issue reappear in *The Piano*. There it was a strong concern in the planning and production phases and even more so when it came to reviews. For the moment, I shall use *Crush* as a first occasion for raising the ideological question: who can tell this story?

> At the Film Commission they were very hesitant about the script in the beginning. They felt it was not appropriate. I mean this is an ongoing debate for pakehas to write scripts in which there were Maori characters at all, just as a few years ago it was not appropriate for men to write scripts in which there were female protagonists.[19]
>
> Many white filmmakers shy away from any representations of Maoris. It is like a minefield; you are damned if you include them in your film and you're damned if you don't.[20]

Fortunately, alternative paths could be found for both difficulties: funding and decisions about Maori characters.

An alternative route for funding

This was the route known as POD (Producer's Own Development Scheme). The Film Commission set up this scheme at the end of the 1980s, as a way to devolve development decision-making from the Commission to producers themselves. For a limited number of producers, the scheme guaranteed income for up to three years. During this time they could develop scripts of their choice. The POD covered all development costs: fees for writers and directors, casting costs, travel, etc. The Commission was then reinvolved in decision-making at the stage of seeking production funding. During the POD period the Commission was also involved in regular, quarterly discussions with the producers as to progression. All creative decisions, however, were left to the producers and directors themselves:

We don't require any approval at all from the lenders of the money at the New Zealand Film Commission as to the content or the nature of what we are developing, subject only that it has New Zealand content and will eventually qualify as a 'New Zealand Film'. If we developed something with a writer outside of New Zealand we would require some sort of permission.[21]

Ikin used the POD scheme to give *Crush* a second chance:

At that point (after the Commission's first refusal for script development) I developed the rest of the project though the POD and didn't give it to them again until it was ready. Then what really swung their response to the script from 'sort of weirdo', 'all over the place', 'not well developed script' to 'yeah, we love it' was Alison being invited to the Sundance Institute (a writing workshop in Utah under the patronage of Robert Redford). Suddenly the Film Commission just leapt on it ...[:] 'somebody else loves it, it must be OK'. It was like a transformation.[22]

The Film Commission, however, was not the only body whose concerns the filmmakers had to keep in mind, and the interests of the several parties were now not identical. Funding for the production of *Crush* came in part from the Film Commission, in part from NZ On Air (roughly the television equivalent of the Film Commission), and in part from the postproduction facility house and lab, Avalon/NFU Studios. The last of these investors was owned by the state broadcaster, TVNZ. Avalon/NFU did not actually put any cash into the project but provided facilities in exchange for a percentage of the rights. Dealing directly with the postproduction facility, however, still allowed considerable freedom. However, TVNZ was not involved with the project at script level: 'We didn't present it to them (the broadcaster) at that level.'[23]

An alternative route for Maori representation

Given the likelihood that whatever you do will not be seen as right by everyone, several alternatives and decisions need to be considered. The first of these has to do with whether to include Maori characters at all. The tempting solution would be to include none of them, staying within the safety of non-Maori characters. If the decision is made that they will be included, the next decision has to do with how they will be represented. Ikin was very clear that they would not follow the pattern of other films made in Rotorua:

It is a very Maori town and the only films that have been made in that town have been sort of touristic, historical, noble savage portrayals.... [A]ll the films that ever have been shot there have had Maoris swinging their *pauas*. You know, folksy, ethnic pieces.[24]

The alternative chosen was to have Maoris appear as more complex characters, in more complex relationships with pakehas than stereotypical representations provide. That, however, raised potential difficulties both in the course of production and when it came to possible distribution and audiences: 'We took a very low profile in Rotorua.... I knew they would hate what we were doing'.[25] The broader concern was partly to do with conventional audiences – Maori or pakeha:

> It is just too challenging. I mean a Maori man masturbating, being masturbated by an underaged girl for a start ...[:] they may find that absolutely shocking. You know the taboo of masturbation, plus being underage, plus the mixed race thing .... Just the tone of it .... It is not the sort of thing that they like to put on Saturday night and they have paid Saturday night money for it.[26]

The concern was also with the way Maori audiences in particular would respond to the film. One outcome would be that it could never be shown in some places. 'I suspect it will never get seen in Rotorua'.[27] Another outcome was that it would be seen but responded to negatively. That expectation was confirmed by the man who was the main Maori character.

> It was with some trepidation that we even cast that character (Horse). I really felt quite wary about it and was surprised that the guy that did it agreed to do it and somehow felt that it was OK .... I think it was quite a bold thing for him to do. It is not a good light role .... When it came to the screening for the cast and crew, even he couldn't deal with it at that level. His family was there and he just ducked out during that scene.[28]

Campion's first feature: *Sweetie*

What we have seen so far is a small set of people on the filmmaking/ film production side: people who already knew one another and whose interests were neatly matched. We have also seen an orientation towards very selective audiences and either a single funding body or a combination of funding bodies that still allowed a great deal of freedom and did not demand control over the filmmaker's choices. To a large extent this was the same for *Sweetie*. The filmmakers were Campion and her co-writer (Gerard Lee). They had made the short *Passionless Moments* together and wanted to extend what they had learned during that project:

> One of our discoveries during the making of *Passionless Moments* was what we called 'the power of the mundane'. We saw that when ordinary people and everyday events were filmed they became transformed by the magic of the silver screen. Suddenly, they looked 'amazing'. The most ordinary human behaviour became bizarre. Everyday objects had an unusual quality .... [W]e began working on a story of an ordinary bank clerk, Kay, who falls in love with another ordinary bank clerk, Louis.[29]

Campion describes some further original aims. She wanted to make a film about love and romance, sex and family. 'I wanted to provoke, but at the same time touch people.'[30] She also wanted the film to be entertaining: 'I like to be entertained in the cinema, and I feel I have a responsibility to entertain audiences and, at the same time, challenge them'.[31]

Into those initial plans entered a third party. In the script, she rapidly expanded from a role originally intended to be minor. In Lee's words:

> As Jane and I discussed Sweetie, she began to inflate, to swear, spit, bark, bite, drool and cry. And we let her have her head and do all these things.[32]

Genevieve Lemon, who played the role of Sweetie, added a further touch. She moved the characterization away from being as monstrous as the original script made her out to be:

> Jane's initial vision of Sweetie was much darker than she turned out to be. She wanted Sweetie to be angry: I'm not an angry person and Jane constantly encouraged me to make her as angry as possible.[33]

The further background circumstance was again one of funding. To start with, a decision needed to be made as to where the film *Sweetie* would be made – a decision that immediately influenced the potential funding sources. Although classed as part of the New Wave New Zealand films, *Sweetie* was actually made in Australia. Campion had moved to Sydney to study anthropology and later to train at the Australian Film, Television and Radio School. Maynard, a frequent producer of 'New Zealand films', was also in Sydney after moving there to find funding for Ward's second feature, *The Navigator*.

The funding sources now to be sought were Australian. These could be at national level (the Australian Film Commission), state level (the New South Wales Film Office), or in the private money market. International sources were not part of the scene. In Maynard's terms:

> I put that script around a lot amongst foreign distributors and they all came back and said that they loved the script but they could not see any elements in it that could lead them into putting money into the film .... I suppose they could not see enough elements so that they could see a return on their investment.[34]

The first attempt to get developmental money from the Australian Film Commission was also not successful: 'We were advised to shelve it'.[35]

> They just didn't believe in it. They declined to fund it in its early stage and I took it across to the New South Wales Film Office who decided to fund it almost immediately.[36]

The Australian Film Commission did come in at a later point, as did a local pre-saler, FilmPac. FilmPac has since gone bankrupt. Its existence at the time, however, is an opening guide to the importance of distribution possibilities that pre-salers can provide. The combination of funding sources it was part of, however, is a strong reminder of the need to anticipate heterogeneity within the groups often given a collective label: filmmaker, audience, or funding body.

Campion's second feature: *An Angel At My Table*

I shall start again with the interests of the filmmakers, with the advance note, however, that *An Angel at My Table* (*Angel*) brings a change in who contributes to a script. Campion has usually been scriptwriter (often with Gerard Lee) as well as director. For *Angel*, however, that was not the case. In time, Laura Jones became the scriptwriter. Her screenplay became a publication in its own right. Both she and Campion, however, were working from material that had already been written: Janet Frame's autobiography, *Owls Do Cry*.[37] In addition, Frame was at that time alive, only in her sixties, and again back in her native New Zealand after time overseas: circumstances reinforced the sense of a need to respect the original source.

Respect to Frame was also a starting point for both Campion and for the film's producer, Ikin (Maynard was co-producer). All three regretted the general lack of awareness of Frame's work, especially within New Zealand. In Ikin's words:

> Janet Frame was not well known in New Zealand .... It was mostly women who read her books .... [I]t was one of my great hopes for the film that it would become part of the curriculum .... Now the first part of the autobiography and the first part of the film are on the school curriculum.[38]

Campion adds a concern with the style in which they wanted to tell the story: 'I didn't want to make it into an obscure art piece.'[39] She also had in mind that it would be made for television:

> It's perfect for it. It's a very intimate portrait of someone so I'll stick up real close to the audience ...[,] really hug Janet Frame most of the time, and shoot for that. Shoot simple and not complicate what in truth is a very simple, heartfelt story. I think that the result is that you do get involved with the story.[40]

At the same time, Campion wanted to avoid any complete, step-by-step account of what happened and why. It is the story of a life, but Campion wanted to bring out the kind of feeling she felt Frame's books generated:

> I wanted to give an interpretation of Janet's life, not an exact portrayal of what happened to her and why. I was looking for the feeling.[41]

The end result was a series that met with this goal:

It feels tight, feels similar to the quality I was getting from the books; I think it is very emotional and charming and frightening too. It's a very small tale but in the end tells of a whole life. You start from her as a baby and leave her at about 40 years old, and so see the shape of her life. It has an epic quality in a tiny fashion.[42]

Part of that advance awareness of style shaped even the choice of photographer. Previously, Campion had worked almost exclusively with Sally Bongers, the Australian cinematographer with whom she had developed the quirky style of *Sweetie*. Now she changed to Stuart Dryburgh:

I hadn't worked with him before, but I wanted a completely different look .... I preferred to work with a New Zealander and I didn't want a very self-attention-grabbing style.[43]

Decisions about the style, however, did not answer all the questions about the story being about Frame's life:

Every now and then we would pinch ourselves and say 'we're telling this person's life and she's alive ...[':] it's such an intrusion, it's so strange.[44]

The question was how to involve Frame. First they needed to meet her. Frame did not readily give interviews. The smallness of New Zealand society was at this point an advantage. Campion's godmother was a friend of Frame's sister and a meeting was arranged via these go-betweens. That meeting Campion approached with trepidation: 'It was ages before I made *Sweetie* so she was very trusting to let me do it.'[45] In fact, Campion's lack of the usual credentials proved to be an asset:

At this stage we didn't have anything behind us. I'd just finished film school, hadn't got any prizes ... which might have given me a guarantee of some respectability. Janet just said you seem adventurous, and I like adventurous people doing my work.[46]

That same degree of trust was important for more than the beginning. It was critical also when it came to the psychiatric hospital scenes. The autobiography was short on detail on this score but the scenes needed to be covered as part of Frame's life.[47] 'I was a bit scared you know, worried that she might think I was grossly misrepresenting her, and the things in her life which were hurtful and painful'.[48] Campion's hope was that she could draw from other material: 'I read *Faces in the Water* [Frame's fictional account of this period] and asked Janet if we could include some stuff from it.'[49] Frame agreed.

Frame played a further role. She was as well an audience during the New Zealand stage of the shoot. She visited the set and watched the film being made. This could have been a major problem for the filmmakers, and Campion credits Frame with making it a feasible experience for all involved:

> She's distanced from our adaptation, she doesn't see it as her life. She sees it as a story using some of her life as a basis. I think she had the courage to turn her life into an autobiography, one of the most lyrical and poetic I've ever read. I think she's an artist, and artists tend to understand the artistic process and respect it.[50]

Frame in fact achieved more than this comfortable distancing. In Campion's description, Frame first sat at a great distance but eventually took a position directly behind the camera: 'She seemed to be enjoying it and afterwards apparently said she didn't think she would ever get back to earth again.'[51]

Was it then easy to get *Angel* funded and distributed? The answer is 'no'. What was being proposed was a television miniseries shot on film, and that meant a comparatively large budget (Campion describes *Angel* as costing $AUS. 2.5 million dollars). The main players did have some credibility, some background behind them. It was Ikin's first feature production, but Maynard, the co-producer, had several films already to his credit. Campion had made *Sweetie* and that had received considerable acclaim but this was to be a very different production in style, audience, and budget. Ikin's first approach was to a group of merchant bankers:

> It took me a year. It was by far the biggest thing I had done to date .... I did try to finance it through the merchant banking world ...[:] the woman that I was dealing with was actually quite excited about it but it was around the time that the stock-market crashed .... I don't think they even bothered reading the script. With people like that it's just a tax deal they are looking at .... Part of the problem was that we were presenting it as a television series and the financial returns from a television series are small. At most it can only just break even. If we had been presenting it as a film as well they probably would have been more interested. A film would have offered the most tax benefits.[52]

A second route was more successful. It was to a combination of television channels and the New Zealand Film Commission. Two television channels came in quickly. These were TVNZ and Channel Four in the United Kingdom:

> We were lucky with *Angel* because the particular woman who was buying it (at TVNZ) was an intellectual, which is unusual ... and she is definitely not there anymore.[53]

> 'She was a dedicated fan of Janet Frame's.'[54]

The New Zealand Film Commission's reaction was initially tentative. They saw *Angel* as too local a story. They were also concerned that *Angel* was initially scripted for television:

They thought that it was of limited audience appeal and it took them almost a year, and repeated applications from me .... They saw it as very specifically New Zealand and didn't think it would travel .... Basically their charge was to fund features and they just couldn't find a way to feel comfortable with television and didn't think that it would ever get a release beyond television.[55]

Gaining a third source of funding also took time and a change of opinion. The approach now was to the Australian Broadcasting Corporation (ABC). Several questions were raised: was the story of Janet Frame appropriate as a film? Was Frame the kind of character that should be presented in current times? The feeling of Sandra Leavy, a producer at the ABC, was that Janet Frame was *'an inappropriate heroine for the nineties'*: '[s]he was too shy and reserved ...[:] a victim'.[56] The ABC turned it down. Only after much discussion and proven support from Channel Four and New Zealand interests did the gatekeepers at the ABC change their minds.

How, then, did material designed as a three-part television series and funded on that basis become a full-length film? The answer was demand:

I never really thought about it as a feature originally but at the Cannes Film Festival ... we had video cassettes of it and people were flocking to see it, asking if they could get it for cinema.[57]

That demonstrated market then made it easier for *Angel* to be recut and distributed as a film.

That history brings out especially clearly some points that apply to many films. Brought out again is the need to break down any of the singleness suggested by labels such as 'the filmmaker' (or even 'the filmmakers') or 'the funding body'. Those groups are usually made up of two or more individuals. For work to go well they need to have common goals. Brought out also is the need to break down perceptions of 'the audience'. Both *Kitchen Sink* and *Sweetie* were made for cinema. Drawn, however, was a distinction between audiences that were 'cinema literate' and audiences that were not. With *Angel* there emerges more strongly a distinction between television and film audiences. Now a distinction between audiences was also tied to sources of funding and to the requirement from the beginning that what was produced would be in line with what was seen as the nature of those two audiences. We shall meet those circumstances again when we turn to *The Piano*.

Campion's third feature: *The Piano*

Campion's own interests will again provide a starting point. She did not want to 'make ten *Sweeties* in a row'.[58] She also wanted to place the film in an historical setting, to make a love story with a sexual motif, and to include both pakeha and Maori culture within it: 'I wanted to write a love story, a fairly daring one, and set it in a world that I had some particular knowledge of that would be fresh to the rest of the world'.[59] The producer this time was to be Jan Chapman, an Australian. I shall start their story this time with a search for funding: 'In 1990, Chapman and Campion set out on a long fundraising tour. In the end the solution was provided by financial investment from one source, the French company CIBY 2000.'[60]

Before that eventual solution – before the magical rescue – the road was somewhat rocky. The size of the budget – $U.S. 10 million – excluded it from the Australian Film Financing Commission's Trust Fund (a fund that would have allowed a waiver of the requirements for presales). Chapman began discussions and presale negotiations with U.S. distributors. It was at that point that she encountered their strong preferences when it came to casting and control over editing: 'When I was going around talking to the different companies about American pre-sales it was quite horrific.'[61] These companies wanted to specify who the actors should be. They also wanted only stories that would appeal to a wide range of people. And they wanted control over the script. Chapman describes their response to the script as positive. This did not mean, however, that no suggestions would be made. In Chapman's words:

> I don't know what would have been restricted, but, for example, it was difficult to get final cut for Jane. I mean they wouldn't automatically have agreed to that at all. Don't forget she had really only made *Sweetie* and *An Angel* before.[62]
>
> Pre-sales usually work against the films .... People offering a pre-sale usually have far too much control .... For instance, you might sell 30% of the film and you'll lose control of the script and possibly casting just to make sure the film works .... [Y]ou've got to avoid becoming a subsidy agent for international distributors. The final cut is usually the first thing you give away in a pre-sale.[63]

In effect, the economic aspects were again a significant part of the text of society and history. This time, however, the ideological circumstances played an even more important part.

Ideological circumstances

All films call for attention to the nature of the audience. Among the dimensions considered are age, gender, colour, and cinema-literacy. Beneath such dimensions lie differences in the hopes and expectations people bring to any new production (their desire, for instance, for some new tale of love). There are likely to be also differences in the knowledge people have of how to read what is offered (their knowledge, for instance, of past stories with similar labels), and in the 'stances' they have come to take towards what they see.

One of those stances has to do with expectations and ideologies that revolve around who can tell what story and how various groups should be represented. That issue is often cast in terms of men and women. To what extent can men, for instance, tell stories of women that women can accept? Will the 'real stories' emerge only when women produce, direct, and are behind the camera? Until that happens, what is seen as likely to occur is the representation of women in ways that reflect only the views of men.

With *The Piano*, the filmmaker's gender was not expected to be an issue. Here was a film made by a woman. It was also a story about a woman, and it began with an extraordinary sympathy for the right of women to their own voice, for Ada's refusal to speak as others spoke, for Ada's insistence that others accept her communicating by notes, by signs, or by body language.

Dissent was the more anticipated – and received – when it came to representation of Maoris. Whenever a filmmaker comes from one social group and the audience from another – groups whose political history is far from serene, and whose versions of history are likely to differ – there is likely to be tension between them as to the nature of proper representation. In New Zealand, the two groups are Maori and pakeha. The Maori are the original population. The pakeha are the colonizers who have maintained a larger share of the power and, in past New Zealand films, have simply left Maoris out of the picture. That way of proceeding is no longer acceptable. Maori voices are more widely heard. Omitting them completely from a film is promptly criticized. It is also felt by the pakeha themselves to be no longer acceptable. At the same time, Maoris have become increasingly concerned about the ways in which they are represented and the extent to which this reflects only the perceptions of the colonizing group.

That kind of concern becomes all the more of a problem when a film is set at a time of early colonization, and the filmmakers wished to make clear their recognition that there were two distinct cultures. Campion's choice of that historical time came partly from her own historical interest and from a sense of some particular contrasts between the people already in place and the new arrivals:

> I became more interested in ... who my ancestors were, how they were, how it must have been for them, a very puritanical society, going to a place like New Zealand which was so astonishingly different, not only physically from England but also culturally in the sense of what the Maori culture was like .... Maori culture is incredibly at ease sexually .... There isn't a sense of privacy about it which is, of course, incredibly different for Europeans from England around that time.[64]

Campion's approach was to first decide about the language to be used by the Maori characters. The original decision was that they would speak pidgin English. Campion's Maori advisors objected to this and a change was made to Maoris speaking Maori with subtitling in English:

We hadn't thought that we were being patronising or insulting, but then we thought, 'well why can't they speak Maori and we'll use subtitles'.[65]

That still left a sense of concern with whether or not this 'created an impression of lack of sophistication or something like that, which is not what we were really aiming at. You know – the noble savage or something'.[66]

In addition, Campion added further checks. In Chapman's description: 'First of all she rewrote most of her original dialogue' with two Maori script advisors – named by Leonie Pihama as Waihoroi Shortland and Selwyn Muru:

> and then we went to New Zealand with some of the cast and started screentesting with that dialogue and they thought it was a problem and we rewrote it again. We got someone else in who went through all of the sentences. They weren't changed fundamentally. I don't think the spirit of it had changed.[67]

The 'spirit' of the sentences may well have not been changed. The point had been made, however, that Maoris had decided how the voice of Maoris would be represented. It was then cause for some sense of wryness, on the part of the filmmakers, to hear that some of the Maori actors felt they had functioned only as 'black background'.[68] They do function as part of the main story theme: the opposition of openness and physicality with the buttoned-up world of the Scots-born settlers. Being only part of the contrast, however, was seen by several Maoris as meaning that their 'own' story was far from being centre stage.

Those concerns about the nature of representation were more widely public in the form of reviews. The nature of those comments, and the significance of representations, is especially brought out in a paper by Leonie Pihama (a Maori).[69] Cherryl Smith and Pihama had briefly reviewed *The Piano* shortly after its release. Their comment was that it was 'a nice white story'.[70] At a later date (2000) Pihama brought together comments from sources both within and outside New Zealand. Pihama's concern is not only with the particular nature of representations but also with the contexts within which they are read and with the 'discourses' or 'meanings' that underlie the representations.

Part of that context consists of the extent to which the audience has any other knowledge of the people represented:

> Maori images are now broadcast to the world through the media of film and television. The construction of those images becomes even more crucial, given that for many readers of such texts this will be the first and possibly only representation of Maori that they will ever see.[71]

More broadly:

> The historical, cultural, social, economic, and political contexts all play a role in how representations of Maori may be viewed and read. Images are not separate

from the context within which they are positioned .... For Maori, as for other indigenous peoples across the world, developments through colonisation brought about fundamental shifts in representation .... [C]olonial imperialism ... assumed that the territories it colonised were open for exploitation .... Ideologies of race ... enabled immigrant settlers to defend their oppression of indigenous people ... on intellectual grounds.[72]

In all, Pihama quotes reviews that range from no concern with Maori representation to those that reject completely the images that *The Piano* presents and their implications. The range covers the following specific issues.

No attention to the way Maoris were represented. 'The Piano received rave reviews in New Zealand ... on the whole ...[;] there was limited discussion relating to Maori or to the overall colonial depiction of this country.'[73] More often, there was discussion on the extent to which this should be called a 'New Zealand film' or an 'Australian film'.

Recognition that both Maoris and pakehas were included rather than Maoris being ignored or excluded. 'Generations of both Maori and pakeha have been raised in a social context' with 'only selective aspects of Maori society being permitted in the public domain'.[74]

Recognition of Campion's turning to Maori advisers. There was also, however, a sense that it then 'becomes even more perplexing that the representations of Maori in the film persisted in the way they did'.[75] Pihama notes that Campion turned to a Maori advisor, Waihoroi Shortland, as a consultant for the film. She 'clearly attempted to seek some form of authenticity in the representation of Maori'.[76]

A view of The Piano *as reflecting only the colonial gaze.* In Pihama's words:

> The Piano is a film that is very much linked to a colonial gaze. It neither criticises nor challenges the stereotypes that have been paraded continuously as 'the way we were'. The representation of Maori as 'uncivilised' 'lounging-around-doing-nothing natives' merely affirms limited ideas of our people. We are left with the notions that Maori women cook and talk continually about sex and that Maori men carry pianos around in the bush, are irrational, and are unable to control their 'native war-like instincts'.[77]

For Pihama it is the colonial gaze that gives rise to 'constructions (that) range from the "happy-go-lucky native" to the sexualised Maori woman available at all times to service pakeha men'.[78]

A view of history as romanticized. Here Pihama cites bell hooks: 'The 19th century world of the white invasion of New Zealand is utterly romanticised in this film (complete with docile, happy darkies – Maori natives – who appear to not have a care in the world).'[79] hooks also 'writes critically of the ways in which *The Piano* represents violence against Maori, land, and women as "natural" with violence constructed as "the inevitable climax of conflicting passions"'.[80] She also sees one of the white characters – Baines – as a stereotyped representation.

A misappropriation of Maori identity by a pakeha. Baines wears on his forehead part of a moko. That tattooing on the forehead is, among Maoris, 'a form of identification. It carries your *whakapapa*, your genealogical links, visibly on your face. It is a powerful statement of being Maori. The moko locates Baines as the Tarzan of *The Piano*.'[81] It is also a major misappropriation of Maori identity. In Pihama's analysis, Baines is simply part of a genre in which a white is presented as 'the antithesis of the uptight, colonial, controlling white man of the type represented by Kevin Costner in *Dances with Wolves'*.[82] Here there is no simple statement of empathy with Maori culture.

An emphasis on the need for non-Maori sources. 'Very few films/videos, outside of those made by political Maori filmmakers, construct Maori people in anything other than the "you do not exist", "you are no good" categories or are located within stereotyped assertions of who we are.'[83]

Some noncritical voices from Maori sources. 'The conservative Maori author of *Once Were Warriors*, Alan Duff ...[,] wrote scathingly of the country's failure to appreciate Campion's achievement.'[84] *Once Were Warriors* is not only a film for which the scriptwriter and director were Maori, but in contrast to *The Piano*, it is also a contemporary story with an urban setting. Within it, the pakeha are almost irrelevant to the representation of Maori society as bound up with concerns about recovering their past identity as warriors and with issues of class and social hierarchy. That makes Alan Duff's comments on the reviews of *The Piano* more interesting.

Is it then impossible to work from anything other than the colonial gaze? Maynard has found it possible to hand over complete control:

> I've just produced six one-hour documentaries about Polynesia made by Polynesians. As a policy I haven't read their scripts though I gave them processes by which they could have their scripts evaluated. I haven't seen the cuts yet. The first are due in about a week ...[;] it's been an absolute hands off .... I've always been concerned that it will be rather conservative, but if they wish to represent themselves in that manner then it's not up to me to interfere.[85]

Maynard is nonetheless optimistic: 'The day is passed in which Maoris wish to represent themselves as perfection.'[86] The decision 'not to interfere', however, may mean that the group originally in control now has to watch itself replaced by others, both from within and outside the country:

> Mainstream filmmakers like Spike Lee have an enormous effect on these people. I mean anyone from a minority culture who has been able to make an important film ... and reached not only their own audience but audiences beyond them has started to have that effect ...[;] there is a very big complex international indigenous filmmakers' network. They meet regularly, they swap ideas and occasionally they will swap directors. There is a lot of interchange and interface now.[87]

In effect, the group called 'the filmmakers' becomes all the more heterogeneous in nationality but perhaps less marked by discrete viewpoints of the stories to be told.

Cross-cutting themes

Presented so far is a film-by-film account of some particular ways in which multiple interests and perspectives affected the shape of representation and the nature of interpretation. To capture more generally the way in which multiple interests and perspectives come together, Kristeva uses the term 'productivity', Bakhtin the term 'dialogue', Gledhill – with a particular interest in films – the term 'negotiations'. All three imply meanings and intentions that are fluid, that cannot be grasped by focusing on one party only (the author, for instance, or the audience), and that must take account of fluctuating relationships and changes in position for all of those involved.

At stake are ways of adding to Kristeva's accounts of the text of society and history. Cutting across the detailed histories are four general additions that could be applied to any film or any representation. The first three of these have been noted also by Gledhill. The fourth comes from McAfee's composite view of Kristeva and Arendt.

The significance of the spectator

The significance of the spectator has come up several times in the detailed histories: in the concern, for example, over the understanding that various audiences may bring to films that are 'different' and in the extent to which various spectators will reject what is offered on the grounds that the story presented reflects only 'a colonial gaze' and the misappropriation of stories that are 'theirs'.

Gledhill's analysis pulls together those observations on the need to ask who the spectator is, and what 'stance' may be brought to a film. Gledhill's sees the work of Kristeva, Cixous, and Irigaray as having 'made possible considerable revisions to the cine-psychoanalytic construction of the classic narrative text, facilitating attempts to take account of the "female spectator"'.[88] She notes as well that the spectator's position is not static. For one thing, 'the viewing or reading site affects the meanings and the pleasures of a work'.[89] We see films in particular places, and we see them with others: others who may also vary from time to time or from site to site. These features make viewing and reading then a form of social practice which will differ from one group or one historical period to another. For another, spectators may read into a text a number of unintended meanings, or may see – at one time – a meaning not noticed earlier. Films intended to be funny are not always received as funny. And what counts as 'funny' or 'tragic' may vary with the time and place. Old films, Gledhill points out, are constantly being reread, with the classics of one era being regarded as minor works at other times, while the neglected works of those times may be discovered later and resurrected.

The relevance of power

The detailed histories have brought out several times the need to consider who seeks or holds relative degrees of power over various phases: the script, the production and its timing, the distribution and selection of audiences. For countries marked by population movement, where one group arrives and another is already in place, Ahmed adds, 'who gets constructed as the host who welcomes the stranger … is an effect of relations of power that cannot be willed away by the "goodwill" of the nation'.[90]

One general way of considering the place of power is offered by Gledhill's emphasis on the nature of hegemony. Gledhill takes as a baseline concept Gramsci's notion of hegemony: a view of society in terms of a dominant ideology that is always being contested and that continually has to be reestablished. In Gledhill's restatement of this widely adopted view of society:

> Hegemony describes the ever shifting, ever negotiated play of ideological, social, and political forces through which power is maintained and established. The culture industries of bourgeois democracy can be conceptualized in a similar way: ideologies are not simply imposed – although this possibility always remains an institutional option through mechanisms such as censorship – but are subject to continuous (re-)negotiation.[91]

As part of this argument, Gledhill points to the way in which the concerns of various audiences are constantly being taken up by the media, with change in the process both to those ideas and to what is produced:

> [T]he potential market represented by groups emerging into new public self-identity and its processes invariably turn alternative life-styles and identities into commodities, through which they are subtly modified and recuperated for the status quo. Thus the media appropriate images and ideas circulating within the women's movement to supply a necessary aura of novelty and contemporaneity. In this process, bourgeois society adapts to new pressures, while at the same time bringing them under control.[92]

Negotiations as central

The detailed histories have covered several times the negotiations that occur in the course of finding funding, determining what the story will cover, and who the actors might be, and making decisions about distribution.

Gledhill sees as a general issue the need for still closer attention to the ways in which tension and appropriation may be worked out. For Gledhill, the issue is not one of any simple contradiction of creative with commercial interests. To any contradiction we need to add a more detailed account of the negotiations that are an intrinsic part of any compromise or any steps forward:

> Negotiation at the point of production is not, however, simply a matter of potential contradiction between the needs of the media industries and user groups .... Such conflict is, indeed, part of the ideology of creativity itself. Aesthetic practice includes, as well as formal and generic traditions, codes of professional and technical performance, of cultural value and, moreover, must satisfy the pressure towards contemporary renewal and innovation. These traditions, codes and pressures produce their own conflicts which media professionals must attempt to solve.[93]

The end result, then, is not any simple assertion of power or any easy acceptance of contradiction. It is instead one of continual negotiations among multiple interests.

The significance of rights to the story

This aspect of representations comes up especially in relation to the representation of Maoris in *Crush* and in *The Piano*. It is an issue that appears in relation to the narratives and images constructed by people who have misappropriated, distorted, or – even in the unlikely occurrence of their content being accurate – failed to respect the importance of who can tell a particular story.

Conceptually, the account I find closest to this kind of issue comes from McAfee's merging of proposals from Arendt and Kristeva. McAfee starts by noting Arendt's emphasis on the importance of our constructing narratives that 'put a biography into words'; that allow us to see meaning in our lives ('we must tell the story of our lives, then, before we can ascribe meaning to it'); that effectively draw 'attention to a who', to an individual; that 'can partake in ... the politics of a memory that is opened, renewed, and shared'. McAfee adds the need to look more carefully at the ways in which a narrative is 'shared' and allows us to be capable of thinking about horror. [94]

She starts from the wish to reconsider the function and purposes of testimonies and narratives proffered in the public sphere, in what Arendt calls 'the space of appearance'.[95] To do so, she adds Kristeva's emphasis on the speaking subject and then extends the mix to examine the impact of narratives that cannot be publicly spoken and, using South Africa's Truth and Reconciliation Commission as an example, become known in all their horrifying detail. In South Africa we can see vividly the importance of a public audience:

> The narrative meaning expressed through testimony can draw on the pain, tension, and trauma that have, in silence or without a public audience, had nowhere to go .... [T]he victim who survives is not only neutralized and stripped of her title as a citizen with dignity, she is robbed also of a community of aid .... The Truth and Reconciliation Commission setting begins to reverse this double trauma: at one and the same time it helps to reinstate her subjectivity and her membership in the community .... [A] witness does seek some kind of acknowledgement, validation, and bestowal of dignity from the community.[96]

That kind of account moves us toward a deeper understanding of why stories have to be told, especially by the actors themselves and often about themselves. (In the Truth and Reconciliation Commission case, they may be victims or perpetrators.) We are still some distance from understanding what kinds of stories by others about oneself are more objectionable than others. The emphasis on shared narratives and the place of a public addressee, however, are major steps toward our understanding.

All told, here are ways to build on Kristeva's account of the text of society and history, both written large in the form of a storehouse of stories and genres accumulated over time, and written small in the form of the mix of circumstances that provide the more proximal backgrounds for any piece of work.

Taken up in the next chapter (the final chapter) are again some general questions about Kristeva's concepts: questions that cover especially the position of women.

Notes

1. Christine Gledhill (1988) 'Pleasurable negotiations'. In E.D. Pribram (Ed.) *Female spectators: Looking at film and television*. London: Verso, p.77.
2. 'Cinema and fantasy', in Julia Kristeva (2002a) *Intimate revolt*. New York: Columbia University Press, p.80.
3. Ibid., pp.79–80.
4. Ibid., p.79.
5. 'Giotto's joy', in Julia Kristeva (1980) *Desire in language: A semiotic approach to literature and art*. New York: Columbia University Press, p.233.
6. Ibid., p.211.
7. Mary Colbert (1993) 'The NZ connection'. In *The Sydney Morning Herald*, 9 August, p.22.
8. Alison Maclean (1992), in *Press Release for Crush*, p.2 of interview.
9. Ikin in interview with K. Goodnow (December, 1992).
10. Ibid.
11. Ikin in interview with K. Goodnow (August, 1993).
12. These background interests are drawn from a taped interview with John Maynard by K. Goodnow (August, 1993). The theme he brought to this particular script might be regarded as one with overtones of his family's history. Ward's mother was a 'foreigner' to the country. She married Ward's father when he was a soldier based in Egypt and she was working as an Army driver. German by nationality and Jewish by religion, she was apparently working her way towards Palestine. Instead, she came to live on a remote New Zealand farm. That background may have contributed to the theme of 'culture

contact' that also runs through Ward's later films (*The Navigator, Map of the Human Heart*). Whether that is so or not (Maynard suggests that it was a factor), Ward is part of Kristeva's contemporary world: a world in which encounters with strangers, and the experience of being a stranger, are increasingly common.
13. Ibid.
14. It has been argued in New Zealand and Australia that these tax breaks led to a flood of poorly developed films that may or may not have a release but whose production guaranteed the investors with a profit. The breaks were discontinued in both countries.
15. New Zealand Film Commission (1992) *Annual Report*. July, Wellington, p.5.
16. Ibid., p.5.
17. Maynard in interview with Goodnow (August, 1993). More difficult was Ward's future after leaving Australia. Gledhill (1988, p.89) comments on the way in which 'the media appropriates images and ideas'. Appropriated also are new voices. The need to generate 'new' stories leads Hollywood to attract a wide range of writers and directors who have had success on the independent circuit, such as Vincent Ward. Ward was coopted to direct the latest of the Alien films. He was seen as having a 'new' and the innovative approach after the independent success of *Vigil* and *The Navigator*. As John Maynard describes, in interview with Goodnow (August, 1993), voices such as Ward's, however, are expected to restrict their forms of expression to preset ideas of the studio/distributor:

> Vincent found it very hard. Like putting a square peg in a round hole. He said he didn't like the script well enough and he pitched for another one which was basically the script for *Alien 3*. I think it was probably the fear that someone else might think that it was a good idea and so on that they decided to weld it in. It was never a good relationship and they parted company.

18. Ikin in interview with Goodnow (August, 1993).
19. Ikin in interview with Goodnow (December, 1992).
20. Ikin in interview with Goodnow (August, 1993).
21. Maynard in interview with Goodnow (August, 1993).
22. Ikin in interview with Goodnow (August, 1993).
23. Ibid.
24. Ibid. *Paua* are abalone shells used for decoration.
25. Ibid.
26. Ikin in interview with Goodnow (December, 1992).
27. Ibid.
28. Ibid.
29. Gerard Lee and Jane Campion (1989) *Sweetie: The screenplay*. Brisbane: Queensland University Press, p.vii.
30. Ibid., p.ix).
31. Ibid., p.xi.
32. Ibid., p.viii.
33. Cited in Ibid., p.xi).
34. Ibid.
35. Ibid., p.vii.
36. Maynard in interview with Goodnow (August, 1993).
37. Janet Frame (1957) *Owls do cry*. Christchurch: Pegasus Press.
38. Ikin in interview with Goodnow (December, 1992).
39. Jane Campion (1990b) in interview with Peter Castaldi: 'Castaldi on Campion'. In *Culture*, issue 9, October, p.10.
40. Ibid.
41. Jane Campion (1990a) in interview with Candida Baker: 'The sweet smell of direct success'. Review of *An Angel at My Table*. *The Age*, 22 September, Section 2, p.6.
42. Jane Campion (1990g) in interview: 'Being brave'. In *Follow Me*, July, p.54.
43. Ibid., p.54.

44. Campion (1990b, p.10).
45. Jane Campion (1990f) in interview with Katherine Tulich: 'Jane's film career takes wing'. In *Daily Telegraph Mirror*, 21 September.
46. Campion (1990g, p.54).
47. Mistakenly diagnosed as schizophrenic in her early adulthood, Frame was hospitalized, given a long series of electric shocks and – as a further part of therapy – scheduled for a lobotomy that was also a favoured feature of that time. Frame's reprieve came about only when, still hospitalized, a newspaper reported that her writing had met with a major prize.
48. Ibid., p.54.
49. Ibid., p.54. Janet Frame (1961) *Faces in the water*. Christchurch: Pegasus Press.
50. Campion (1990b, p.10).
51. Ibid., p.54.
52. Ikin in interview with Goodnow (August, 1993).
53. Ikin in interview with Goodnow (December, 1992).
54. Ikin in interview with Goodnow (August, 1993).
55. Ibid.
56. Ibid., emphasis added.
57. Campion (1990f).
58. Campion (1990g, p.55).
59. Ibid., p.24.
60. Press Release for *The Piano* (1993, p.4).
61. Chapman in interview with Goodnow (August, 1993).
62. Ibid.
63. Maynard in interview with Goodnow (August, 1993).
64. Jane Campion (1993a), in interview with Lyndon Barber: 'Playing it low-key'. In *The Sydney Morning Herald*, 3 August, p.24.
65. Chapman in interview with Goodnow (August, 1993).
66. Ibid.
67. Ibid.
68. Ikin in interview with Goodnow (August, 1993).
69. Leonie Pihama (2000) 'Ebony and ivory: Constructions of the Maori in *The Piano*'. In H. Margolis (Ed.) *Jane Campion's* The Piano. Cambridge: Cambridge University Press.
70. Leonie Pihama and Cherryl Smith (1994) 'A nice white story: Reviewing *The Piano*'. *Broadsheet* 200.
71. Pihama (2000, p.121).
72. Ibid., p.117.
73. Ibid., p.125.
74. Ibid., p.131.
75. Ibid., p.131.
76. Ibid., p.131.
77. Ibid., p.130.
78. Ibid., p.128.
79. Pihama (2000, p.126) cites bell hooks (1994) 'Gangsta culture – Sexism, misogyny'. In *Outlaw culture: Resisting representation*. New York: Routledge, p.119.
80. Pihama (2000, p.125) cites hooks (1994, p.119).
81. Pihama (2000, p.127).
82. Ibid., p.128.
83. Leonie Pihama (1994) 'Are films dangerous? A Maori woman's perspective on *The Piano*'. In *Hecate: An interdisciplinary journal of women's liberation*, issue 20(2), p.239. Cited in Pihama (2000, p.120).
84. Harriet Margolis (Ed.) (2000) *Jane Campion's* The Piano. Cambridge: Cambridge University Press, p.34. The Duff article was entitled 'Another Tall Poppy Emerges' and appeared in *The Eastland Sun*, 3 August 1994: p.4. Cutting down the tall poppies is a New Zealand

term used to refer to 'a tendency New Zealanders have to cut down to size anyone who seems to stand out from the ordinary' (Margolis, 2000, p.4).
85. Ibid.
86. Ibid.
87. Ibid. Also Pihama (2000, p.39).
88. Gledhill (1988, pp.66–67).
89. Ibid., p.70.
90. Sara Ahmed (2005) 'The skin of the community: Affect and boundary formation'. In T. Chanter and E. Plonowska Ziarek (Eds) *Revolt, affect, collectivity: The unstable boundaries of Kristeva's polis*. Albany: State University of New York Press, p. 96.
91. Ibid., p.68.
92. Ibid., p.89. The argument for such 'recuperative strategies' on the part of mainstream cinema, Gledhill notes, has also been made strongly by several authors in: Peter Steven (Ed.) (1985) *Jump cut: Hollywood, politics and counter-cinema*. New York: Præger.
93. Ibid., p.69.
94. Noëlle McAfee (2005) 'Bearing witness in the *Polis*: Kristeva, Arendt, and the space of appearance'. In Chanter and Ziarek. The material quoted is from Kristeva's account of Arendt's life and work: Julia Kristeva (2001a) *Hannah Arendt*. New York: Columbia University Press, respectively from pages 43, 69, 74, 95, and 96.
95. Arendt, cited by McAfee (2005, p. 114).
96. McAfee (2005, p.121).

Chapter 9

WOMEN AND SOCIAL CHANGE

As a way of bringing out the value of understanding and extending Kristeva's concepts, I have turned to analyses of horror, strangers, and love. Noted also have been gaps that, if filled, would make her concepts even more valuable.

The gap of particular concern in the previous chapter had to do with aspects of the text of society and history that are close to the production of any work. Kristeva gives primary attention to the storehouse of narratives and images that the past provides. Less well brought out – almost set aside after their recognition as important – are the economic and ideological circumstances that, closer to the time of production, shape the form of what emerges.

This chapter looks at a different kind of gap. It has to do with two interrelated issues: the position of women (especially in comparison with men) and the extent to which Kristeva actually moves toward the social change that she emphasizes as essential and that she sees herself as contributing to.

The lack of clear and productive positives on these issues limits the extensions of Kristeva's proposals to any content area. The area of film analysis provides an example. Here there is a widespread concern with the extent to which a film simply respects existing stereotypes and assumptions. The representation of gender is one of the major bases to that judgement. Barbara Creed, for example, saw *Alien* 'as an attempt to shore up the symbolic order by constructing the feminine as an imaginary "other" which must be repressed and controlled in order to secure and protect the social order'.[1] Robin Wood has divided horror films into those that are 'reactionary' and those that are 'progressive' or 'apocalyptic'. (The latter are films in which all that a dominant ideology has repressed 'explodes and blows it apart'.)[2] The journal *Cahiers du cinéma* has offered a seven-point scale for categorizing and rating any film for the extent to which it is complicit with the status quo or challenges it.[3] The representation of women is a key part to those divisions and ratings.

There has been no shortage of criticisms of Kristeva's proposals on these issues. Noëlle McAfee has offered a succinct view of them, and I shall not go through them one by one.[4] Cutting across them, however, are several concerns. One of these is Kristeva's position with regard to feminist theory and feminist proposals for change. A second is her lack of attention to the work of women. A third is her emphasis on the significance of women as able to create a new life: an emphasis that has been read as making pregnancy and motherhood a major difference between men and women and a necessary part of women's development.

As a starting point, I shall take Kristeva's description of 'three generations of feminist theory'.[5] Taken up then are proposals related to men and women, with particular emphasis on motherhood. The section that follows takes up Kristeva's proposals on women's voices, women's writing, and women's genius. This section includes proposals from a trilogy of books that focus on the lives and works of three particular women: Hannah Arendt (2001), Melanie Klein (2001), and Colette (2004).[6] It remains true that two earlier books – *Tales of Love* and *About Chinese Women*[7] – contain the main building blocks for understanding Kristeva's views of women. To those, however, we now need to add later work. The more recent books, however, offer a modified view of her earlier proposals about men and women and about motherhood. They also add to her descriptions about the ways in which social and political contexts shape the work produced. The final two sections sum up some remaining reservations about Kristeva's proposals (mainly in the form of gaps) and provide a reminder of the alternative features of her work.

Kristeva's 'generations' of feminist theory

In her essay on 'Women's Time', Kristeva speaks of three 'generations' of thought:[8] generations that Ann Kaplan has linked to particular kinds of film.[9] The essay makes it clear that Kristeva did not ignore feminist theory, even though she remained cautious about involvement in any particular group. (In her view, movements that start as dedicated to 'freedom' often end up being repressive, placing more emphasis on following a particular line than on encouraging questioning and new ideas.) By 'generations' she means a change in perspective, 'a shift that may be related loosely to chronological time but has more to do with the place from which one speaks'.[10]

> My usage of the term 'generation' ... does not exclude – quite the contrary – the parallel existence of all three in the same historical time, or even that they be interwoven with one another.[11]

What are these generations and how do they alter representations of women? The first concentrates on the

> political demands of women; the struggle for equal pay for equal work, for taking power in social institutions on an equal footing with men; the rejection, when necessary, of the attributes traditionally considered feminine or maternal.[12]

It is from this perspective, Kaplan points out, that film analysts make content analyses of texts, asking about the kind of work that women are represented as doing and the extent to which they occupy any place that is centre-stage. It is from this perspective also that questions are asked about the extent to which women are, in life as well as in texts, in positions of power: the extent to which they are producers, directors, cinematographers, etc. It is presumably as part of this phase also that women have searched for their history (or 'herstory', as some have written it) and considered the ways in which past generations resisted domination or exercised some degree of power.

Kristeva places 'radical feminism' as a 'current' within this first generation. Here are heard calls for women to form groups that separate themselves from male societies. In Kristeva's description:

> Then there are the more radical feminist currents which ... make of the second sex a counter-society ...[:] a sort of alter ego of the official society, in which real or fantasized possibilities for *jouissance* take refuge ...[. T]his counter-society is imagined as harmonious, without prohibitions, free and fulfilling.[13]

From this perspective, Kaplan notes, the 'focus is on women-identified women, on striving for autonomy and wholeness through communities of women, or at least through intense relating to other women'.[14] Women become 'valorized'.

> The essential aspects of women, repressed in patriarchy, are often assumed to embody a more humane, moral mode of being which, once brought to light, could help change society in beneficial directions. Female values become a standard for critiquing the harsh, competitive, and individualistic 'male' values that govern society: they offer an alternate way not only of seeing but of being.[15]

Female values also become a focus for action: 'because of their essential humaneness', they 'should be resurrected, celebrated, revitalized'.[16]

Film analysts who take this point of view may then be critical of 'the depiction of family life as the solution for all ills ...[;] the forced heterosexual coupling in most narrative films ...[;] the discrepancies between images of marriage in popular culture and in real life'; or 'the failure of popular culture to address women's positive ways of relating to one another and the portrayal of men as 'naturally' dominant'.[17] This last line of interest has been particularly enduring. The calls for societies or communities of women may have diminished, but there has remained a strong interest in the way women relate to one another, in either a 'free' or 'patriarchal' society. Relationships between sisters, mothers, and daughters, or co-workers, then attract particular attention. They become either the main theme of a text, or a subtheme we should consider both as a critical part of a narrative and as a potential source of pleasure to women readers or spectators. Linda Williams's discussion of the relationships in *Stella Dallas* between Stella

Dallas, her daughter, and the second Mrs Dallas, provides a classic example, arguing for these relationships as a major theme rather than as a minor part of Stella Dallas's own decline and fall as a *nouvelle* member of upper-class society.[18]

In Kristeva's second generation, interest shifts to analysis of the methods and the processes by which definitions of 'masculine' and 'feminine' are constructed. In this wave,

> linear temporality has been almost totally refused, and as a consequence there has arisen an exacerbated distrust of the entire political dimension .... Especially interested in the specificity of female psychology and its symbolic realizations, these women ... have undertaken a veritable exploration of the dynamic of signs.[19]

There are two parts to this statement by Kristeva. One refers to interest in 'the specificity of female psychology': that is, to differences between men and women in their interests, fears, pleasures, and upbringing. The other has to do with the analysis of signs and their construction. The 'specificity of female psychology' I shall set aside until I consider in more detail Kristeva's views on differences and similarities between men and women. The 'dynamic of signs', however, warrants some expanded comment at this point.

What does interest in the 'dynamic of signs' propose as essential steps for text analysis and political action? Kaplan provides an answer. In her terms, a necessary step 'as we attempt to bring about change beneficial to women' is an analysis of 'the language order through which we learn to be what our culture calls "women" as distinct from a group called "men"'.[20] As part of that approach, 'scholars analyze the symbolic systems – including the filmic and televisional apparatuses – through which we communicate to one another and organize our lives.[21]

It is the dissection of 'apparatuses' within film that then draws attention to the nature of gaze (the camera's gaze and the spectator's gaze).[22] The dissection of 'apparatuses' calls for attention to

> elements including the machine itself (its technological features – the way it produces and presents images); its various 'texts' – ads, commentaries, and displays; the central relationship of programming to the sponsor ...; and the now various sites of reception, from the living room to the bathroom .... Scholars might focus on problems of enunciation, that is, of who speaks a text and to whom it is addressed, or they might look at the manner in which we watch TV ...[:] the 'flow' of the programs.[23]

The dynamic of signs sounds like a generation or a perspective within which one might well place Kristeva. Why then does she place herself as belonging to a third generation? And what are its characteristics?

In this third attitude, which I strongly advocate ..., the very dichotomy man/woman as an opposition between two rival entities may be understood as belonging to metaphysics. What can ... 'sexual identity' mean in a ... scientific space where the very notion of identity is being challenged?[24]

In Kristeva's view, this third generation of thought will take as central three interrelated issues. One is the 'interiorization of ... the socio-symbolic contract ... its cutting edge into the interior of every identity, whether subjective, sexual, ideological, or so forth.'[25] The second again cuts across persons: 'the analysis of the potentialities of *victim/executioner* which characterize each identity, each subject, each sex'.[26] The third is an indication that not all social problems are being set aside:

> The new generation of women is showing that its major social concern has become the socio-symbolic contract as a sacrificial contract ... [and] women are today affirming ... that they are forced to experience this sacrificial contract against their will.[27]

In short, Kristeva by no means ignores feminist theory. She has also a concern with many of the issues that mark feminist theory: a concern with the presence of particularity and individuality among men or women, the nature of interconnections between the symbolic and the social order, and the need to look carefully at the dichotomies 'men' and 'women', avoiding any essentialist view of their differences and at the same time recognizing that both similarities and differences exist.

On men and women

Kristeva's views on similarities and differences have changed from one time to another, and it is important to note the date of most pronouncements. The main contrast, however, is between two positions. The later position is an emphasis on the particularity and individuality of people (male or female): an emphasis accompanied by resistance to laying out differences between the two groups, or even considering them in group terms. The other is an interest in laying out significant differences. As an indication of the first kind of position, I shall start with a statement made by Kristeva in 2001: 'I am not interested in groups; I am interested in individuals'.[28] More fully:

> My reproach to some political discourses with which I am disillusioned is that they don't consider the individual as a value .... That's why I say that, of course, political struggles for people that are exploited will continue, but they will continue maybe better if the main concern remains the individuality and particularity of the person.[29]

The second kind of position – the comparison of groups – is at the core of Kristeva's comments on: (a) the social position of women (their possible marginality, and their need for alliance in relationships that can offer support and protection); (b) the course of development for men and women (in particular, significance of being able to give 'birth', of being mothers); and (c) the significance of women's writing.

A difference in social position?

One of the differences Kristeva has described between men and women has been not in their 'essence' but, instead, in their place in society. That emphasis takes two main forms. One of these is the description of women as socially marginal, occupying positions that are similar to those of other oppressed groups. Moi quotes Kristeva: 'Call it "woman" or "oppressed classes of society", it is the same struggle, and never one without the other'.[30] That kind of proposal, Moi adds, 'conveniently chooses to overlook the differences among the "dissident" groups she enumerates':[31]

> In so far as women are defined as marginal by patriarchy, their struggle can be theorized in the same way as any other struggle against a centralized power structure. Thus Kristeva uses exactly the same terms to describe dissident intellectuals, certain avant garde writers, and the working class.[32]

A subtler version of 'weak' place in society has to do with the nature of links to an existing social order. Women are often described by Kristeva as especially in need of the support and protection that the social order can present and as especially vulnerable to any 'collapse' of the social order. If collapse occurs, a woman may take pleasure in imagining that she 'is' the sublime, repressed forces which return through the fissures of the order. But she can just as easily die from this upheaval.[33] At particular risk are women with children:

> [R]egardless of the body sciences and changes in manners ...[,] women shall need the couple, especially during the fertile period of their lives, in order to have a certain reliability. Motherhood ... needs a support.[34]

Motherhood or 'the maternal passion'

Kristeva has a sustained interest in the significance and consequences of motherhood. She has, for example, described the feminist movement as having taken the 'rejection of tradition ... to excess' with 'the most troublesome example' being 'the perception of motherhood as the ultimate proof that women have been exploited by every imaginable form of patriarchy'.[35] She claims the significance of 'motherhood ...[:] the most essential of the female vocations ...[;] an all-consuming and irreplaceable vocation' has been ignored.[36]

That kind of statement, in a work published in 2001, easily revives earlier concerns that Kristeva was regarding her own needs for motherhood as relevant to all women,[37] or that she looks at women's sexuality only 'from a position of sanctioned heterosexuality …. [C]ultural subversion is not really her concern'.[38]

The later material still emphasizes the importance of motherhood, and the emphasis still falls mainly on pregnancy and birth. There are, however, three changes. In one, motherhood is considered in terms of its significance to society as a whole. Mothers may be the one group of people who cherish and nourish the lives of individual others:

> At a time when the quality and the value of an individual's life are coming to be regarded as less important than the economic value of their labour and as easily replaceable, will mothers be our only safeguard against the wholesale automation of human beings?[39]

In a second change, the emphasis on motherhood begins to give way to an emphasis on 'natality'. The critical experience is one where we have the direct and vivid sense of giving birth or rebirth to something new and valuable, something that helps both ourselves and others take a new step. That birth, that sense of 'natality', need not necessarily take the form of giving birth to a child: a move perhaps prompted in part by writing a volume (the first of the trilogy) about the life and work of Hannah Arendt – a woman who did not have children, who did not write about either the particular position of women or about motherhood, but who did write about the importance of maintaining a commitment to the value of human life.

The third change lies in Kristeva's 2005 argument that what we need to understand and appreciate is the nature of 'the maternal passion'.[40] Here is a kind of love that is critical both for the mental life of the individual and for society as a whole. What we need to do, then, is 'to sharpen our understanding of this passion …[:] this is what motherhood lacks today'.[41]

In Kristeva's analysis, this 'passion' has several features. It is marked by a deep concern for the value of another's life and for the state of their well-being. It is marked also by a strong sense of a beginning. It is not confined to physically giving birth:

> Women can also live out … maternal passion without gestation or birth (through adoption, surrogate mothers and other fertility techniques … or on another level through care-taking, teaching, long-term relationships or in communal/ community work). For most, however, … maternal passion generally concerns mothers and remains the prototype of the love relation.[42]

This 'maternal passion' also combines both love and hate. This mix is the case for all relationships but 'motherhood in particular makes us experience more sharply' both sides of the coin. It also allows space for the other to grow. In a view that parallels one proposed by Melanie Klein, what occurs is there is then both a passionate attachment and a 'depassioning', a sublimation of the first forms of that attachment into allowing the other to learn to think, feel, and act for himself or herself, and allowing the mother herself to 'make room for pleasure, for the child, for thought .... to disappear'.[43]

This kind of position avoids the limitations imposed by an earlier preoccupation with motherhood only in the form of pregnancy and childbirth. Here instead is a view of mothering that can be extended throughout the course of parenting. Here also is the placement of 'the maternal passion' within other forms of love, and room for men to experience the same kind of passion, avoiding a sharp division that seems at first to have only a physical basis.

Women's voice, women's writing, women's genius

Kristeva's early views on women's writings were far from positive. Alice Jardine, in her translator's comments on *Women's Time* (1987), suggests that Kristeva's references to *'écriture féminine'* are to a particular genre popular in France at a particular time.[44] Even if one takes this qualification into account, however, and discounts Kristeva's apparent attraction to the provocative comment, statements such as the following (made in 1981) are difficult to accept:

> In women's writing, language seems to be seen from a foreign land; it is seen from the point of view of an asymbolic, spastic body .... Estranged from language, women are visionaries, dancers who suffer as they speak.[45]

Behind this kind of statement, however, is a larger view of how language and communicative skill arise. They depend, in Kristeva's argument, on affiliation with sources of power:

> We cannot gain access to the temporal scene, that is, to the political and historical affairs of our society, except by identifying with the values considered to be masculine (mastery, superego, the sanctioning communicative word that institutes stable social exchanges).[46]

If we are not willing to move into the 'communicative word' of the dominant order, Kristeva asks, what are the alternatives? The poorest choice, she argues, is to 'refuse this role and sullenly hold back, neither speaking nor writing ..., occasionally punctuated by some kind of outburst: a cry, a refusal, "hysterical symptoms"',[47] perhaps remaining 'forever ... in a sulk in the face of history, politics, and social affairs..[48]

The wiser choice, Kristeva argues, is one of becoming part of the prevailing social order but doing so warily and sceptically. Faced with a choice between becoming 'the most passionate servants of the political order' and 'forever ... in a sulk', Kristeva proposed, in 1986, a third route:

> Let us refuse both these extremes …. But how can we do this? By listening; by recognizing the unspoken in all discourse, however Revolutionary, by emphasizing at each point whatever remains unsatisfied, repressed, new, eccentric, incomprehensible, that which disturbs the mutual understanding of the established powers.[49]

These statements seem oddly patriarchal and gratuitously negative. They also easily give rise to the feeling that Kristeva's concepts are at some points defences of her own social position. She is, as Moi points out, a member of the French 'establishment'. (The photographs on the back covers of her recent books, if they are not intended as satire, are certainly conventional images of a carefully groomed woman in a studio portrait pose). It is with all the more relief then that we find Kristeva turning to the work of three women who did not simply hold sceptical but unspoken views. Instead, they openly argued for other views of the world and, in Colette's case, for other ways of speaking and writing. The three are Hannah Arendt, Melanie Klein, and Colette. To each Kristeva dedicated a volume in a three-volume set with the title *Female Genius: Life, Madness, Words – Hannah Arendt, Melanie Klein, Colette*.

Why consider the books on Arendt, Klein, and Colette?

The reasons are several.

They are about women. Kristeva has argued for the significance of women. At the same time, most of the work she has referred to and used as sources or examples are by men. Where, then, is the work of women?

They are recent. As McAfee notes, much of what was written about Kristeva's position on women was based on her early work. The recent work, however, allows us to see more readily what is new and what is a maintained position.

They reveal a clearer picture of the ways in which lives and work are interwoven, and of the impact of sociopolitical contexts. Each of these women lived at particular times and particular places. Their theoretical positions and their perceptions of possible steps forward reflect those times and places.

They are surprisingly readable. Kristeva can write for a broad audience. At an earlier point, for example, she rewrote – for a broader audience – her conceptual analysis of strangers (the transposition of *Strangers to Ourselves* and *Nations Without Nationalism*.[50] That transposition I found impressive and reassuring. More often, I had found the style in which she writes about her own concepts a distraction from the brilliance of her ideas. These three books, however, are examples of a capacity to examine in depth, and with an eye more to understanding than to criticism, the works of others, for the most part setting aside her usual use of a more inventive style.

Let me start with what Kristeva sees the three as having in common, and then consider briefly each of the three, with an emphasis on the contexts they experienced and on their proposals about our readiness and our capacity to question, challenge, revolt, and come up with something that is the beginning of a new way of thinking, writing, or living.

What is common to Arendt, Klein, and Colette?

Kristeva comments on several features.

They are all 'women of revolt'. Despite their differences, the three are women of revolt, with revolt used in the sense of a sustained questioning and challenging of any established way of thinking.[51] In this respect, and in their demonstration of 'particularity' and 'individuality', they may well be regarded as members of Kristeva's possible 'third generation'.

Each is a 'genius'. The term is used to refer to people who 'have left their mark on the increasingly diverse pursuits of our time',[52] and have come to be recognized as 'extraordinary' rather than as simply equal to everyone else.[53] The three writers meet these criteria. They also demolish any suggestion that only men can be geniuses. Kristeva cites, for example, statements to the effect that women have only a 'genius of ... patience'.[54] Here, in contrast, are women whose approach is one of 'living the life of the mind ...[,] able to work toward unique, innovative creations and to remake the human condition'.[55]

They cannot be simply assigned to a group labelled 'women' or 'Woman'. They cannot be regarded as 'members of a group with a capital W'[56]: 'In the end, the particular accomplishments of each woman and her personality ... cannot be reduced to the common denominator of a group or a sexual identity'.[57]

Their genius is of a kind especially likely to be shown, by women, to be a 'female genius'. Marking these women are moves toward new ways of thinking and of being: moves that are likely to have an underlying awareness of women as offering a denial of the future as entirely one of disasters, death, and endings, and focusing instead on the drama of 'beginnings'.[58] For all three, questioning and challenging formed a necessary step toward the possibility of psychic life and of a 'rebirth' of ideas: ideas that could break old ways of writing, thinking, or feeling.

They lived in nonsupportive contexts but they did not succumb to unproductive anger, melancholia, or withdrawal and disappearance. They lived and worked at times when women were not expected to engage strongly in 'the life of the mind' and were often seen as unable to do so. They lived 'outside the norm'[59] and their 'geniuses ... came at a price: ... they pay for it by being ostracized, misunderstood, and disdained'.[60] In contexts such as these, it would be easy to give in, to waste one's energy in sad regret or in anger.

Instead, each proposed some ways forward: ways by which all of us may move forward and make a different future a possibility.

Arendt: Context and proposals

Kristeva's analysis of Arendt's life and work is chronologically the first of the three volumes. Arendt's work is also at the end of a range when it comes to style. She admired the apparently minimalist style of Franz Kafka, a style that never distracted from the meaning of the narrative: 'style in any form, through its own magic, is a way of avoiding the truth'.[61] Her proposals as well are the most explicitly linked to a political world.

Arendt's life (1906 to 1975) progressed from that of a philosophy student in Heidelberg to political activity and arrest, followed by a forced flight in 1933 (part of a Jewish exodus that soon became close to impossible), and a later career as a political theorist with an academic appointment at Princeton. Her work still prompts close attention and debate. It has also prompted a small set of papers linking her concepts to Kristeva's.[62] A keen observer of political change and its impact, Arendt kept track of events in Germany, Israel, and Russia, and drew from all of these a concern with 'dark times'[63] and their impact on the people who lived through them.

In essence, what did she see as the nature and the impact of these 'dark times'? They are times when the value of human life is especially downgraded. The rise of technology, with its emphasis on people as easily replaced, diminishes that value. A sharper downgrading comes with totalitarian regimes. To Arendt, 'Nazism and totalitarianism are two sides of the same horror, because they both partake in the same 'contempt for the *value of human life* ...[and are systems] in which all men have become equally superfluous'.[64] People themselves could then come to feel that they no longer had value, and could lose 'interest in their own well-being'.[65]

In the face of this threat, what ways forward are there? One way was mentioned at the end of Chapter 8. This was the development of a narrative: a story of one's life that gave meaning to it or, when written by others, gave meaning to a series of events. These narratives, I noted, need to become publicly shared: not kept to oneself or to a few others. This public address then serves two purposes. It acts as a protection against the ease with which a narrative could disappear in the course of the inevitable frailty of social order. It is also an essential bridge between the individual and the social. Only when a narrative is developed and its meaning shared with others can democracies, and participation in them, come about.

Three further steps forward are essential to note. One is to maintain 'the life of the mind', a life marked by constant challenging and rethinking, and a search for understanding (one way of avoiding a 'banality of evil' that we come to take for granted). Another is the maintenance of one's own identity: one's own sense of value, of not being superfluous. A third was the development of forgiveness. Without a capacity to forgive others for what they have done, there can be no way forward, no hope for a future. Instead, we would be tied only to a past that could not be undone.

Forgiveness is a concept that has attracted increasing attention.[66] I shall note here only its core function (the maintenance of hope for a possible future) and some of the qualifications Arendt added. What is forgiven, she proposed, is the person, not the act.Some people, however, are unforgiveable. Eichmann, for example, was unforgiveable: he emerged at his trial as a robot-like bureaucrat who lacked judgement and who would, if allowed to, return and continue with the same actions as before.[67] Some actions are also unforgiveable. These are 'willed evils', outside 'the realm of human affairs and the potentialities of human power'. In contrast are actions that may be labelled as 'trespass'. They may be forgiven 'in order to make it possible for life to go on by constantly releasing men from what they have done unknowingly'.[68]

In effect, at the core of Arendt's work is a concern, similar to Kristeva's, with how anything 'new' is seen as possible and how it emerges. We might ask whether women are especially susceptible to the feeling of being superfluous or, as Kristeva might argue, more likely to see themselves as always needed for humanity to survive. Arendt, however, sees all people as threatened by 'dark times', as potentially able to move forward, and as responsible for doing so.

Klein: Context and proposals

Klein's life (1882–1960) contained some of the elements contained in that of Arendt. She moved from Europe to England (1926), after an earlier move to Budapest (where she began analysis with Sandor Ferenczi). Political upheavals and war, however – events so pivotal for Arendt – were of less significance to Klein than involvement in the intensive rivalries and disputes among several psychoanalytic groups. Kristeva reports, with some amusement, Donald Winnicott's comment during one of these debates: 'I would like to point out that an air raid is going on'.[69] For Klein, the more significant events appear to have been a closely controlling mother, an unhappy early marriage, and observations of the feelings and fantasies that very young children act out in the course of play. These events seem to have prompted Klein's interest in autonomy, her particular description of motherhood, and her awareness of envy, cruelty, destructiveness, and guilt as early parts of psychic life. In Kristeva's description,

> a restless dissidence, one that emerged during an era of conformity and of planned transgressions, reflects the view of a human being governed by a death drive that

is readily transformable into creativity as long as he or she is given a bit of innate luck, a capacity for love, and 'a good enough mother' (as Winnicott puts it …).[70]

Kristeva offers an account of the changes in analytic theory that Klein proposed and of the ways in which some of her concepts have been taken up by social theorists.[71] The concept of particular relevance to views of women and motherhood is the concept that Winnicott called 'the good enough mother'. This mother ceases to regard the child as her double. She meets the child's basic needs but also allows room for the child's exploration and independent thought and, at the same time, some room for her own growth and pleasure. Here is a model, some argued, for the growth of 'democracy in which the state tends to social needs without hindering individual liberties'.[72] Its opposite is the tyrannical mother: the epitome of any tyrannical authority that we absorb into ourselves and make part of ourselves. In a sense, there is then no real mother. There is instead an internalized model of her: one that can change.

These are mother figures and forms of change or transformation that add to those prepared by Kristeva. We might well look for them in film. Some have already appeared. *Now, Voyager* provides an example. Charlotte Vale's mother is presented first as the tyrant mother. After her voyage, however, Charlotte is ready both to resist control and to recognize that the mother really does not have the power that Charlotte had attributed to her. Here, then, are a mother who leaves little room for growth and a daughter who comes to recognize that her image of her mother and her mother's power were in part her own construction.

Colette: Context and proposals

The span of time (1873–1954) again overlaps the span for Arendt and for Klein. Unlike Arendt and Klein, however – 'two restless women tested by the upheavals of their age', in Kristeva's description[73] – Colette remained in place. Her home was always France, with the main transition being from rural Burgundy to Paris. Her second husband – Dutch and Jewish in background – spent part of the occupation period in Free France, and part in hiding in the Paris apartment, but Colette stayed in Paris. War and politics were not a major concern to her. The stronger aspect of context, I suggest, is the picture of restrictions and entrapment contained in her story of 'The Nightingale and the Rose' (adapted from a story by Oscar Wilde): part of a 1908 work with the title *Tendrils of the Vine*.[74]

In brief, the nightingale starts as a conventional singer: 'It had a gentle wisp of a voice'. It began singing in the morning, 'went to bed at seven … and did nothing but snooze till the next day'. The change came when it woke one morning to find itself trapped:

During its sleep ... the tendrils of the vine ... grew so thick ... that the nightingale awoke tied down, its feet entangled in forked bonds, its wings powerless. It thought it was dying, struggled, escaped only with tremendous difficulty, and swore to itself not to sleep all spring so long as the tendrils of the vine were growing. The very next night, it sang to keep itself awake ..., fell in love with its own voice, [and] became the frantic, intoxicated, and gasping singer to which one listens ... with ... delight.

The story then extends the theme to the writer's own discovery that 'the tendrils of a bitter vine had bound me .... I fled'. Now:

I feverishly cry out what is usually kept quiet .... I would like to say, say, say everything I know, everything I think ...[,] everything that enchants me, wounds me and astonishes me .... I no longer know happy sleep, but I no longer fear the tendrils of the vine.[75]

I use that story as a capsule description of both Colette's context and her intent. She 'knew nothing of politics, dreamt only of revealing feminine *jouissance*', and believed that there is 'no emancipation of women without a liberation of women's sexuality, which is fundamentally a bisexuality'.[76] She wrote a long series of novels, was engaged in scripts, subtitles, and adaptations of her books into film, and was often a film critic. The novels in themselves, Kristeva notes, are not remarkable for their plots (they are 'repetitive and rather commonplace' and 'have not aged well').[77] What has survived well, however, is a sense of deliberate freedom and the quality of her use of words and images. 'Look!' was one of Colette's basic messages, and her writing often covers the magic and the pleasure of what one sees. She describes her mother as less attentive to her daughter than to watching the magical opening of a cactus rose.[78] This core concern, Kristeva argues, was a large part of Colette's 'ease with the unfurling of images that was ... to characterize the twentieth century, from the illustrated book to cinema'.[79]

Words, however, were also major sources of pleasure. What counted was not the factual information they might convey. Words were, to Colette, 'the world's flesh'.[80] In their own sounds, they should bring out the feelings we are experiencing: 'Harsh: now that's a good plastic word, fashioned like a rasp'.[81]

Words should bring out also the rhythm of experience, the sensual pleasure of what one sees or hears. In short, words themselves carry Colette's belief in what life was about or should be about: a level of freedom and pleasure that women especially should struggle to attain, breaking free from 'the tendrils of the vine'. In short, a different view again of women and of women's lives.

Some reservations

It will be clear by now that I find Kristeva's work of major interest. Nonetheless, some questions remain. These have to do with what is covered (the place of images and her view of silence) and the links to social change.

The place of images

Kristeva sees current society as a world that has become a 'universe of the image that invades us through film and television'.[82] It has become also a world in which the 'universe of the image', combined with aspects of a contemporary family (the lack of relationships, lack of authority and so on), leads to 'phantasmic poverty', to 'new maladies of the soul'.[83]

There are, Kristeva agrees, films that are not so trivial or so negative in their impact. She is nonetheless surprised by Colette's fascination with film: her early purchase of a television set, and her praise of documentaries, for the way they captured events and mixed those descriptions with 'enchantment, marvels, and indisputable miracles'.[84] 'Some day there will undoubtedly be no other method besides film for teaching children and young people'.[85]

Kristeva came to see some of the positives that Colette perceived. In her description of Colette's work with film, for instance, she sees put into effective practice Colette's insistence that we look at any event, from the rise of a seagull on the wind to the birth of a plant or the action of people, and the expressions of emotion in their faces or their bodies. This suggests that Kristeva herself was gaining sensitivity to the power and the potential of what is presented visually as well as in words. Kristeva notes as well the positive use Colette made of silence: of images without words.

In effect, Kristeva was not completely insensitive to the pleasures and values of film images. Only some films, however, had the features she saw as needing to be present. These films went beyond 'the gaze by which I identify an object, a face'.[86] They tap directly into our emotions. They use every aspect of what is presented visually in ways that convey the meaning of the narrative. Eisenstein, she felt, produced such films: 'Eisenstein's message ... was clear: the drama, the conflict must be interiorised ...[:] every element of the visible must be saturated with conflict.'[87]

Kristeva, however, sees those features as present only in a few films. In fact, they are a major part of what is contained in many films: films such as those I have used as a focus. To take a few examples, in *Vigil* the narrative of 'strangers' in a landscape to which they do not belong in the film is captured not only by the narrative but also by the way the hills loom over the small section of farmed land, often covered with fog, inhabited only by hawks, and by the absence of any scene shot from above. In *Kitchen Sink* the notion that a casual attitude may be taken toward the life or death of another – toward whether one gives it life or throws it away – is underlined by its black and white style, its everyday setting (a kitchen, a suburban house, everyday activities), and its use of silence and no signs of surprise or concern. Kristeva recognized the effectiveness of that kind of style in Solzhenitsyn's writing. The degradation and destruction of human life in Russian detention camps are made all the more stark by the use of banal stories and a style that is 'dull, drab, but full'.[88] That same off-setting and underlining is also present in film.

In time, Kristeva's recognition of positives may lead to a view of film as able to give rise to a rich level of fantasy, a rush of feeling, a revived search for meaning and a renewed questioning and rethinking. With more exposure to film (it seems so far to range from Eisenstein to Godard and Chaplin), Kristeva might well see the qualities she values present in a wider set of films than she has considered, and consider women as producers not only of words but also images. For the moment, however, we must make those extensions ourselves.

Kristeva's view of silence

Kristeva's description of silence covers two forms. It is at times a 'sullen sulk'. At others, it is quite the opposite. The foreigner's silence, for instance, is a silence that Kristeva describes as often chosen, as a position of pride, allowing a sealed-off self that can withstand the onslaughts of others' speech. Moreover, Kristeva devotes an entire chapter in *Tales of Love* to someone who does not speak: Jeanne Guyon.[89] This is the only woman to be given such space. The choice is all the more surprising because Kristeva sees Guyon as advocating a means other than speech to communicate with God (an 'ineffable silence'). Communicating with God may call for different means than those called for by a change in a literary or social order. More probably, Kristeva distinguishes between silences that are imposed and silences that are chosen out of anger or preference.

The fact remains that Kristeva's occasional endorsement of refusal as a means of not perpetuating the status quo is outweighed by her more frequent insistence that only a voice that speaks from the centre and uses the language of power is likely to be heard and to produce change.[90] I would have hoped, for instance, to find within Kristeva's writings a base from which to consider films in which silence is expressed as a preference, as a refusal (*The Piano, Persona, Children of a Lesser God*).[91] These are, moreover, films in which the refusal comes from women (I know no film in which an equivalent refusal comes from a man). One of those films (*Children of a Lesser God*) also stands out in stark contrast to an earlier film devoted to a deaf woman (Helen Keller) in which speech was unequivocally presented as a gift to be deeply appreciated (*The Miracle Worker*). I can understand that for a psychoanalyst speech occupies a special position: in analysis 'words take the place of frozen terror and desire'.[92] Nonetheless, to my regret, I do not find as yet within Kristeva's works a strong basis for considering the source or the impact of representations of silence, a major limitation when it comes to the analysis of film.

An acceptance of the status quo?

There is no doubt that Kristeva is an advocate of social change: change, for example, in the form of reducing the disadvantage experienced by minority groups, stopping the drift – in France – away from the sense of a common nation, and altering the position of women. Any advocate of social change, however, may be taken to task if it appears that he or she is really aligned with the status quo. Any suggestion that one's writings are complicit with the established order undercuts one's status as producing a text that is new in social terms, however novel the surface style may be. In addition, any advocate of social change needs to ask how social change comes about and what may be done to make change more likely.

Kristeva is not always seen as meeting these criteria. Her position has, in fact, been seen as 'politically unsatisfactory', as 'an apology for the establishment of sociality at the cost of women's equality'.[93] Such comments appear to stem partly from the social position that Kristeva occupies as a person. In Moi's terms:

> Kristeva, with her university chair in linguistics and her psychoanalytic practice, would certainly seem to have positioned herself at the very centre of the traditional intellectual power structures of the Left Bank.[94]

More disturbing to me – all the more so because statements on this score appear more than once – are Kristeva's comments on women as needing to maintain the status quo. Those needs would surely argue against change. They also seem to set aside the possibility that 'collapse' in the existing social order may have benefits for women. Of concern to me also is the importance Kristeva gives to women becoming members of central groups: to their never being 'marginalized' or seen as an outsider. On the one hand, this being central may make it more likely that one's voice will be heard. On the other, it is also likely that one will raise fewer objections to the established order. Doing so may threaten the extent to which one is accepted as a full member of a governing group.

Some degree of marginality may in fact be desirable. It can have the political value of being seen as able to change. It can also give the individual the sense of being able to change by shifting to a new setting or new set of circumstances. That kind of change may well be easier to achieve than the radical overhaul of a fixed identity or a fixed position.

Where does Kristeva stand when it comes to the specific ways by which change may come about? Kristeva's argument has always been for change in the symbolic order: in the end of her essay on three 'generations', Kristeva describes as one essential step for the third generation as being the need to question or reject the forcibly sacrificial quality of the sociosymbolic contract offered to women. Noted also has been her advocacy of subversion of the symbolic order by changing the use of language, breaking through conventional linguistic structures.

These steps might seem insufficient to analysts who see political change as stemming only from steps that directly change a legal or occupational structure. Such doubts, however, seem to underplay the social significance of changes in language practice or narrative practice. To take but one example, a general awareness of assumptions about gender has certainly followed a shift in practice such as the avoidance of 'he' as covering both males and females in any textbook or public document. To take another – an example drawn from one of the films I have reviewed – there have been changes in New Zealand after the production of *An Angel at My Table*. New Zealanders have come to know that they possess a national treasure. Frame's books, along with the film, have become part of the official school curriculum. And people of all ages have acquired (or have had articulated for them) a scepticism towards official medicine and an awareness that those who are diagnosed as 'mad' or 'incurably mad' may not be so at all.

Doubts may still remain about the links between changes in an individual's psychic life and what occurs in one's life with others. That kind of gap seems to be part of the move toward developing psychoanalytic theory that incorporates both: see Kelly Oliver's chapter on revolt and forgiveness, for example.[95] In time, I would expect to see Kristeva's views of such links to become more clearly and more fully articulated.

A reminder of positives

I have organized this chapter around some general questions and reservations that have been expressed about Kristeva's views on women and social change. Let me end by reminding the reader of the positives that led to my choice of her as a base for film analysis.

I might, for instance, have chosen – from among the French feminists – theorists such as Cixous or Irigaray. Cixous has been an astute observer of the dichotomies (male/female, rational/emotional, etc.) that sustain 'rational' thought and social order.[96] Irigaray offers an analysis of maternity and, unlike Kristeva, sustained attention to the nature of sexual love between women. (Kristeva's comments on this score, and on love between men, are sporadic and minor as well as often negative).[97] Outside of France, I might have started from Kaplan's analysis of representations of motherhood (an analysis that strongly elaborates the sacrificial contract)[98] or from Tania Modleski's combined use of the theories of Kristeva and those of Nancy Chodorow to account for the affective impact of horror movies.[99]

All of these theorists offer potential bases for film analysts. Kristeva has the special advantage of combining three features. She offers at the same time a particular position on women, a broad conceptual sweep, and a particular emphasis on two issues of major interest to film analysts: the affective impact of various representations, and the ways in which the emergence of a new text reflects the texts that have preceded it and the circumstances of a given time.

Kristeva's position on women contains some arguable features. Constant throughout, however, is an insistence that 'femininity', like 'masculinity', is a construct: that is, any difference cannot be attributed to biology or to some 'essential', unchangeable difference between men and women. Like Moi, I find this emphasis attractive:

> If, as Cixous and Irigaray have shown, femininity is defined as lack, negativity, absence of meaning, irrationality, chaos, darkness – in short, as non-being – Kristeva's emphasis on marginality allows us to view this repression of the feminine in terms of *positionality* rather than of essences. What is perceived as marginal at any given time depends on the position one occupies.[100]

In effect, borders and the people seen as occupying border positions may be constantly redefined.

The broad conceptual sweep is part of a position marked by several disciplines and by a strong sense of historical change. It is also a position that effectively brings together contributions from several disciplines. To Kristeva's broad historical sweep I have felt the need to add an account of history that is closer to the time of production, but the broader account of past texts into which any current text is inserted is an essential base.

The relevance to film analysis is a feature that I would hope to need little further statement at this point. To make a general comment, however, let me note that any account of the way a film is received can benefit from the analysis of affective experience and its forms. Kristeva offers an account in which affect, to take one example, is strongly related to instability, and instability stems both from the nature of human development (e.g., from the persistence of feelings and rhythms of early childhood set aside but not entirely abandoned) and from the quality of signs (their inherent instability and the need to regard any meaning as a production involving speaker and addressee). When one combines a coherent position that covers a variety of affective experiences with a special interest in the way texts are related to one another, and a focus on the way new texts emerge, the appeal to film analysts becomes still stronger.

These are not, however, the only qualities that have attracted me to Kristeva. Attractive to me is a position that McAfee notes as important also to her. Here there is no sharp dividing line drawn between the semiotic and the symbolic orders. Rhythms, feelings, and motives do not simply disappear or become suppressed when words come in. Instead, the two remain intertwined.[101]

Attractive also is Kristeva's insistence upon always asking: what is missing here? What is essential? What is not accounted for? That approach – one Kristeva has consistently taken – adds a quality of conceptual excitement to her work. It is, for instance, refreshing to turn from linguists' emphases upon syntax and referential meaning to Kristeva's insistence that in poetry, the order of words does matter ('Jack hit John' and 'John was hit by Jack' may have the same referential meaning but the impact of one phrase is not the same as the other). The position of the word on the page also matters, as does the sound of the word itself.[102] Kristeva's approach says, 'Look at the subtext', but it also does more than this. It tells us what the subtext is that we should look for, listen for: the experience of being a stranger, the ways in which passion may be combined with caring, and the fascination that accompanies horror.

The power of this type of questioning is further illustrated by the way it has been used to considerable effect by feminists in many areas, asking: who is missing from these histories, these landscapes? It has even been turned back upon Kristeva: why are there so few women among the writers she considers? Where is Virginia Woolf or Gertrude Stein? In short, it is by no means socially ineffective to say that one of the ways in which women (and men) can contribute to changes in theory and practice is by listening to, and actively asking about, what is not said, not represented, or by considering new texts in terms of whether they begin to fill some of those silences.

Attractive also is the dynamic quality to Kristeva's insistence upon the tension that always exists between competing views of events. It is true that analyses of society have often leaned towards the perception of competing forces, with some of these being dominant, or hegemonic, in Gramsci's term. What needs to be done, however, is to specify the competing ideologies that are relevant to any particular event or any particular representation, and to provide examples of the way in which the competition has been played out at various times. Kristeva, for instance, is by no means the first to refer to the tension between an ethos of universalism and an ethos of particularism, but she stands out for her analysis of the forms this tension has taken, and the variety of resolutions that it has engendered over a range of historical occasions. To read her account, for instance, of the way the speakers for the French Revolution framed their concept of rights and fluctuated in their treatment of foreigners, is to see academic tension between universalism and particularism brought to life.

In similar fashion, Kristeva manages to articulate the ways in which traditional representations bind us in a sociosymbolic contract that, for all that it is challenged, nonetheless persists. 'Stabat Mater', to take a particular case, is a powerful articulation of the way a sacrificial contract becomes concretized in images (the Mater Dolorosa, or the serene, nursing Madonna) that meet some particular needs of men and women but make it difficult to question the contracts and the omissions they contain. In this type of analysis, the nature and implications of the sociosymbolic contract come to life, prompting one to search – as Kristeva suggests – for alternatives (not just any alternatives, but alternatives that allow more freedom in what one does or how one feels).

Do more positives still need to be added? I personally like Kristeva's insistence upon not being typecast, her refusal to be placed under one 'ism' or another. At a time when in theory one argues against restrictions imposed by traditional categorizations and dichotomies, her refusal to be placed – whatever its rationale – is a practice in line with what she preaches. I like as well the mixture of perspectives from literary theory, psychoanalysis and political theory. It is a mixture that could easily become unmanageable. It results, instead, in an abstractable set of past propositions that is coherent and that yields new propositions to be used as a basis for further analysis. The concern with coherence is one that arose for me on turning from the first piece of work that I read by Kristeva (*Powers of Horror*) to the books on strangers and on love. It is, however, a concern that I came to set to rest. I hope that I have done so also for others.

All told, here is a base, a perspective, that prompts a variety of questions that may be brought to many film texts. To demonstrate that this is possible, and rewarding, has been my purpose in bringing Kristeva's concepts to bear upon the analysis of a specific set of films. (It is otherwise all too easy to say that the concepts are 'relevant'.) The concepts Kristeva proposes are not always fully elaborated. The language in which she clothes them makes them often not easily accessible. The rewards for struggling with the difficulties, however, are major.

Notes

1. Barbara Creed (1985) 'Horror and the monstrous-feminine: An imaginary abjection'. In *Screen*, issue 27(1), p.169.
2. Robin Wood (1985) 'An introduction to the American horror film'. In B. Nichols (Ed.) *Movies and methods*, vol. 2. Berkeley: University of California Press, p.215.
3. Robert Lapsley and Michael Westlake (1988) *Film theory: An introduction*. Manchester: Manchester University Press, p.9.
4. See Noëlle McAfee (2004) *Julia Kristeva*. New York: Routledge, pp.76–90.
5. Julia Kristeva (1981) 'Women's time'. In *Signs*, issue 7(1), p.13.
6. The three books were published in English under the general title: *Female genius: Life, madness, words – Hannah Arendt, Melanie Klein, Colette*. Julia Kristeva (2001a) *Hannah Arendt*. New York: Columbia University Press; Julia Kristeva (2001b) *Melanie Klein*. New York: Columbia University Press; Julia Kristeva (2004) *Colette*. New York: Columbia University Press. French versions were published by Fayard: *Le Génie féminin*, tome I, *Hannah Arendt*, 1999 (Folio «Essais» n° 432); *Le Génie féminin*, tome II, *Mélanie Klein*, 2000 (Folio «Essais» n° 433); *Le Génie féminin*, tome III, *Colette*, 2002 (Folio «Essais» n° 442).
7. Julia Kristeva (1986a) 'About Chinese women'. In T. Moi (Ed.) (1986) The Kristeva reader. Oxford: Basil Blackwell; Julia Kristeva (1987b) *Tales of love*. New York: Columbia University Press.
8. Julia Kristeva (1981, p.13).

9. E. Ann Kaplan (1987) 'Feminist criticism and television'. In R.C. Allen (Ed.) *Channels of discourse*. London: Methuen.
10. Kristeva (1981, p.13).
11. Ibid., p.33, emphasis in original.
12. Ibid., pp.18–19.
13. Ibid., p.27.
14. Kaplan (1987, p.217).
15. Ibid., p.217.
16. Ibid., p.217.
17. Ibid., p.226.
18. Linda Williams (1984) '"Something else besides a mother": Stella Dallas and the maternal melodrama'. In *Cinema Journal*, issue 24(1).
19. Kristeva (1981, p.19).
20. Kaplan (1987, p.216).
21. Ibid., p.229, emphasis added.
22. Ibid., pp.228–229.
23. Ibid., p.229.
24. Kristeva, (1981, p.34)., emphasis in original.
25. Ibid., p.35.
26. Ibid., p.35, emphasis in original.
27. Ibid., p.25.
28. Quoted in Rosalind Coward (1984) 'Julia Kristeva in conversation with Rosalind Coward'. In L. Appagnanesi (Ed.) *Desire*. London: ICA documents, p.24.
29. Ibid., p.27.
30. Toril Moi (1985) *Sexual/textual politics*. London: Methuen, p.164.
31. Ibid., p.171.
32. Ibid, p.164. The same central interest in marginality, in Moi's view, occurs in the way Kristeva brings together the feminine and the semiotic. The two are not similar in the sense that the semiotic is a female world, while the symbolic is exclusively male. The semiotic Mother encompasses both masculinity and feminity: 'the opposition between masculine and feminine does not exist in pre-Oedipality' (p.165). 'Femininity and the semiotic do, however, have one thing in common: their marginality. As the feminine is defined as marginal under patriarchy, so the semiotic is marginal to language. This is why the two categories, along with other forms of "dissidence", can be theorized in roughly the same way in Kristeva's work' (p.166).
33. Kristeva (1986a).
34. 'Romeo and Juliet', in Kristeva (1987b, p.227).
35. Julia Kristeva (2001a) *Hannah Arendt*. New York: Columbia University Press, p.xiii.
36. Ibid., p.xiii–xiv.
37. See, for example, Jacqueline Rose (1986) *Sexuality in the field of vision*. London: Verso, p.142.
38. Judith Butler (1993) 'The body politics of Julia Kristeva'. In K. Oliver (Ed.) *Ethics, politics and difference in Julia Kristeva's writing*. New York: Routledge, p.172.
39. Kristeva (2001a, p.xiii).
40. Julia Kristeva (2005) *Motherhood today*. At www.kristeva.fr.
41. Ibid.
42. Ibid.
43. Ibid.
44. See Alice Jardine's footnote in her introduction to 'Women's time': Alice Jardine (1981) 'Introduction to Julia Kristeva's *Women's time*'. In *Signs*, issue 7, p.16, n.16.
45. Kristeva cited in E. Grosz (1989) *Sexual subversions: Three French feminists*. Sydney: Allen and Unwin, p.64.
46. Kristeva (1986a, p.155).
47. Ibid., p.156.

48. Ibid., p.156.
49. Ibid., p.156.
50. Julia Kristeva (1991a) *Strangers to ourselves*. New York: Columbia University Press; Julia Kristeva (1993) *Nations without nationalism*. New York: Columbia University Press.
51. The comment comes from Julia Kristeva (2002b) *Revolt, she said*. Interviews with Julia Kristeva, edited by Sylvère Lotringer. Los Angeles: Semiotext(e) Foreign Agents Series, p.95.
52. Kristeva (2001a, p.xv).
53. Ibid., p.x.
54. Ibid., p.xii.
55. Ibid., p.xv.
56. McAfee (2004, p.100).
57. Kristeva (2001a, p.xix).
58. Ibid., p.xiv.
59. Ibid., p.xiii.
60. Ibid., p.xix.
61. Ibid., p.93.
62. The links between Kristeva and Arendt have been commented on in Peg Birmingham (2005) 'Political affections: Kristeva and Arendt on violence and gratitude'. In T. Chanter and E. Plonowska Ziarek (Eds) *Revolt, affect, collectivity: The unstable boundaries of Kristeva's polis*. Albany: State University of New York Press.
63. Hannah Arendt (1971) *Men in dark times*. New York: Harcourt.
64. Ibid., p.7, emphasis in original.
65. Ibid., p.7.
66. See, for example, Birmingham (2005).
67. Kristeva (2001a, p.233).
68. Arendt, cited by Kristeva (2001a, p.232).
69. Cited in Julia Kristeva (1991b) in interview with Ebba Witt-Bratström: 'Främlingskap – intervju med Julia Kristeva'. In *Kvinnovetenskaplig tidskrift*, issue 3(91), p.218.
70. Ibid., p.231.
71. Ibid., pp.230–241.
72. Ibid., p.233.
73. Julia Kristeva (2004) *Colette*. New York: Columbia University Press, p.5.
74. Referred to in Kristeva (2004, p.483). In French: *Les vrilles de la vigne*.
75. Colette cited by Kristeva (2004, pp.120–122).
76. Kristeva (2004, p.11).
77. Ibid., p.15.
78. Colette quoted in Kristeva (2004, p.13).
79. Kristeva (2004, p.341).
80. Kristeva (2004). Part of the title to volume 3 of the trilogy: 'Words, Colette or the world's flesh'.
81. Ibid., p.3.
82. Julia Kristeva (2002a) *Intimate revolt*. New York: Columbia University Press, p.68.
83. Ibid., p.68.
84. Kristeva (2004, p.352).
85. Ibid., p.352.
86. Ibid., p.73.
87. Ibid., p.76.
88. Kristeva refers to Solzhenitsyn in Julia Kristeva (2000a) *Crisis of the european subject*. New York: Other Press.
89. 'A pure silence: The perfection of Jeanne Guyon', in Kristeva (1987, pp.297–317).
90. I take the term 'dissecting' from Kristeva's comparison between Virginia Woolf and Joyce. 'Virginia Woolf describes suspended states, subtle sensations and, above all, colors ... but she does *not* dissect *language* as Joyce does' (Kristeva cited by Grosz, 1989, p.64).

91. Ann Kaplan draws attention to Marguerite Duras's representation of women's silence as a deliberate refusal in the film *Nathalie Granger*: E. Ann Kaplan (1983) *Women and film: Both sides of the camera*. New York: Methuen.
92. Julia Kristeva (1987a) *In the beginning was love: Psychoanalysis and faith*. New York: Columbia University Press, p.17.
93. The description 'politically unsatisfactory' comes from the French Marxist-Feminist Literary Collective, and is cited by Moi (1985, p.170). The second statement comes from Creed (1985, p.54).
94. Moi (1985, p.169).
95. Kelly Oliver (2005) 'Revolt and forgiveness'. In Chanter and Ziarek.
96. For Cixous, Moi (1985, pp.102–121) offers a useful introduction.
97. For Irigaray, Moi (1985, pp.127–149) offers one introduction; Grosz (1989, pp.146–183) offers another. Grosz offers as well a comparison of Kristeva with Irigaray, regarding Kristeva as the 'dutiful daughter' of Lacan while Irigaray serves as the 'defiant daughter': Elizabeth Grosz (1990) *Jacques Lacan: A feminist introduction*. Sydney: Allen and Unwin, pp.147–187. Among the most accessible pieces, for English readers, is also an article in *Signs*, 1980, pp.69–79 ('When our lips speak together'). Butler (1993) reviews Kristeva's comments on female homosexuality.
98. E. Ann Kaplan (1992) *Motherhood and representation: The mother in popular culture and melodrama*. London: Routledge.
99. Tania Modleski (1986) 'The terror of pleasure: The contemporary horror film and postmodern theory'. In T. Modleski (Ed.) *Studies in entertainment: Studies in mass culture*. Bloomington: Indiana University Press.
100. Moi (1985, p.166), emphasis in original.
101. McAfee (2004).
102. Julia Kristeva (1980) *Desire in language: A semiotic approach to literature and art*. New York: Columbia University Press.

BIBLIOGRAPHY

Aaron, Michele (2007) *Spectatorship: The power of looking on*. London: Wallflower Press.

Ahmed, Sara (2005) 'The skin of the community: Affect and boundary formation'. In T. Chanter and E. Plonowska Ziarek (Eds) *Revolt, affect, collectivity: The unstable boundaries of Kristeva's polis*. Albany: State University of New York Press.

Arendt, Hannah (1971) *Men in dark times*. New York: Harcourt.

Baker, Candida (1990) 'The sweet smell of direct success'. Review of *An Angel at My Table*. In *The Age*, 22 September.

Birmingham, Peg (2005) 'Political affections: Kristeva and Arendt on violence and gratitude'. In T. Chanter and E. Plonowska Ziarek (Eds) *Revolt, affect, collectivity: The unstable boundaries of Kristeva's polis*. Albany: State University of New York Press.

Bobo, Jacqueline (1988) '*The Color Purple*: Black women as cultural readers'. In E.D. Pribram (Ed.) *Female spectators: Looking at film and television*. London: Verso.

Butler, Judith (1993) 'The body politics of Julia Kristeva'. In K. Oliver (Ed.) *Ethics, politics and difference in Julia Kristeva's writing*. New York: Routledge.

Campion, Jane (1990a) in interview with Candida Baker: 'The sweet smell of direct success'. Review of *An Angel at My Table*. In *The Age*, 22 September.

—— (1990b) in interview with Peter Castaldi: 'Castaldi on Campion'. In *Culture*, issue 9, October.

—— (1990c) in interview with Susan Chenery: 'A real sweetie'. In *GH* (Good Housekeeping), June.

—— (1990d) in interview with Alexander McGregor: 'Women in prime'. In *Blitz*, May.

—— (1990e) in interview with David Stratton: 'An interview with Jane Campion'. In D. Stratton, *The avocado plantation: Boom and bust in the Australian film industry*. Sydney: Pan Macmillan.

—— (1990f) in interview with Katherine Tulich: 'Jane's film career takes wing'. In *Daily Telegraph Mirror*, 21 September.

—— (1990g) in interview in article entitled: 'Being brave'. In *Follow Me*, July.

_____ (1991) in interview with David Stratton: 'Preface'. In G. Lee, and J. Campion, *Sweetie: The screenplay*. St. Lucia: Queensland University Press.

_____ (1993a) in interview with Lynden Barber: 'Playing it low-key'. In *The Sydney Morning Herald*, 3 August.

_____ (1993b) in interview with Milo Bilbrough: 'Jane Campion – The Piano'. In *Cinema Papers*, issue 93, May.

Chanter, Tina (2005) 'The exoticization and universalization of the fetish, and the naturalization of the phallus: Abject objections'. In T. Chanter and E. Plonowska Ziarek (Eds) *Revolt, affect, collectivity: The unstable boundaries of Kristeva's polis*. Albany: State University of New York Press.

Chanter, Tina and Ziarek, Eva Plonowska (Eds) (2005) *Revolt, affect, collectivity: The unstable boundaries of Kristeva's polis*. Albany: State University of New York Press.

Chodorow, Nancy (1978) *The reproduction of mothering: Psychoanalysis and the sociology of gender*. Berkeley: University of California Press.

Clover, Carol J. (1992) *Men, women and chain saws: Gender in the modern horror film*. Princeton: Princeton University Press.

Colbert, Mary (1993) 'The NZ connection'. In *The Sydney Morning Herald*, 9 August.

Coombs, Felicity and Gemmell, Suzanne (Eds) (1999) *Piano lessons: Approaches to* The Piano. Sydney: John Libbey.

Coward, Rosalind (1984) 'Julia Kristeva in conversation with Rosalind Coward'. In L. Appagnanesi (Ed.) *Desire*. London: ICA documents.

Coward, Rosalind and Ellis, John (1977) *Language and materialism*. London: Routledge & Kegan Paul.

Creed, Barbara (1985) 'Horror and the monstrous-feminine: An imaginary abjection'. In *Screen*, issue 27(1).

_____ (1993) *The monstrous-feminine: Film, feminism, psychoanalysis*. London: Routledge.

Derrida, Jacques (1973) *Speech and phenomena and other essays on Husserl's theory of signs*. Evanston: Northwestern University.

Douglas, Mary (1966) *Purity and danger: An analysis of concepts of pollution and taboo*. London: Routledge & Kegan Paul.

Duff, Alan (1994) 'Another tall poppy emerges'. In *The Eastland Sun*, 3 August.

Dyer, Richard (1982) 'Don't look now: The male pin-up'. In *Screen*, issue 23(3–4).

Eagleton, Terry (1983) *Literary theory*. Oxford: Blackwell.

Ellis, John (1982) *Visible fictions: Cinema, television, video*. London: Routledge & Kegan Paul.

Fletcher, John and Benjamin, Andrew (Eds) (1990) *Abjection, melancholia, and love: The work of Julia Kristeva*. London: Routledge.

Foucault, Michel (1980) *Power/knowledge: Selected interviews and other writings 1972–1977*. Brighton: Harvester Press.

Frame, Janet (1957) *Owls do cry*. Christchurch: Pegasus Press.
―――― (1961) *Faces in the water*. Christchurch: Pegasus Press.
Fraser, Nancy and Lee Bartky, Sandra (Eds) (1992) *Revaluing French feminism: Critical essays on difference, agency, & culture*. Bloomington: Indiana University Press.
Freud, Sigmund (1964) 'The uncanny'. In J. Strachey (Ed.) *The Standard edition of the complete psychological works of Sigmund Freud*, vol. 18. London: Hogarth Press.
Gaines, Jane (1984) 'Women and representation: Can we enjoy alternative pleasure?' *Jump Cut 29* (Spring, 1984). Reprinted in 1987 in D. Lazere (Ed.) *American media and mass culture: Left perspectives*. University of California Press; and in 1990 in Patricia Erens (Ed.) *Sexual strategms: Issues in feminist film criticism*. Bloomington: Indiana University Press,
Gledhill, Christine (1988) 'Pleasurable negotiations'. In E.D. Pribram (Ed.) *Female spectators: Looking at film and television*. London: Verso.
Goffman, Erving (1971) *The presentation of self in everyday life*. Harmondsworth: Penguin.
Goodnow, Katherine (1991a) *Alien/Aliens: Analyzing the forms and sources of horror*. Bergen: University of Bergen.
―――― (1991b) 'Mødre, fødsle, og den kvinnelige tilskuer'. In Z, Issue 38.
―――― (2006) 'Bodies: Taking account of viewers' perspectives'. In K. Goodnow and J. Lohman (Eds) *Human remains and museum practice*. Paris: UNESCO.
Grant, Barry Keith (Ed.) (1996) *The dread of difference: Gender and the horror film*. Austin: University of Texas Press.
Grosz, Elizabeth (1989) *Sexual subversions: Three French feminists*. Sydney: Allen and Unwin.
―――― (1990) *Jacques Lacan: A feminist introduction*. Sydney: Allen and Unwin.
Hardy, Ann (2000) 'The last patriarch'. In H. Margolis (Ed.) *Jane Campion's The Piano*. Cambridge: Cambridge University Press.
Hauser, Arnold (1982) *The sociology of art*. London: Routledge & Kegan Paul. Translated by Kenneth J. Northcott.
hooks, bell (1994) 'Gangsta culture – Sexism, misogyny'. In *Outlaw culture: Resisting representation*. New York: Routledge.
Irigaray, Luce (1980) 'When our lips speak together'. In *Signs*, issue 6 1
Jardine, Alice (1981) 'Introduction to Julia Kristeva's *Women's Time*'. In *Signs*, issue 7.
Jones, Laura (1990) *Screenplay for An Angel at My Table*. London: Pandora.
Kaplan, E. Ann (1983) *Women and film: Both sides of the camera*. New York: Methuen.
―――― (1987) 'Feminist criticism and television'. In R.C. Allen (Ed.) *Channels of discourse*. London: Methuen.
―――― (1992) *Motherhood and representation: The mother in popular culture and melodrama*. London: Routledge.

Kristeva, Julia (1975) 'The system and the speaking subject'. In T. Sebeok (Ed.) *The tell-tale sign: A survey of semiotics*. Lisse, Netherlands: The Peter de Ridder Press.

_____ (1980) *Desire in language: A semiotic approach to literature and art*. New York: Columbia University Press.

_____ (1981) 'Women's time'. In *Signs*, issue 7(1).

_____ (1982) *Powers of horror: An essay on abjection*. New York: Columbia University Press. Translated by Leon S. Roudiez.

_____ (1984) *Revolution in poetic language*. New York: Columbia University Press.

_____ (1986a) 'About Chinese women'. In T. Moi (Ed.) *The Kristeva reader*. Oxford: Basil Blackwell.

_____ (1986b) 'A new type of intellectual: the dissident'. In T. Moi (Ed.) *The Kristeva reader*. Oxford: Basil Blackwell.

_____ (1986c) 'Freud and love'. In T. Moi (Ed.) *The Kristeva reader*. Oxford: Basil Blackwell.

_____ (1986d) 'Psychoanalysis and the polis'. In T. Moi (Ed.) *The Kristeva reader*. Oxford: Basil Blackwell.

_____ (1986e) 'Stabat mater'. In T. Moi (Ed.) *The Kristeva reader*. Oxford: Basil Blackwell.

_____ (1987a) *In the beginning was love: Psychoanalysis and faith*. New York: Columbia University Press.

_____ (1987b) *Tales of love*. New York: Columbia University Press.

_____ (1989) *Language the unknown: An initiation into linguistics*. New York: Columbia University Press.

_____ (1990) 'The adolescent novel'. In J. Fletcher and A. Benjamin (Eds) *Abjection, melancholia, and love: The work of Julia Kristeva*. London: Routledge.

_____ (1991a) *Strangers to ourselves*. New York: Columbia University Press.

_____ (1991b) in interview with Ebba Witt-Bratström: 'Främlingskap – intervju med Julia Kristeva'. In *Kvinnovetenskaplig tidskrift*, issue 3(91).

_____ (1992) *The samurai*. New York: Columbia University Press.

_____ (1993) *Nations without nationalism*. New York: Columbia University Press.

_____ (1995) *New maladies of the soul*. New York: Columbia University Press.

_____ (2000a) *Crisis of the European subject*. New York: Other Press.

_____ (2000b) *The sense and non-sense of revolt*. New York: Columbia University Press.

_____ (2001a) *Hannah Arendt*. New York: Columbia University Press.

_____ (2001b) *Melanie Klein*. New York: Columbia University Press.

_____ (2002a) *Intimate revolt*. New York: Columbia University Press.

_____ (2002b) *Revolt, she said*. Interviews with Julia Kristeva, edited by Sylvère Lotringer. Los Angeles: Semiotext(e) Foreign Agents Series.

―――― (2004) *Colette*. New York: Columbia University Press.
―――― (2005) *Motherhood today*. At www.kristeva.fr.
Lacan, Jacques (1977) *Écrits*. London: Travistock.
Lapsley, Robert and Westlake, Michael (1988) *Film theory: An introduction*. Manchester: Manchester University Press.
Lechte, John (1990) *Julia Kristeva*. London: Routledge.
Lee, Gerard and Campion, Jane (1991) *Sweetie: The screenplay*. St. Lucia: Queensland University Press.
MacKinnon, Kenneth (1999) 'After Mulvey: Male erotic objectification'. In M. Aaron (Ed.) *The body's perilous pleasures: Dangerous desires and contemporary culture*. Edinburgh: Edinburgh University Press.
Maclean, Alison (1992) interviewed in press release for *Crush*.
Margaroni, Maria (2003) 'Jane Campion's selling of the mother/land: Restaging the crisis of the postcolonial subject'. In *Camera Obscura*, issue 18(2).
Margolis, Harriet (Ed.) (2000) *Jane Campion's* The Piano. Cambridge: Cambridge University Press.
McAfee, Noëlle (1993) 'Abject strangers: Toward an ethic of respect'. In K. Oliver (Ed.) *Ethics, politics and difference in Julia Kristeva's writing*. New York: Routledge.
―――― (2004) *Julia Kristeva*. New York: Routledge.
―――― (2005) 'Bearing witness in the Polis: Kristeva, Arendt, and the space of appearance'. In T. Chanter and E. Plonowska Ziarek (Eds) *Revolt, affect, collectivity: The unstable boundaries of Kristeva's polis*. Albany: State University of New York Press.
Modleski, Tania (1982) *Loving with a vengeance*. New York: Methuen.
―――― (1986) 'The terror of pleasure: The contemporary horror film and postmodern theory'. In T. Modleski (Ed.) *Studies in entertainment: Studies in mass culture*. Bloomington: Indiana University Press.
―――― (1988) *The women who knew too much: Hitchcock and feminist theory*. New York: Methuen.
Moi, Toril (1985) *Sexual/textual politics*. London: Methuen.
―――― (Ed.) (1986) *The Kristeva reader*. Oxford: Basil Blackwell.
Moruzzi, Norma Claire (1993) 'Julia Kristeva on the process of political self-identification'. In K. Oliver (Ed.) *Ethics, politics and difference in Julia Kristeva's writing*. New York: Routledge.
―――― (2000) *Speaking through the mask: Hannah Arendt and the politics of social identity*. Ithica, N.Y.: Cornell University Press.
Mulvey, Laura (1989) *Visual and other pleasures*. Basingstoke: Macmillan.
Neale, Steve (1993 [1983]) 'Masculinity as spectacle: Reflections on men and mainstream cinema'. In S. Cohan and I.R. Hark (Eds) *Screening the male: Exploring masculinities in Hollywood cinema*. London: Routledge.
New Zealand Film Commission (1992) *Annual report*. July, Wellington.

Nowell-Smith, Geoffrey (1991) 'On Kiri Te Kanawa, Judy Garland, and the Culture Industry'. In J. Narremore and P. Brantlinger (Eds) *Modernity and Mass Culture*. Indiana University Press.

Oliver, Kelly (Ed.) (1993a) *Ethics, politics and difference in Julia Kristeva's writing*. New York: Routledge.

―――― (1993b) *Reading Kristeva: Unraveling the double-bind*. Bloomington: Indiana University Press.

―――― (2005) 'Revolt and forgiveness'. In T. Chanter and E. Plonowska Ziarek (Eds) *Revolt, affect, collectivity: The unstable boundaries of Kristeva's polis*. Albany: State University of New York Press.

Pihama, Leonie (1994) 'Are films dangerous? A Maori woman's perspective on *The Piano*'. In *Hecate: An interdisciplinary journal of women's liberation*, issue 20(2).

―――― (2000) 'Ebony and ivory: Constructions of the Maori in *The Piano*'. In H. Margolis (Ed.) *Jane Campion's* The Piano. Cambridge: Cambridge University Press

Pihama, Leonie and Smith, Cherryl (1994) 'A nice white story: Reviewing *The Piano*'. *Broadsheet* 200.

Pinedo, Isabel C. (2004) 'Postmodern elements of contemporary horror film'. In S. Prince (Ed.) *The horror film*. New Brunswick: Rutgers University Press.

Pribram, E. Deidre (Ed.) (1988) *Female spectators: Looking at film and television*. London: Verso.

Prince, Stephen (2004) 'Dread, taboo, and *The Thing*: Toward a social theory of the horror film'. In S. Prince (Ed.) *The horror film*. New Brunswick: Rutgers University Press.

Restuccia, Frances L. (2005) 'Black and *Blue*: Kieslowski's melancholia'. In T. Chanter and E. Plonowska Ziarek (Eds) *Revolt, affect, collectivity: The unstable boundaries of Kristeva's polis*. Albany: State University of New York Press.

Michelle Rosaldo (1974) 'Women, culture and society: A theoretical overview'. In M.Z. Rosaldo and L. Lamphere (Eds) *Women, culture and society*. Stanford: Stanford University Press.

Rose, Jacqueline (1986) *Sexuality in the field of vision*. London: Verso.

Roudiez Léon (1980) 'Introduction'. In J. Kristeva *Desire in language: A semiotic approach to literature and art*. New York: Columbia University Press

Sebeok, Thomas (Ed.) (1975) *The tell-tale sign: A survey of semiotics*. Lisse, Netherlands: The Peter de Ridder Press.

Smelik, Anneke (1999) 'Feminist film theory'. In P. Cook and M. Bernink (Eds) *The cinema book*. London: British Film Institute.

Smith, Anna (1996) *Julia Kristeva: Readings of exile and estrangement*. New York: St Martin's Press.

Sobchack, Vivian (1990) 'The virginity of astronauts: Sex and the science fiction film'. In A. Kuhn (Ed.) *Alien zone: Cultural theory and contemporary science fiction cinema*. London: Verso.

Stacey, Jackie (1994) *Star gazing: Hollywood cinema and female spectatorship*. London: Routledge.

Staiger, Janet (2000) *Perverse spectators: The practices of film reception*. New York: New York University Press.

Stam, Robert, Burgoyne, Robert, and Flitterman-Lewis, Sandy (1992) *New vocabularies in film semiotics: Structuralism, post-structuralism and beyond*. London: Routledge.

Steven, Peter (Ed.) (1985) *Jump cut: Hollywood, politics and counter-cinema*. New York: Præger.

Stratton, David (1990) *The avocado plantation: Boom and bust in the Australian film industry*. Sydney: Pan Macmillan.

Williams, Linda (1984) '"Something else besides a mother": Stella Dallas and the maternal melodrama'. In *Cinema Journal*, issue 24(1).

―――― (Ed.) (1994) *Viewing positions: Ways of seeing film*. New Brunswick, NJ: Rutgers University Press.

Wood, Robin (1985) 'An introduction to the American horror film'. In B. Nichols (Ed.) *Movies and methods*, vol. 2. Berkeley: University of California Press.

FILMOGRAPHY

Organised by chapter in which each film is first mentioned

Preface

Alien – Ridley Scott, 1979
Aliens – James Cameron, 1986
Exotica – Atom Egoyan, 1994
Three Colors: Blue – Krysztof Kieslowski, 1993
The Piano – Jane Campion, 1993
Crush – Alison Maclean, 1992
An Angel at My Table – Jane Campion, 1990
Vigil - Vincent Ward, 1984
Kitchen Sink - Alison Maclean, 1989
Sweetie - Jane Campion, 1989
The Heart of the Stag – Michael Firth, 1984

Chapter 1

Rashomon – Akira Kurosawa, 1950

Chapter 2

The Fly – David Cronenberg 1986 and 1958 original
Aliens 3 – David Fincher, 1992
Dune – David Lynch, 1984
Eraserhead – David Lynch, 1977
Blue Velvet – David Lynch, 1986
Thriller – Michael Jackson, 1984
Black and White – Michael Jackson, 1991
Dr. Jekyll and Mr. Hyde – Victor Fleming, 1941
Creature from the Black Lagoon – Jack Arnold, 1954
King Kong – Peter Jackson, 2005 and 1933 original
Carrie – Brian de Palma, 1976
The Exorcist – William Friedkin, 1973

The Omen – Richard Donner, 1976 and John Moore, 2006
Rosemary's Baby – Roman Polanski, 1968
Psycho – Alfred Hitchcock, 1960
Dressed to Kill – Brian de Palma, 1980
Reflection of Fear – William A. Fraker, 1973
Cruising – William Friedkin, 1980
The Hunger – Tony Scott, 1983
Cat People – Paul Schrader, 1982
Dance of the Vampires – Roman Polanski, 1967
Night of the Living Dead – George Romero, 1968
An American Werewolf in Paris – Anthony Waller, 1997
A Company of Wolves – Neil Jordan, 1984
Gaslight – George Cukor, 1944
Sleep My Love – Douglas Sirk, 1948
The original *Stepford Wives* – Bryon Forbes, 1975
Silence of the Lambs – Jonathon Demme, 1991
Tootsie – Sydney Pollack, 1982
Videodrome – David Cronenberg, 1983

Chapter 3

Silkwood – Mike Nichols, 1983
The Virgin Spring – Ingmar Bergman, 1960
Jaws II – Jeannot Szwarc, 1978
Jaws – Steven Spielberg, 1975
Pygmalion – Anthony Asquith, 1938
Jurassic Park - Stephen Spielberg, 1993
The Color Purple – Steven Spielberg, 1985
Frenzy – Alfred Hitchcock, 1972

Chapter 4

Mississippi Masala – Mira Nair, 1991
My Beautiful Launderette – Stephen Frears, 1985
Camille Claudel – Bruno Nyutten, 1988
Baghdad Café – Percy Adlon, 1987
Lost in Translation – Sofia Coppola, 2003
Dances With Wolves – Kevin Costner, 1990
Thunderheart – Michael Apted, 1992
A State of Siege – Vincent Ward, 1978
In Spring One Plants Alone– Vincent Ward, 1980
Navigator – Vincent Ward, 1988
Map of the Human Heart – Vincent Ward, 1993

Chapter 5

Now Voyager – Irving Rapper, 1942
One Flew Over the Cuckoo's Nest – Milos Forman, 1975
Frances – Graeme Clifford, 1982
Look Who's Talking Now - Tom Ropelewski, 1993

Chapter 6

Passionless Moments - Jane Campion and Gerard Lee, 1983
Peel - Jane Campion, 1982
Stranger Than Paradise - Jim Jarmusch, 1984
The Last Days of Chez Nous – Gillian Armstrong, 1993

Chapter 7

The Good Mother – Leonard Nimoy, 1988
Look Who's Talking – Amy Heckerling, 1989
Look Who's Talking, Too – Amy Heckerling, 1990

Chapter 8

Cagney and Lacey - Barbara Avedon and Barbara Corday, series start 1982
Coma – Michael Crichton, 1978
The Dictator - Charles Chaplin, 1940
Talkback – Alison Maclean, 1987
Rud's Wife – Alison Maclean, 1986
Once Were Warriors – Lee Tamahori, 1994

Chapter 9

Nathalie Granger - Marguerite Duras, 1972
Stella Dallas – King Vidor, 1937
Persona – Ingmar Bergman, 1966
Children of a Lesser God – Randa Haines, 1986
The Miracle – Arthur Penn, 1962

Index

Aaron, Michele, 61n21
abjection, 28–62, 66, 141
addressee, 21–23
Aegyptus, 108
Aeschylus, 73
affect, 9
Ahmed, Sara, 178
Alien, xii, 32, 36–39, 42, 45n31, 52, 57, 184
Aliens, xii, 32, 39–40, 42, 45n27, 45n31
Aliens 3, 36, 45n27, 45n31
Althusser, Louis, 3
ambivalence, 13
American Werewolf in Paris, 36
An Angel at my Table, xii, xiv, 63, 96–113, 118, 146, 201
  production history of, 160, 168–171
ancient Greece, 12
Anglican services, 54
Aphrodite, 108
Aquinas, Thomas, 116, 133
Arendt, Hannah, 177, 179, 185, 190–195
  on Nazism, 194
assimilation, 107–108
Auschwitz, 37
Australia,
  New Zealand and, 91
Australian Aboriginals
  rights to vote, 91
Australian Broadcasting Corporation, 171
Australian Film Commission, 120, 167
Australian Film Financing Commission, 172
Australian Film, Television and Radio School, 167
Avalon Studios, 165

Baby Boom, 155
Baghdad Café, 63
Bakthin, Mikhail, 12–16, 26n54, 76, 177
Band Wagon, 14
barbarians, 72–73
Barthes, Roland, 3, 26, 115
Baslez, Marie-Françoise, 100
Bataille, Georges, 18
Baudelaire, 122
Benveniste, Émile, 20
birth, 190
  images of, 38, 41–44, 45n31
Blessed Virgin, 132
blood, 32, 41
  menstrual, 40
Blue Velvet, 38
Bobo, Jacqueline, 60
Bongers, Sally, 169
bourgeois society, 178
Bowles, Jane, 161
Brontë, Emily, 150
Burgoyne, Robert, 14

Cagney and Lacey, 159
Cahiers du cinema, 184
Camille Claudel, 63
Campion, Jane, xiii, xv in 29, 103, 118–119, 131, 145–146, 149–150, 152–153, 161, 166–177
Camus, Albert, 78
Cannes Film Festival, 171
carnivalesque folklore, 16
Carrie, 32, 41
Cat People, 32, 36
Channel Four, 170–171
Chanter, Tina, xii
Chaplin, Charles, 199
Chapman, Jan, xvin29, 120, 146, 161, 172–175

Chez Nous, 120
Children of a Lesser God, 199
Chodorow, Nancy, 201
Christian traditions, 11
Christianity, 50–51, 53
CIBY 2000, 120, 172
Cixous, Hélène, 6, 177, 201–202
Clover, Carol, 60n1
code violations, 123–124
Colette, 115, 185, 192–193, 196–198
Color Purple, 55, 57
Coma, 159
Company of Wolves, 36
Coombs, Felicity, 138n11
corpse, 30, 33, 47
　living, 32
cosmopolitanism, 100
Costner, David, 176
Coward, Rosalind, 20, 23, 26n62
Creature from the Black Lagoon, 32
Creed, Barbara, xii, 31, 33, 49–50, 184
Cronenberg, David, 35
Cruising, 32
Crush, xii, xiv, 69, 71–72, 74–75, 77–78, 81–86, 88, 91–92, 129, 179
　production history of, 164–166

Danaïdes, 73, 108
Dance of the Vampire, 32
Dances with Wolves, 63, 176
Davis, Bette, 111
death, 30–31
　rituals surrounding, 47–48, 51
DeGaulle, Charles, 67
Derrida, Jacques, 3, 25n19
dialogue, 13, 177
Dictator, 159
Diderot, Denis, 76
Disney, 162
Don Juan, 122
Dostoevky, Fyodor, 38
Douglas, Mary, 46–47
Dressed to Kill, 32, 42
Dr. Jekyll and Mr. Hyde, 32, 36
Dryburgh, Stuart, 169
Duff, Alan, 176
　composites, 37–38
　dialogism, 13
　duplicity and treachery, 38–39

Eagleton, Terry, 25n21
Eastern Europe, 67
Eichmann, Adolf, 195
Eisenstein, Sergei, 198–199
Ellis, John, 20, 23, 26n62, 27n77
England, 91
Eraserhead, 36
Euripedes, 73
European politics, 64
excrement, 33
Exorcist, 32
Exotica, xii

F for Fake, 14
Faces in the Water, 169
Fall of the House of Usher, 48
fathers, 143
feminism, 5–6
　generations of, 58, 185–188
　motherhood and, 143
Ferenczi, Sandor, 195
film noir, 14
FilmPac, 167
Flitterman-Lewis, Sandy, 14
Fly, 25, 55
foreigners, 7, 10, 63–113
　establishing better relations with, 133
　the feelings of, 103–107
　the options of, 107–110
　the position of, 100–103
Forrest, John, 101–102, 108
Foucault, Michel, 130
Frame, Janet, 78, 96–113, 168–171, 182n47, 201
France, 12, 90
　immigration and, 90–92
　Kristeva and, 65, 67
　language and, 106
　New Zealand and, 90
　xenophobia and, 4
Frances, 111
Fraser, Nancy, 4–5, 9
French feminists, 2, 99, 201
French Revolution, 12, 83, 203
Frenzy, 56
Freud, Sigmund, 24, 40–41, 59, 79, 81
Freudian theory, 8, 40

Gaslight, 39
Gemmell, Suzanne, 138n11
gender,
  difference, 58–59
  identity, 41
German Romanticism, 81
Giotto, 21–22, 160
Gledhill, Christine, 159, 161, 177–179
Godard, Jean-Luc, 199
Good Mother, 155–156
gothic films, 39
Gramsci, Antonio, 178, 203
Grant, Barry, 60n2
Greenpeace, 90
Grosz, Elizabeth, 5–6, 8, 25n20, 139n50
Guyon, Jeanne, 127, 199

Hall, Stuart, 60
Harden, Marcia Gay, 78
hate, 116
Heartburn, 155
Heart of the Stag, xii
Hegel, 93
hegemony, 178, 203
Heloise and Abelard, 128
Hermes, 108
Hirsch, Marianne, 143
Hitchcock, Alfred, 56, 58
Homer, 72
hooks, bell, 175
horror, 11, 28–60, 141
horror films, 32–33, 35–60, 184, 201
Hunger, 32
Hunter, Holly, 119

Ikin, Bridget, xvin29, 28, 70, 92, 112, 160–162, 164–166, 168–171
  on Maori representation, 74
imaginary, 30
indigenous filmmakers, 176
In Spring One Plants Alone, 70
intertextuality, 12, 14–17
intertextual dialogism, 14
Inuit, 123
Irigaray, Luce, 177, 201–202

jackaroos, 119, 153
Jackson, Michael, 36

Jakobson, Roman, 20
Jarmusch, Jim, 119
John Hopkins Medical School, 102
Jones, Laura, 161, 168
Joyce, James, 18
Judaic traditions, 11
Judaism, 11, 50–51, 53, 80
  women and, 150
Jurassic Park, 55

Kafka, Franz, 18, 194
Kaplan, Ann, 154–156, 158n51, 185–187, 201
Keitel, Harvery, 119
Keller, Helen, 199
King Kong, 32
Kitchen Sink, xii, xiv, 28–57, 198–199
  production history of, 160–162
Klein, Melanie, 185, 190, 192–196
Kooning, Willem de, 108
Kristeva, Julia,
  differences between men and women, 58–60
  feminism and, xi–xii, 2, 185–188
  foreigners, 10
  horror, 28–62
  images: cinema and television, 198–199
  intertextuality, 14–17
  love, 10, 12, 97, 115–158
  Marxism and, 2, 58
  maternal love, 154–156
  men and women, 188–191
  motherhood and creativity, 148
  music, 151
  nationalism, 66–68, 92–93
  order and borders, 2–12, 30–37, 66–68
  position of women, 180, 184–204
  productivity, 19
  revolt, xi
  the semiotic and symbolic order, 30
  silence, 198–200
  strangers and foreignness, 63–114
  women and foreignness, 72
  women's writing, 191–197
Kubrick, Stanley, 14

Index

Lacan, Jacques, 3, 5, 8, 25n21, 30, 41
Lacanian theory, 8, 30, 40–41
language, 20, 106–107, 109, 136
Lapsley, Robert, xiv
Larkin, Frank, 60
Lee, Gerard, 118, 149, 166–168
Lee, Spike, 176
Lemon, Genevieve, 167
Leavy, Sandra, 171
Leviticus, 45n20
Life magazine, 156
linguistics, 8
Look Who's Talking, 156
Look Who's Talking Now, 112, 156
Lost in Translation, 63
love, 12, 115–158
   between adults, 125
   between mother and child, 124–126
   courtly, 123
   difficulties of, 133
   expected course of, 124–126
   marriage and, 130
   motherhood and, 137
   object of, 122–124
   steps towards, 133–138
Lynch, David, 36

Mc Afee, Noëlle, x, 75, 177, 179–180, 184, 192, 202
Maclean, Alison, xvin29, 28, 70, 92, 160–162, 164–166
Maori, xiii, 120–121, 123, 131, 136, 146
   representation of, 74–75, 164–166, 171–176
   rights, 91
Map of the Human Heart, 70
Marat, Jean-Paul, 83
Margolis, Harriet, 138n11
Margaroni, Maria, xii, 138n11
marriage, 122
   ceremonies, 131
   as the enemy of love, 129–130
   mothers and, 137
Marxism, 2
Mater Dolorosa, 58, 131–132, 137, 142, 154, 203
Matisse, Henri, 22, 27n72, 64, 116, 125
Maynard, John, xvin29, 70, 118, 160, 162–163, 167–168, 170

media-specific knowledge, 54–57
Medieval Church, 21
Medieval Europe, 123
melodrama, 158n51
men,
   African American, 60
   Chinese, 58
   as spectators, 57–60
Menippean discourse,
   Bakhtin and, 12, 15–19
Menippus of Gadara, 16
metics, 100–101
Middle Ages, 23, 122
Miracle Worker, 199
Mississippi Masala, 63
Modleski, Tania, 49, 56, 58, 201
Moi, Toril, x, 2, 5, 15, 25n19, 143, 189, 192, 200, 202
moko, 176
monologic texts, 12, 17–18
Moruzzi, Norma Claire, 75
motherhood, 58, 89, 137–138, 144, 155–156, 189–191
   love and, 143
   creativity and, 148
mothers, 43–44, 115
   daughters and, 151–152
   Mater Dolorosa, 58, 131–132, 137, 143, 151
   single, 143
Muru, Selwyn, 174
music, 151
musical texts, 21
My Beautiful Laundrette, 63

Narcissus, 122
nation, 87–88
nationalism, 66–68, 92
Navigator, 70, 167
negotiations, 24, 177–179
Neil, Sam, 119
New South Wales Film Office, 167
New York Times, 118
New Zealand, 90–91
   film industry, xii–xiii, 24, 74, 163
   France and, 90–91
New Zealand Film Commission, 29, 161, 163–165, 170
New Zealand films,
   Maori representation, 74–75

New Zealand On Air, 165
Nicholson, Jack, 14, 112
Night of the Living Dead, 33
Nightingale and the Rose, 196–197
Nilsson, Lennart, 155
Now Voyager, 102, 111–112, 196
Nyman, Michael, 151

Old Testament, 34, 50, 83
Oliver, Kelly, 201
Omen, 32
Once Were Warriors, 176
One Flew over the Cuckoo's Nest, 97, 102, 112
order and borders, 2–12, 30–37, 65–68, 115–116
  disturbance by love, 127
Owls Do Cry, 168

paganism, 50–51
Paine, Thomas, 83
pakeha, xiii, 74, 121, 146, 164, 166, 171, 173–176
Palmed d´Or, 120
parody, 18
particularism, 7, 69, 83, 87, 96
Passionless Moments, 118, 166
Peel, 118
Pentacostal services, 54
Persona, 199
phantasmagoria, 18
Piano, xii–xiv, 118–121, 123–124, 128–129, 131,134–136, 141, 143–146, 149–154, 179, 199
  production history of, 160, 171–177
Picasso, Pablo, xi
Pihama, Leonie, 174–176
Pinedo, Isabel Cristina, 61n18
Plato, 82, 100
Polynesia, 176
polyphonic texts, 12, 17–18
Poseidon, 108
Posssessed, 38
pregnancy, 33–34, 154, 190
productivity, 20, 57, 177
Proust, Marcel, 101
Psycho, 32, 56, 125
psychoanalytic practice, 115
psychoanalytic theory, 40–41, 43, 59, 79, 81

purification ceremonies, 47
Pygmalion, 55

Rainbow Warrior, 90
Raising Arizona, 155
Redford, Robert, 165
Reds, 14
Reflection of Fear, 32
Restuccia, Frances, xii
Riffaterre, Michael, 14
rituals of defilement, 47–53
Romeo and Juliet, 6, 127, 128, 130
Rosaldo, Michelle, 6, 25n18,
Rose, Jacqueline, 25n31, 94n17
Rosemary's Baby, 32
Rotorua, 165–166
Roudiez, Léon, 2–3, 16–17
Rousseau, Jean-Jacques, 83
Rud's Wife, 161

Sargeson, Frank, 101–102, 105
satanic rituals, 51
Saussure, Ferdinand, 8
semiotic
  and symbolic order, 30, 126
Shakespeare, 13
Shelley, Mary, 29, 55
shifters, 20
Shining, 14
Shortland, Waihoroi, 174–175
silence, 109, 127, 136, 198–200
Silence of the Lambs, 36, 40
Silkwood, 47
sin, 51
skin, 34–37, 54
slaves, 89
Sleep My Love, 39
Smelik, Anneke, 57
Smith, Cherryl, 174
Snow White and the Seven Dwarfs, 153
Sobchack, Vivian, 42
sociology of texts, 22–23
Socratic dialogue, 15
Sollers, Philippe, 99
Solzhenitsyn, Aleksandr, 199
Song of Songs, 127
Sophocles, 72
South African Truth and Reconciliation Commission, 179–180

speakers, 21–23
speaking subject, 9
spectators, 49–50, 53, 57–60, 69, 186
  impact of *Angel* on, 110–113
  significance of, 177–178
  stance of the, 177–178
speech,
  refusal of, 135
Spinoza, 138
splitting, 85
Stam, Robert, 14
State of Siege, 70
Stein, Gertrude, 203
Stella Dallas, 186–187
Stendhal, 122
Stepford Wives, 39
Stranger than Paradise, 119
strangers, 63–114
  the feelings of, 103–107
  narrative function of, 86–88
  the options of, 107–110
  the position of, 100–103
structuralism, 15
Sundance Institute, 165
Sweenie Todd, 55
Sweetie, xii, xiv, 118–119, 125, 128, 132, 135, 141, 143–146, 149, 151–153
  production history of, 160, 166–168
symbolic, 30, 126, 142
symbolic order, 30, 41, 136

Talkback, 161
Tarzan, 176
Television New Zealand, 162, 170
Tendrils of the Vine, 196
terra nullius, 91
texts of society and history, 12–19
Thunderhead, 63
Tootsie, 42
transposition, 16, 97
treachery, 39–40

uncanny, 4, 66
unheimlich, 66
universalism, 7, 69, 96
University of Paris, 1

Vale, Charlotte, 196
vampires, 32
Van Gogh, 101, 108
Vanity Fair, 118
Victorian society, 145
Videodrome, 43
Vigil, xii, xiv, 17, 56, 69–71, 73–74, 77–78, 83, 86, 88, 92, 198
  production history of, 160–163
Village Voice, 29, 55
Virgin Mary, 89, 137–138
Virgin Spring, 47
Voltaire, 76

Ward, Vincent, 70, 162–163, 180n12, 181n17
werewolves, 32
Westlake, Michael, xiv
whakapapa, 176
Wild at Heart, 38, 43
Williams, Linda, 186
Winnicott, Donald, 195–196
Witt-Bratström, Ebba, 93n7
Wolf, Hugo, 101, 108
women,
  African American, 60
  Chinese, 58
  fundamentalism and, 92–93
  love and, 142
  representation of, 184
  as spectators, 57–60, 186
Wood, Robin, 184
Woolf, Virginia, 201
Wuthering Heights, xiii, 146, 150

xenophobia, 100
xenos, 66

Yeats, William Butler, 101
Yddish theatre, 14

Zelig, 14
zombies, 32

CPSIA information can be obtained at www.ICGtesting.com
Printed in the USA
LVOW13s1914120214

373445LV00006B/42/P

9 781782 385066